EVERMORE

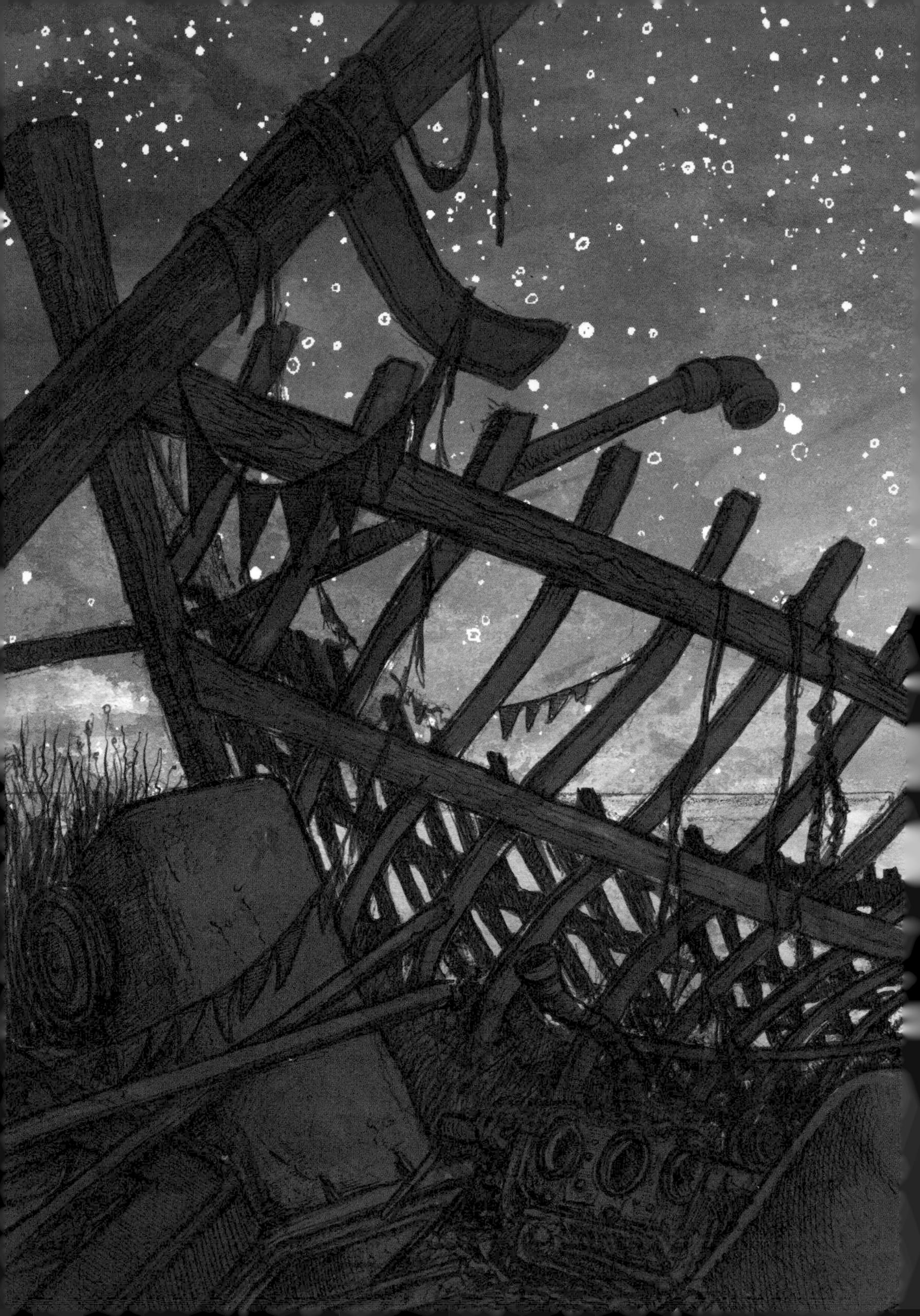

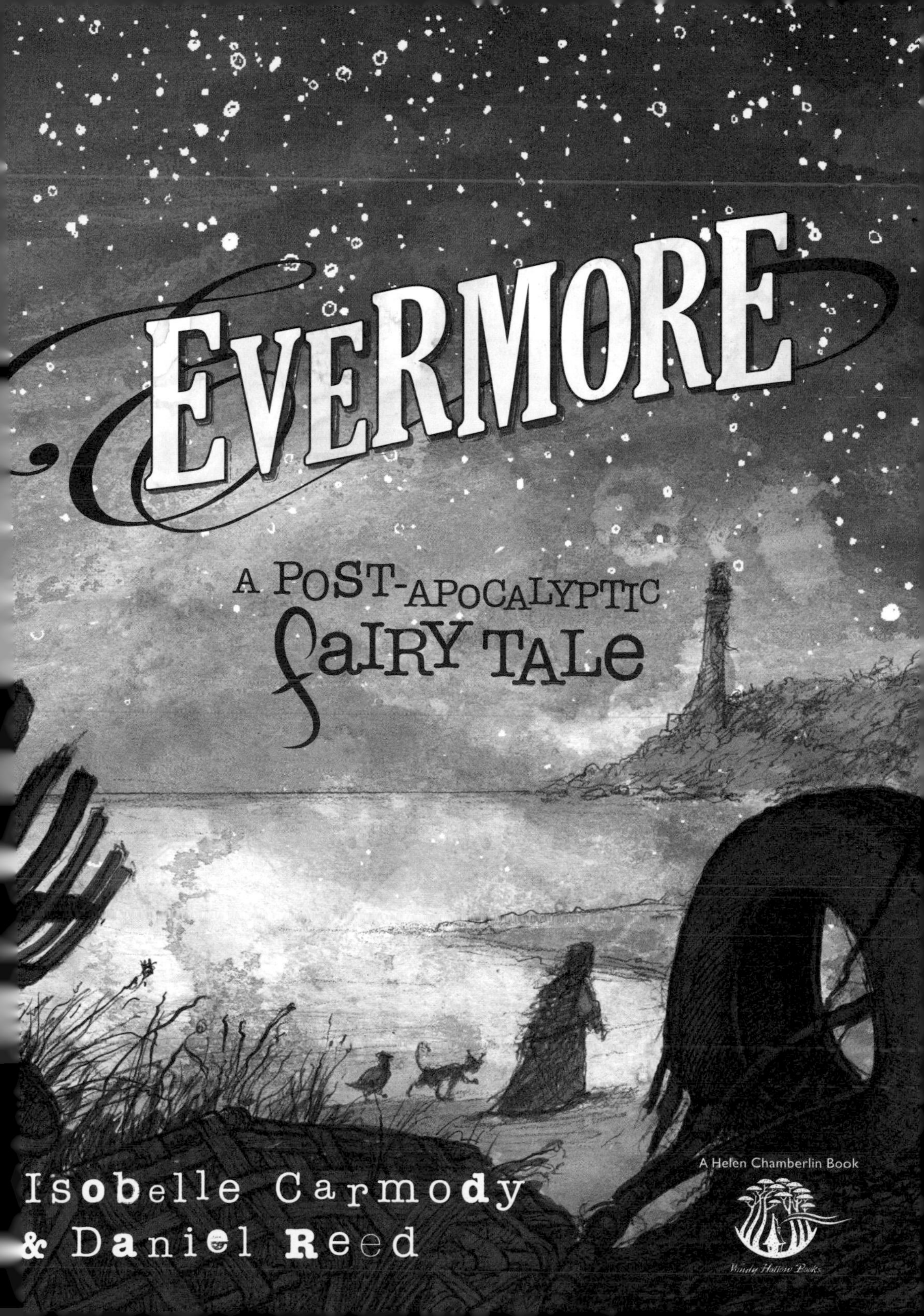
EVERMORE
A POST-APOCALYPTIC FAIRY TALE
Isobelle Carmody
& Daniel Reed
A Helen Chamberlin Book
Windy Hollow Books

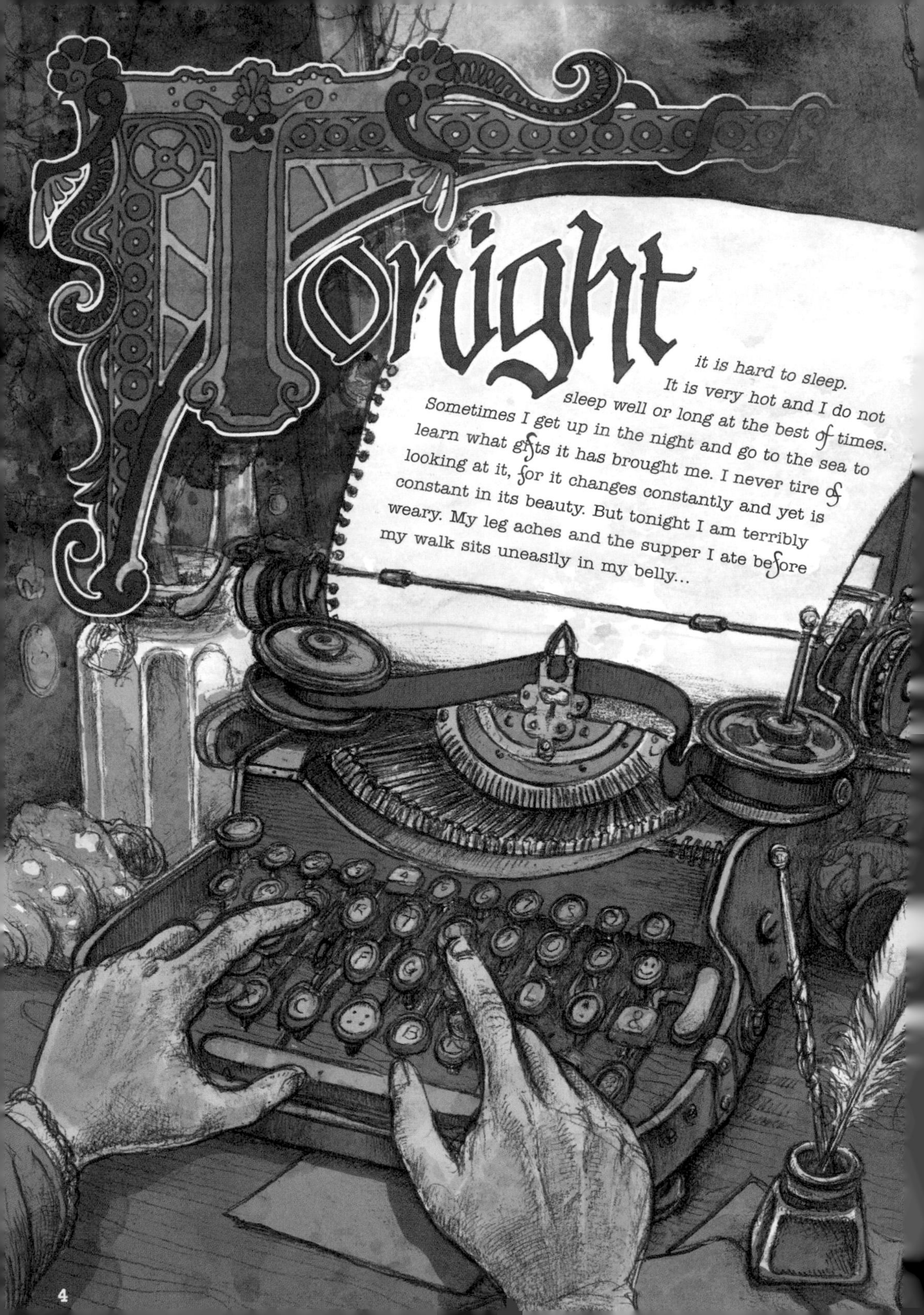

Tonight it is hard to sleep. It is very hot and I do not sleep well or long at the best of times. Sometimes I get up in the night and go to the sea to learn what gifts it has brought me. I never tire of looking at it, for it changes constantly and yet is constant in its beauty. But tonight I am terribly weary. My leg aches and the supper I ate before my walk sits uneasily in my belly...

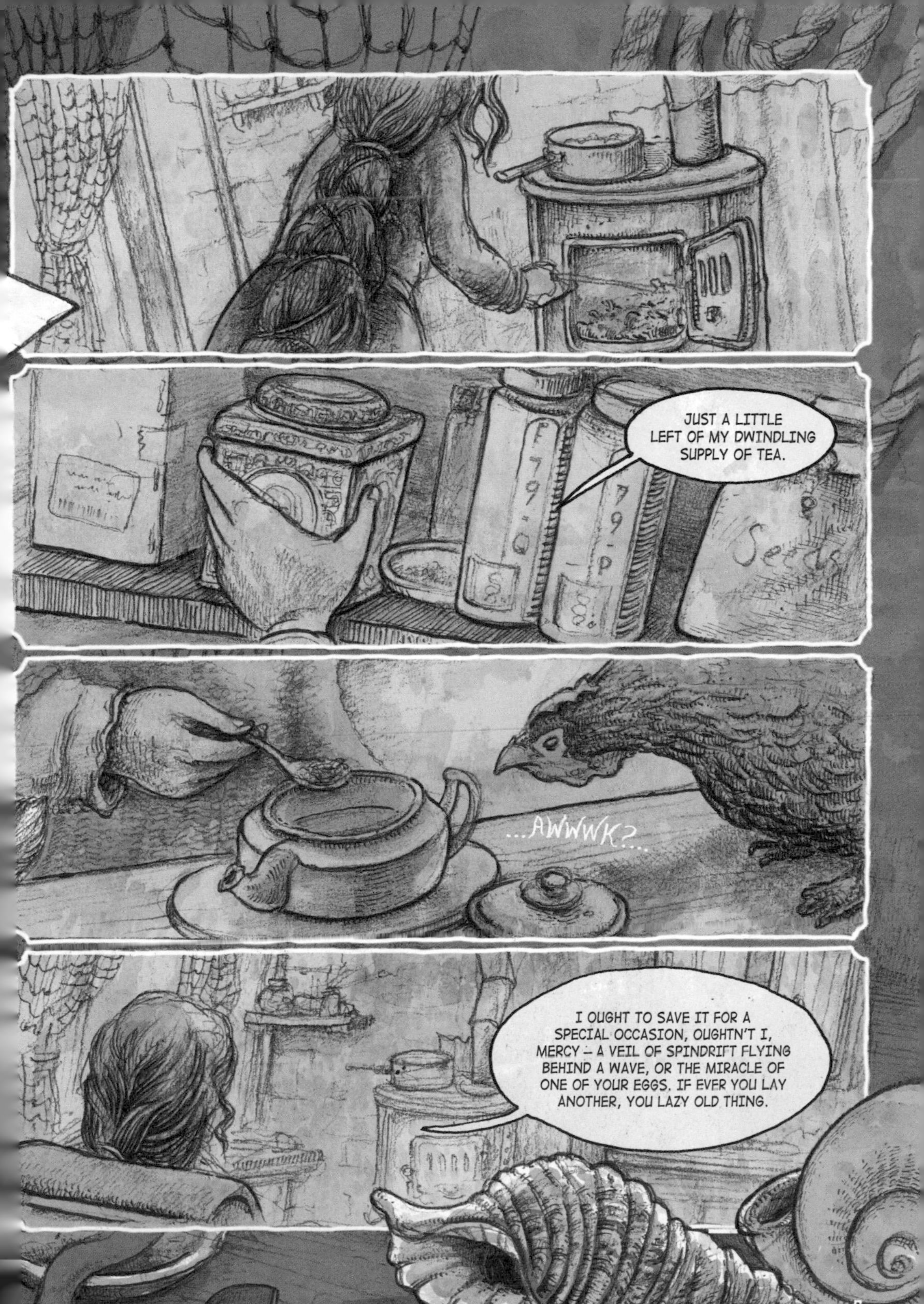
JUST A LITTLE LEFT OF MY DWINDLING SUPPLY OF TEA.
...AWWWK?...
I OUGHT TO SAVE IT FOR A SPECIAL OCCASION, OUGHTN'T I, MERCY – A VEIL OF SPINDRIFT FLYING BEHIND A WAVE, OR THE MIRACLE OF ONE OF YOUR EGGS. IF EVER YOU LAY ANOTHER, YOU LAZY OLD THING.

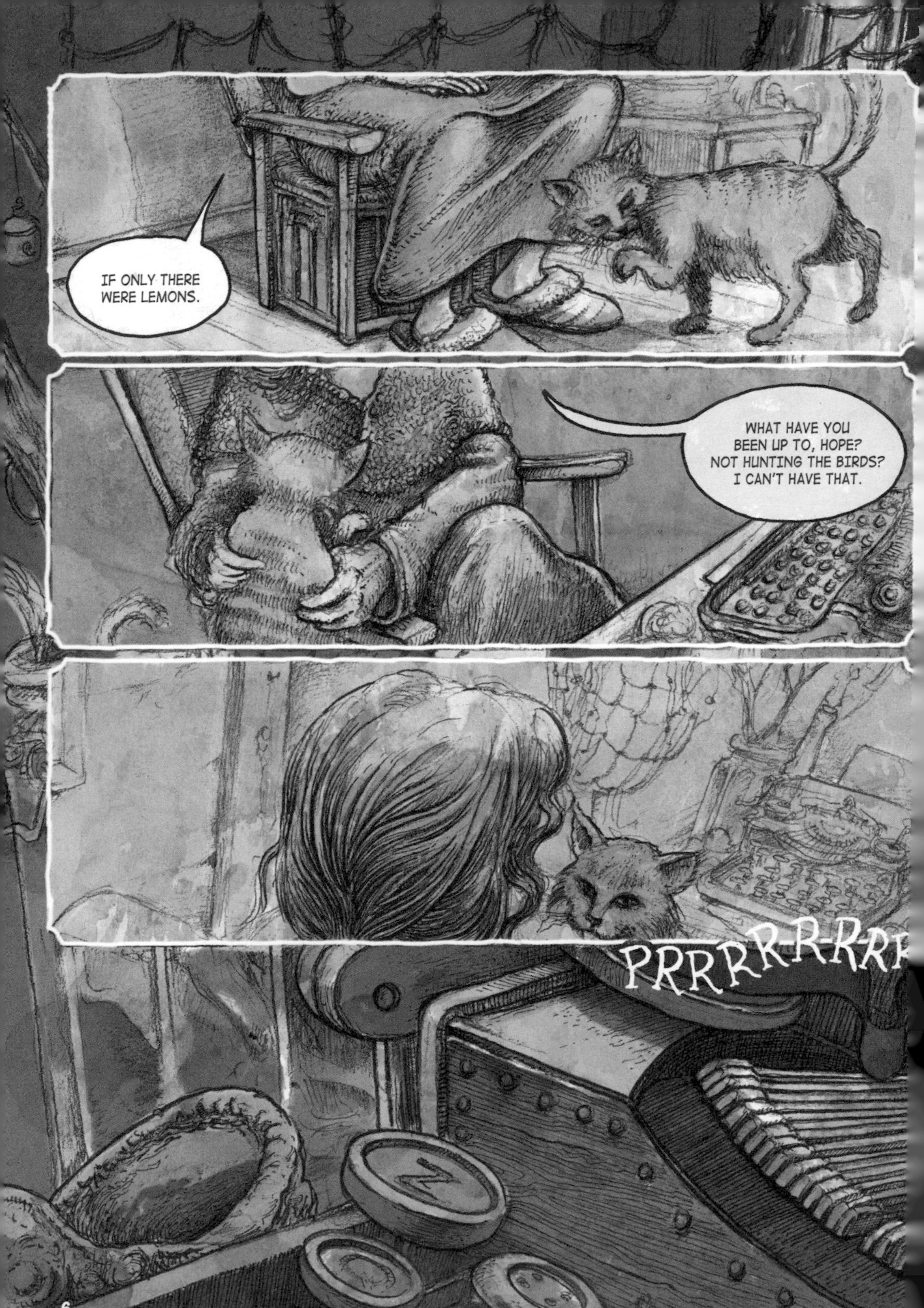
IF ONLY THERE WERE LEMONS.
WHAT HAVE YOU BEEN UP TO, HOPE? NOT HUNTING THE BIRDS? I CAN'T HAVE THAT.
PRRRR-R-RRR

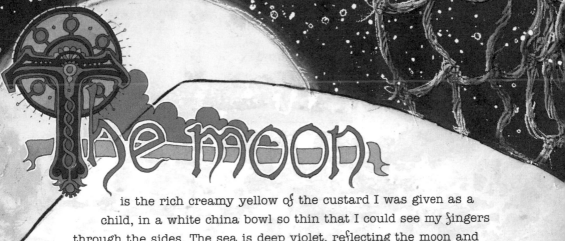

The moon

is the rich creamy yellow of the custard I was given as a child, in a white china bowl so thin that I could see my fingers through the sides. The sea is deep violet, reflecting the moon and a glimmering dust of stars. I know it is not age that keeps me awake tonight, nor the heat. It is the dream I had last night of the tower. It makes me feel as if something is coming to change everything.

But what can change now? I am no longer young and, aside from the cat, nothing has come here to the end of the world since I did, thirty years ago. I am no longer a princess waiting for a prince to come and rescue me.

THAT'S RIGHT, ISN'T IT, HOPE? I HAVE A BACK THAT ACHES AND A KNEE THAT CAN'T BE TRUSTED. I AM TOO OLD FOR ANYTHING BUT DRINKING TEA AND STROKING A CAT.

In this heat and this uneasy wakefulness, my mind drifts. I ride the waves of memory back to that other night, long years past, when I lay in a chamber atop a white tower, between sheets of silk, under impossibly soft quilts; the booty of a lost world. It was very hot that night, too, so that eventually I threw off the quilts.

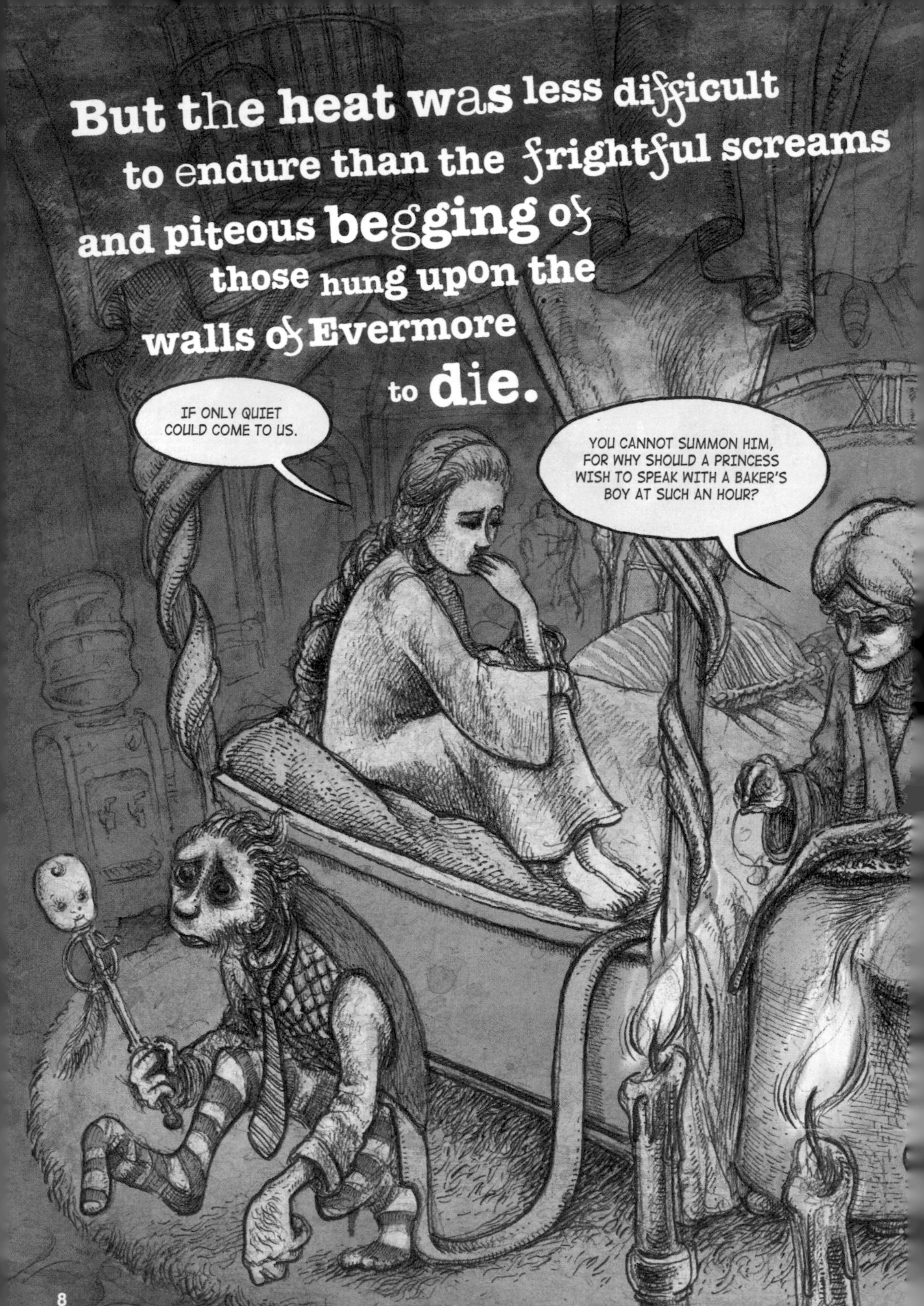
But the heat was less difficult to endure than the frightful screams and piteous begging of those hung upon the walls of Evermore to die.
IF ONLY QUIET COULD COME TO US.
YOU CANNOT SUMMON HIM, FOR WHY SHOULD A PRINCESS WISH TO SPEAK WITH A BAKER'S BOY AT SUCH AN HOUR?

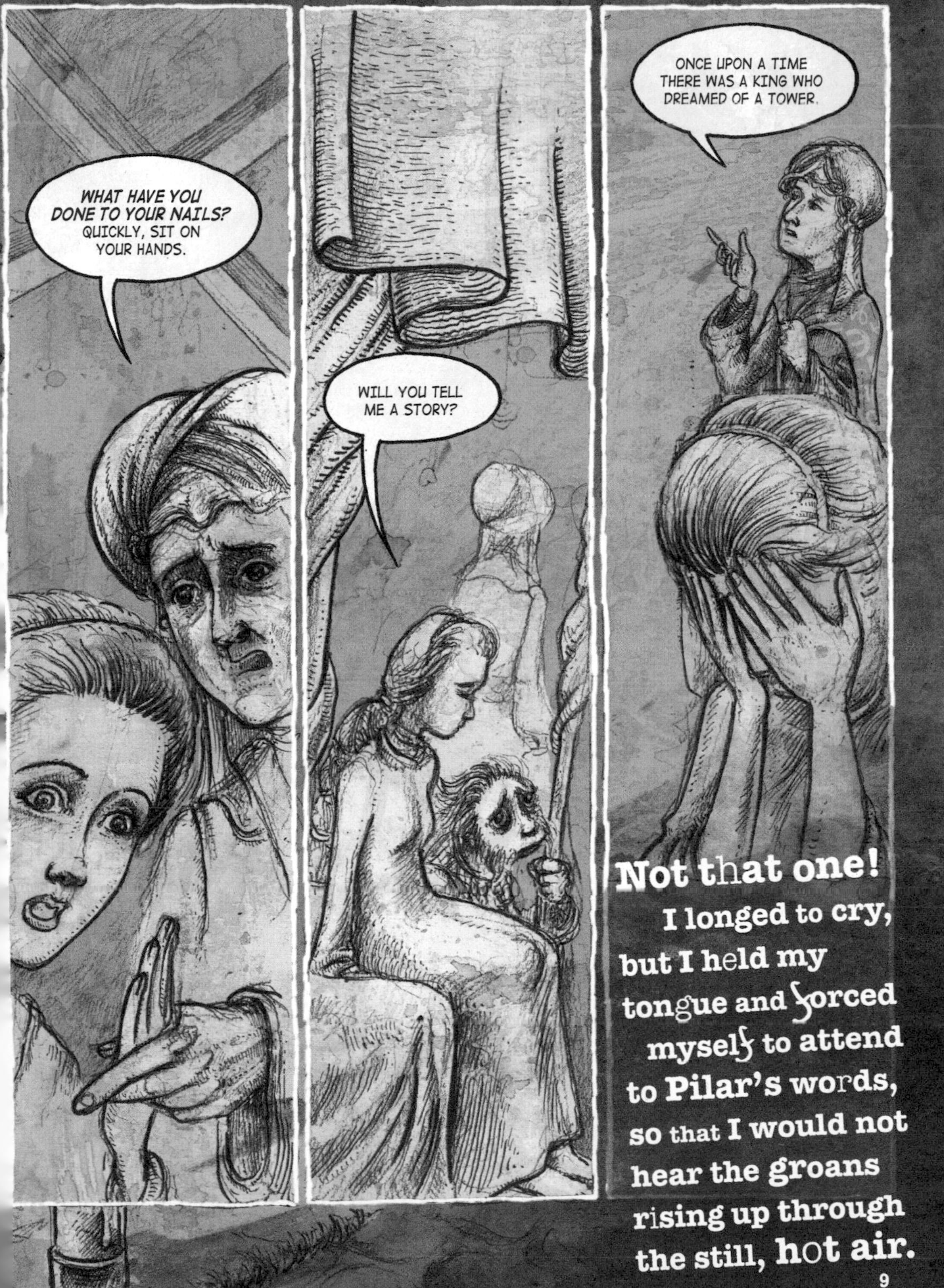
WHAT HAVE YOU DONE TO YOUR NAILS? QUICKLY, SIT ON YOUR HANDS.
WILL YOU TELL ME A STORY?
ONCE UPON A TIME THERE WAS A KING WHO DREAMED OF A TOWER.
Not that one! I longed to cry, but I held my tongue and forced myself to attend to Pilar's words, so that I would not hear the groans rising up through the still, hot air.

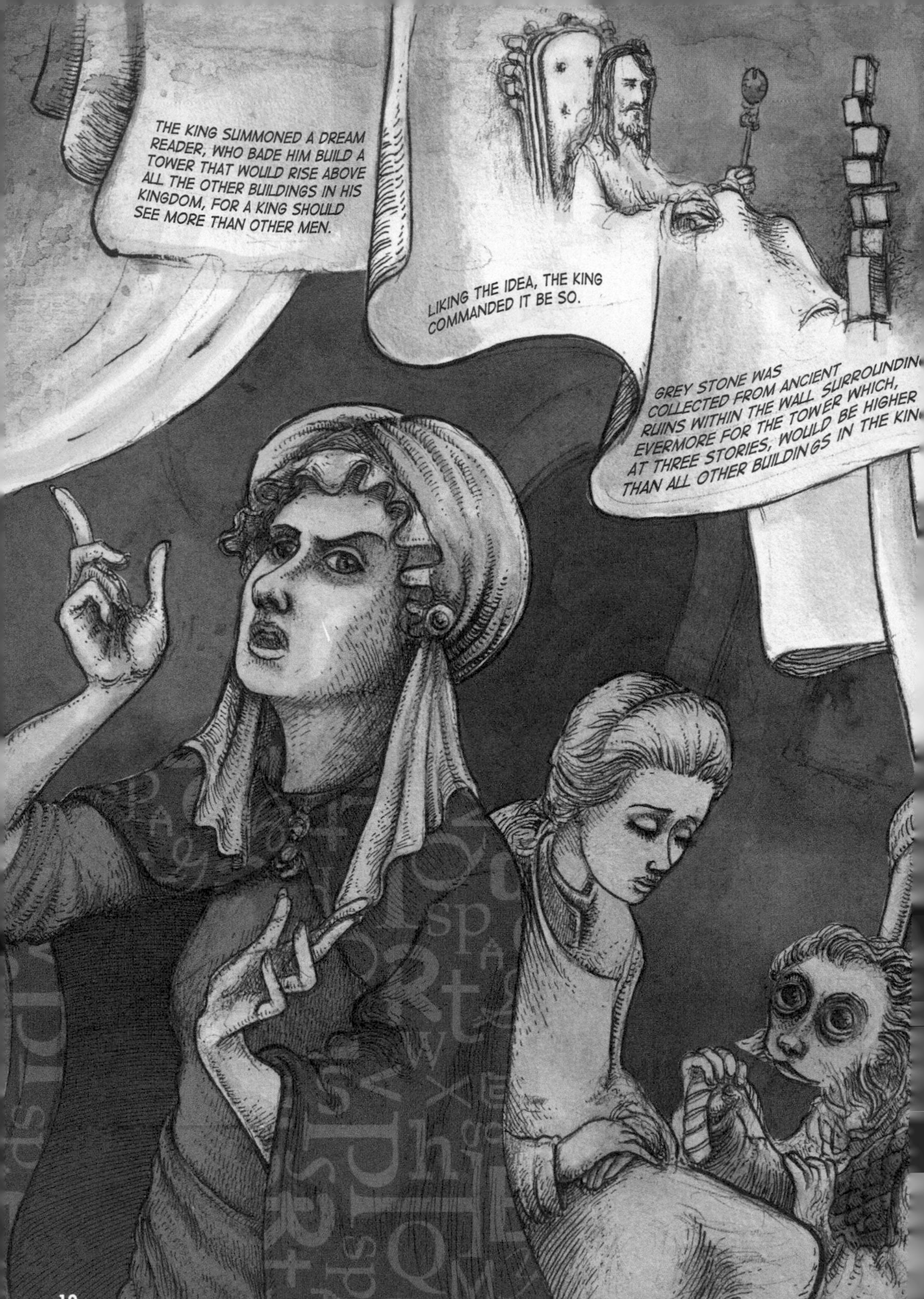
THE KING SUMMONED A DREAM READER, WHO BADE HIM BUILD A TOWER THAT WOULD RISE ABOVE ALL THE OTHER BUILDINGS IN HIS KINGDOM, FOR A KING SHOULD SEE MORE THAN OTHER MEN.
LIKING THE IDEA, THE KING COMMANDED IT BE SO.
GREY STONE WAS COLLECTED FROM ANCIENT RUINS WITHIN THE WALL SURROUNDIN EVERMORE FOR THE TOWER WHICH, AT THREE STORIES, WOULD BE HIGHER THAN ALL OTHER BUILDINGS IN THE KIN

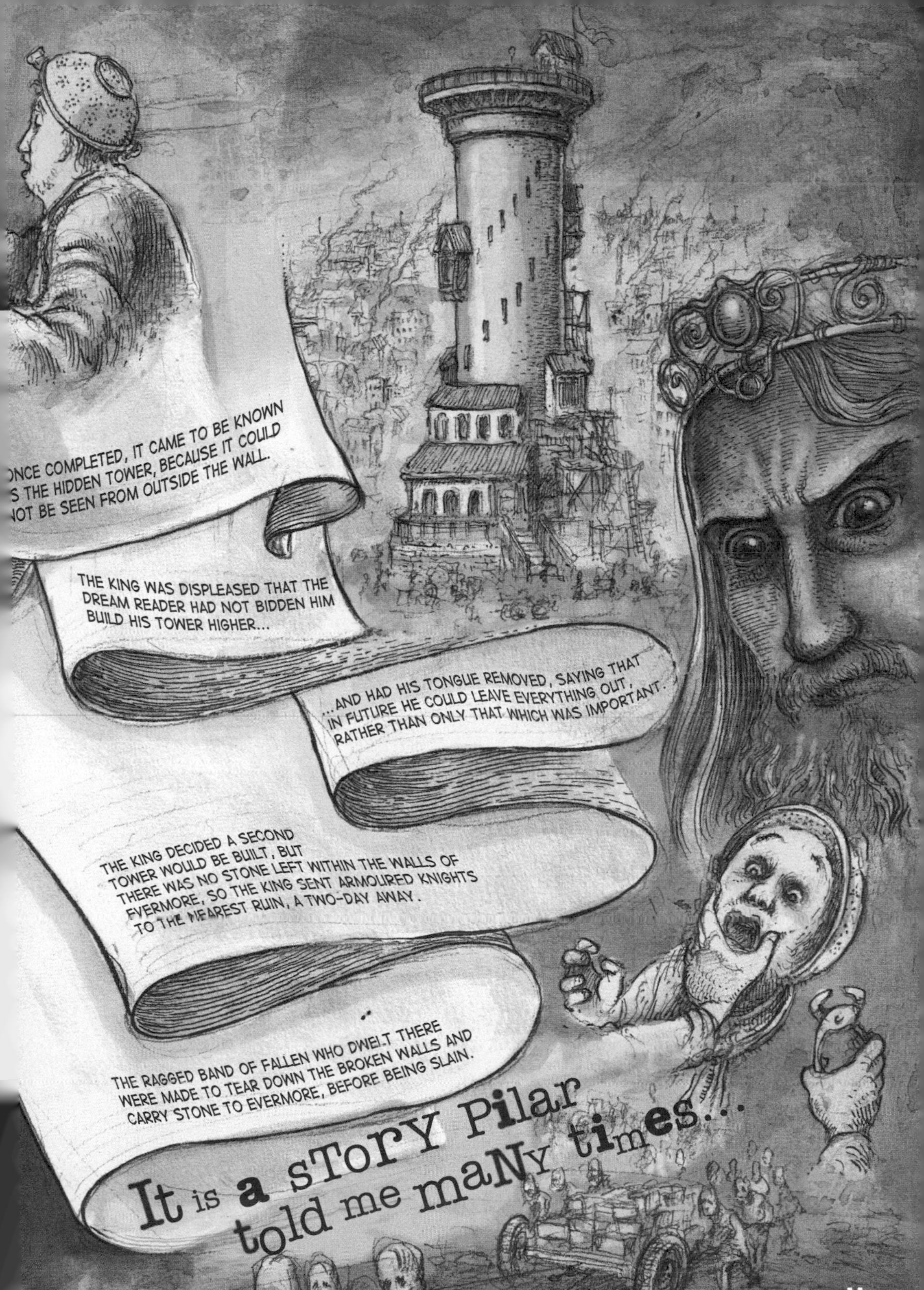
ONCE COMPLETED, IT CAME TO BE KNOWN
S THE HIDDEN TOWER, BECAUSE IT COULD
NOT BE SEEN FROM OUTSIDE THE WALL.
THE KING WAS DISPLEASED THAT THE
DREAM READER HAD NOT BIDDEN HIM
BUILD HIS TOWER HIGHER...
...AND HAD HIS TONGUE REMOVED, SAYING THAT
IN FUTURE HE COULD LEAVE EVERYTHING OUT,
RATHER THAN ONLY THAT WHICH WAS IMPORTANT.
THE KING DECIDED A SECOND
TOWER WOULD BE BUILT, BUT
THERE WAS NO STONE LEFT WITHIN THE WALLS OF
EVERMORE, SO THE KING SENT ARMOURED KNIGHTS
TO THE NEAREST RUIN, A TWO-DAY AWAY.
THE RAGGED BAND OF FALLEN WHO DWELT THERE
WERE MADE TO TEAR DOWN THE BROKEN WALLS AND
CARRY STONE TO EVERMORE, BEFORE BEING SLAIN.
It is a sTorY Pilar
told me maNy times...

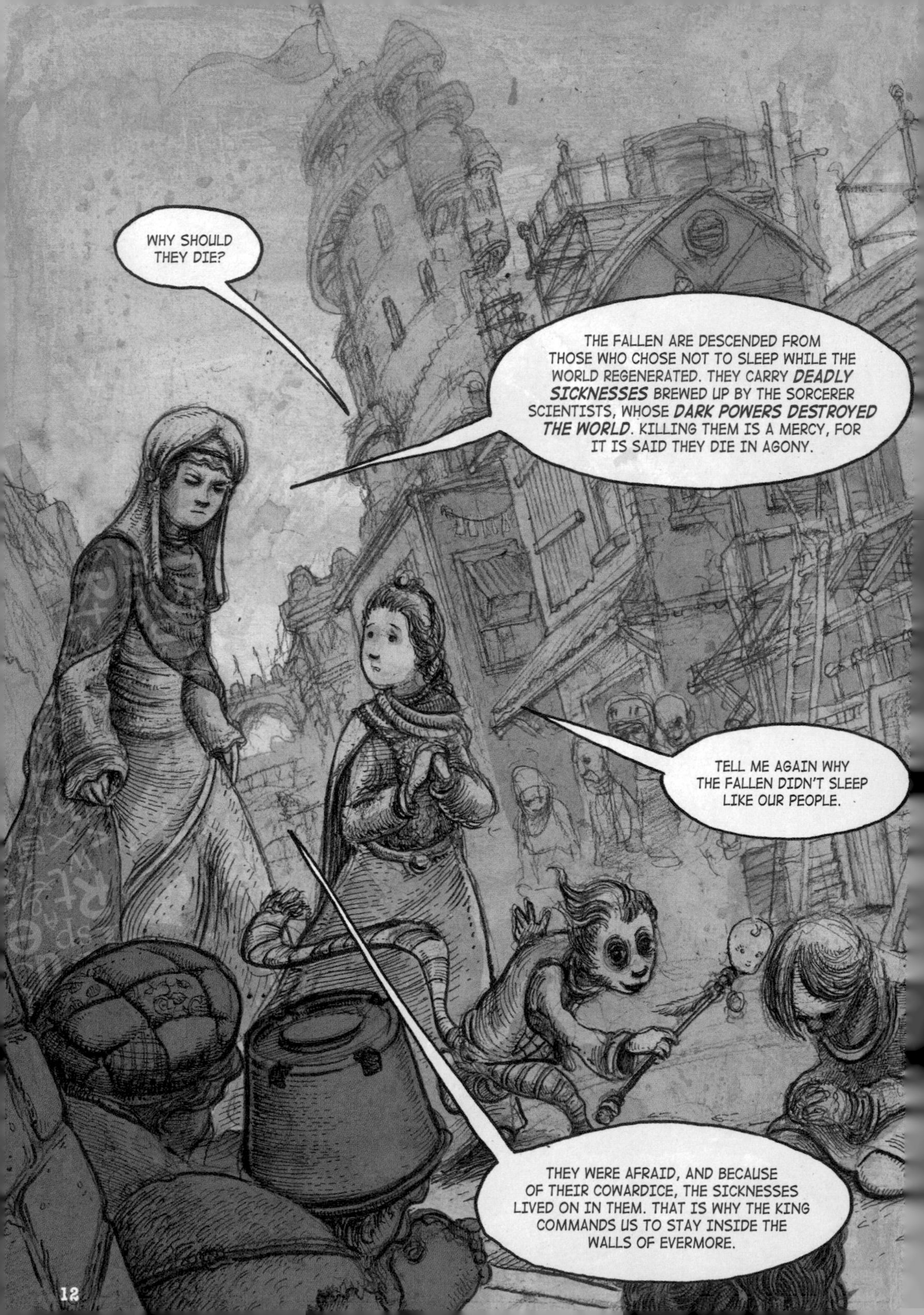
WHY SHOULD THEY DIE?
THE FALLEN ARE DESCENDED FROM THOSE WHO CHOSE NOT TO SLEEP WHILE THE WORLD REGENERATED. THEY CARRY ***DEADLY SICKNESSES*** BREWED UP BY THE SORCERER SCIENTISTS, WHOSE ***DARK POWERS DESTROYED THE WORLD***. KILLING THEM IS A MERCY, FOR IT IS SAID THEY DIE IN AGONY.
TELL ME AGAIN WHY THE FALLEN DIDN'T SLEEP LIKE OUR PEOPLE.
THEY WERE AFRAID, AND BECAUSE OF THEIR COWARDICE, THE SICKNESSES LIVED ON IN THEM. THAT IS WHY THE KING COMMANDS US TO STAY INSIDE THE WALLS OF EVERMORE.

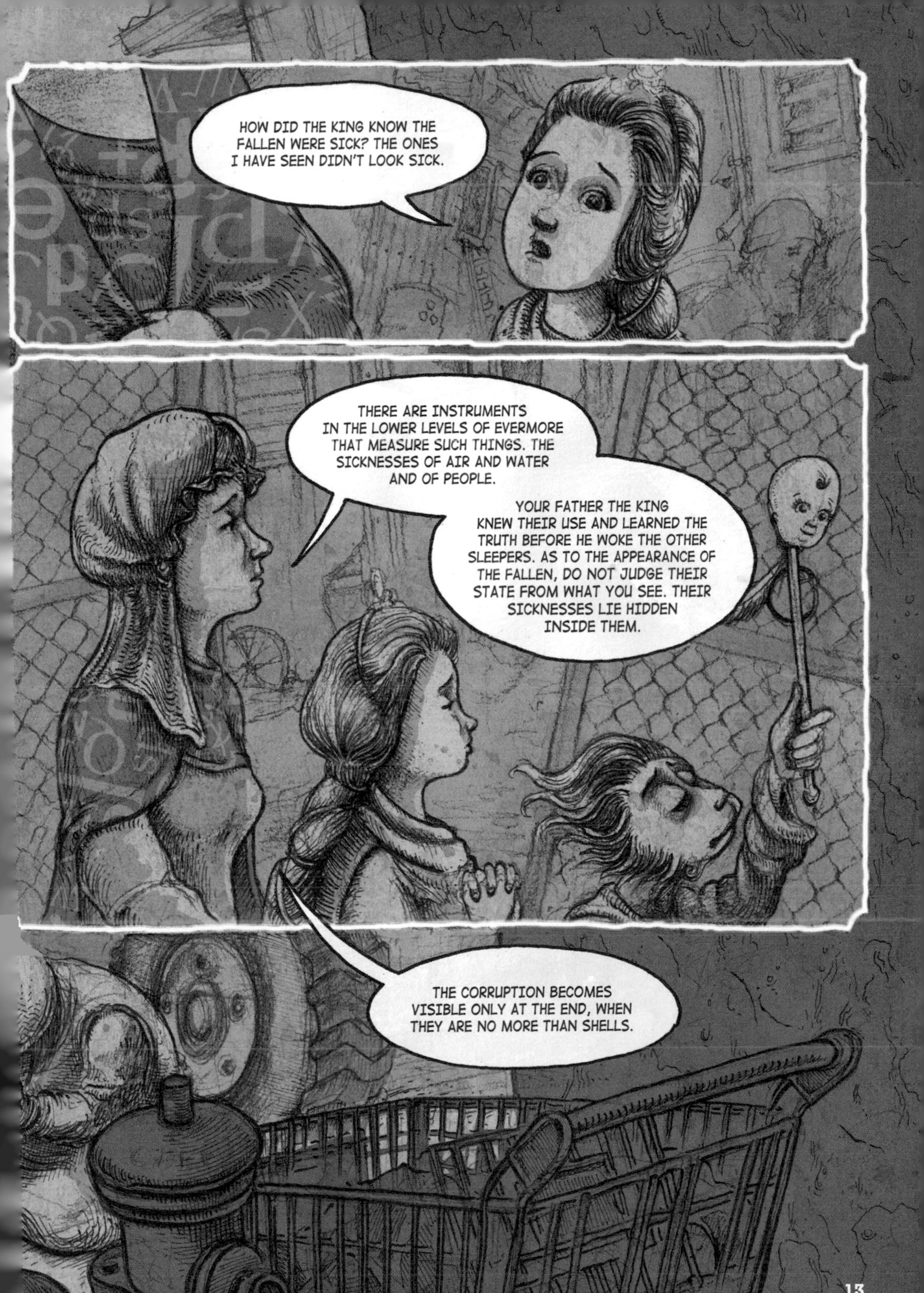

HOW DID THE KING KNOW THE FALLEN WERE SICK? THE ONES I HAVE SEEN DIDN'T LOOK SICK.
THERE ARE INSTRUMENTS IN THE LOWER LEVELS OF EVERMORE THAT MEASURE SUCH THINGS. THE SICKNESSES OF AIR AND WATER AND OF PEOPLE.
YOUR FATHER THE KING KNEW THEIR USE AND LEARNED THE TRUTH BEFORE HE WOKE THE OTHER SLEEPERS. AS TO THE APPEARANCE OF THE FALLEN, DO NOT JUDGE THEIR STATE FROM WHAT YOU SEE. THEIR SICKNESSES LIE HIDDEN INSIDE THEM.
THE CORRUPTION BECOMES VISIBLE ONLY AT THE END, WHEN THEY ARE NO MORE THAN SHELLS.

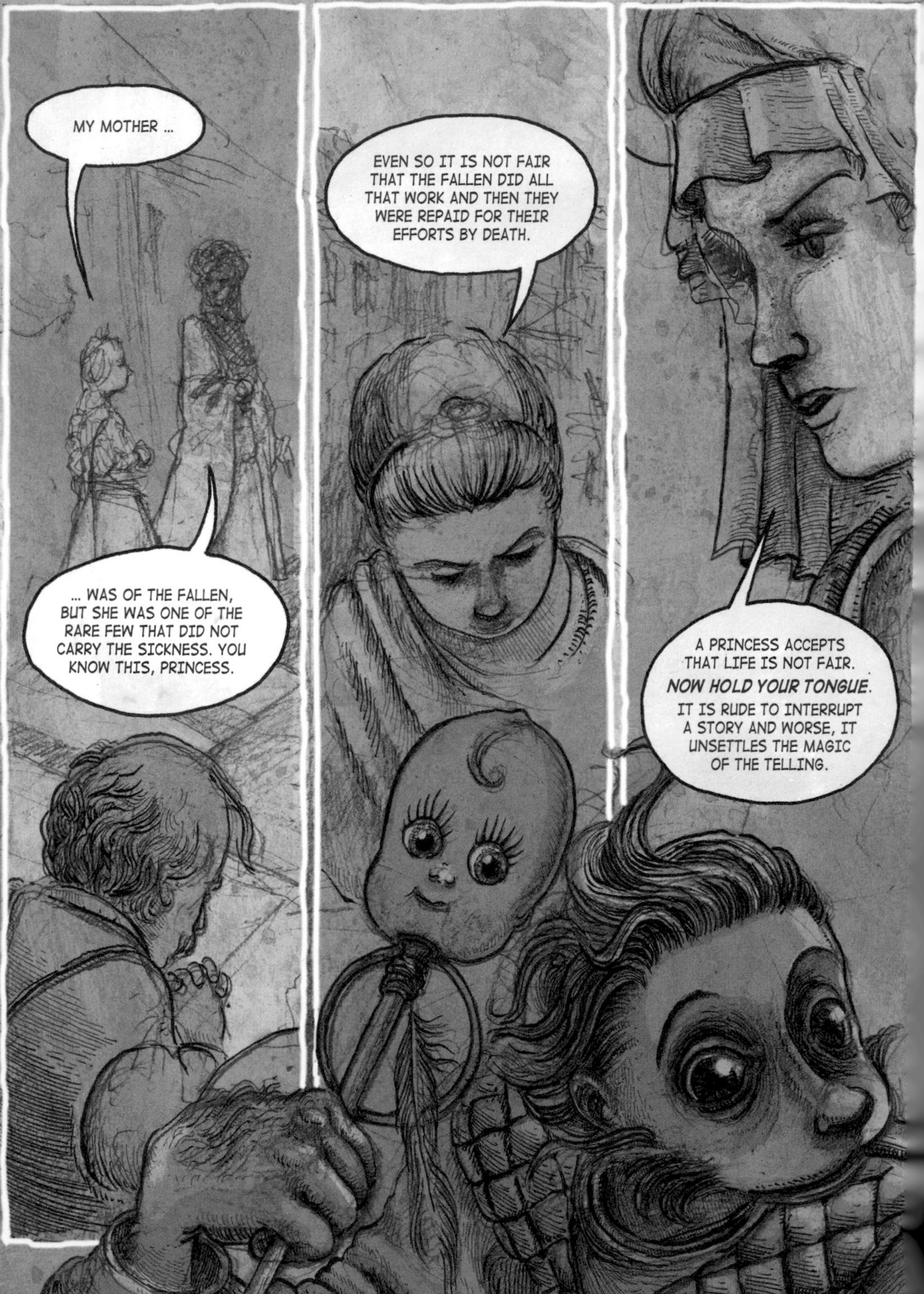

MY MOTHER ...
... WAS OF THE FALLEN, BUT SHE WAS ONE OF THE RARE FEW THAT DID NOT CARRY THE SICKNESS. YOU KNOW THIS, PRINCESS.
EVEN SO IT IS NOT FAIR THAT THE FALLEN DID ALL THAT WORK AND THEN THEY WERE REPAID FOR THEIR EFFORTS BY DEATH.
A PRINCESS ACCEPTS THAT LIFE IS NOT FAIR. *NOW HOLD YOUR TONGUE*. IT IS RUDE TO INTERRUPT A STORY AND WORSE, IT UNSETTLES THE MAGIC OF THE TELLING.

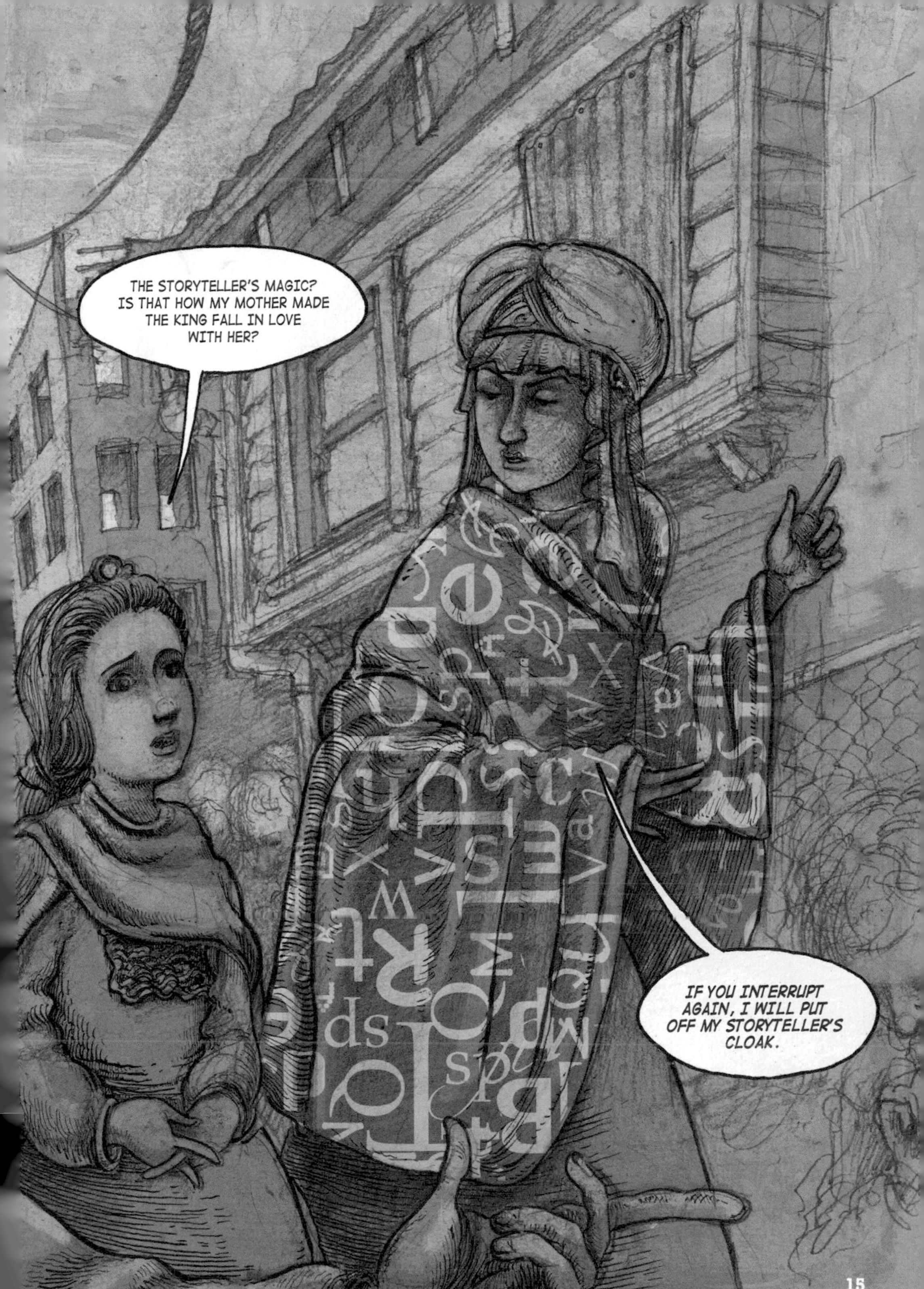
THE STORYTELLER'S MAGIC? IS THAT HOW MY MOTHER MADE THE KING FALL IN LOVE WITH HER?
IF YOU INTERRUPT AGAIN, I WILL PUT OFF MY STORYTELLER'S CLOAK.

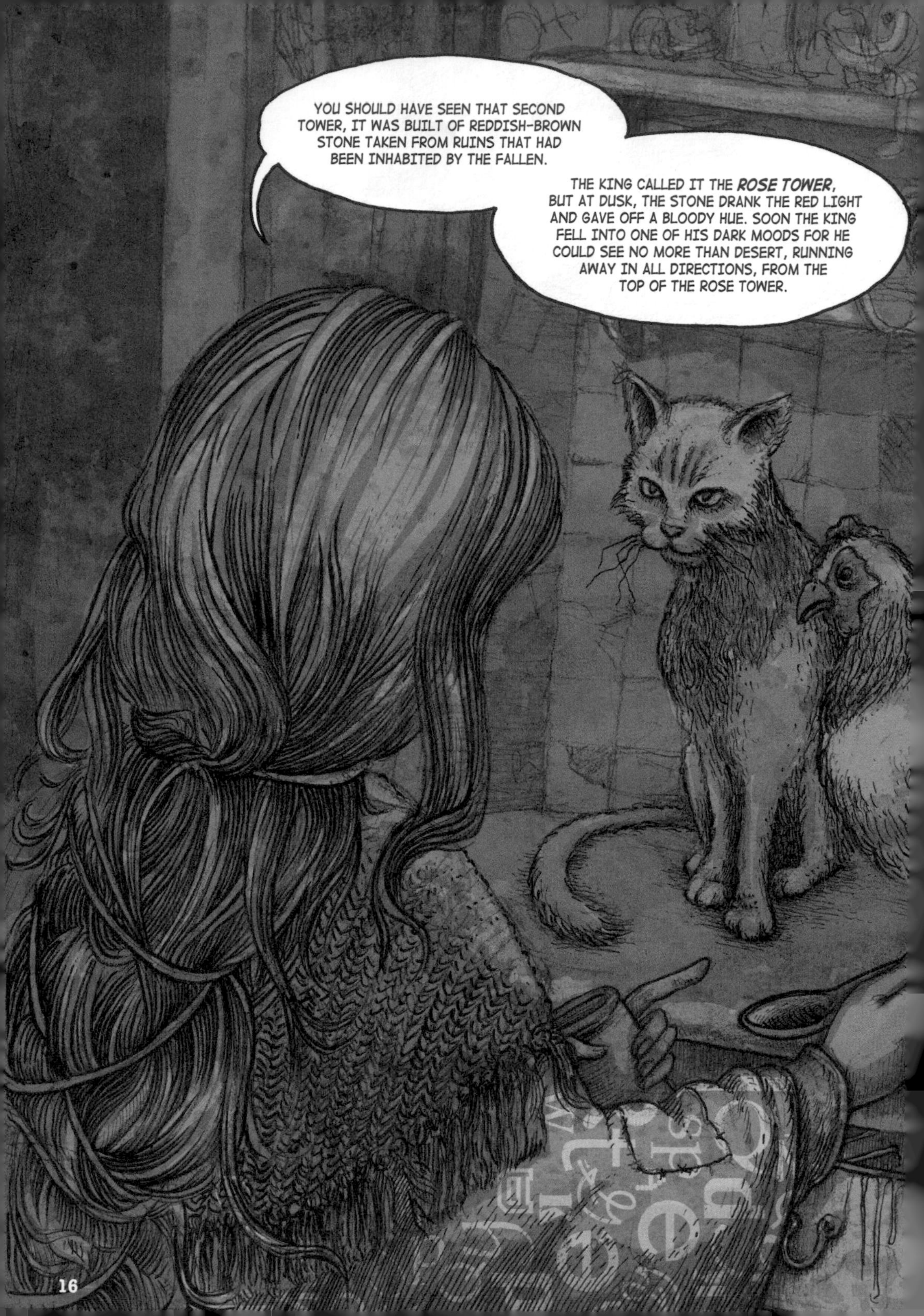
YOU SHOULD HAVE SEEN THAT SECOND TOWER, IT WAS BUILT OF REDDISH-BROWN STONE TAKEN FROM RUINS THAT HAD BEEN INHABITED BY THE FALLEN.
THE KING CALLED IT THE ROSE TOWER, BUT AT DUSK, THE STONE DRANK THE RED LIGHT AND GAVE OFF A BLOODY HUE. SOON THE KING FELL INTO ONE OF HIS DARK MOODS FOR HE COULD SEE NO MORE THAN DESERT, RUNNING AWAY IN ALL DIRECTIONS, FROM THE TOP OF THE ROSE TOWER.

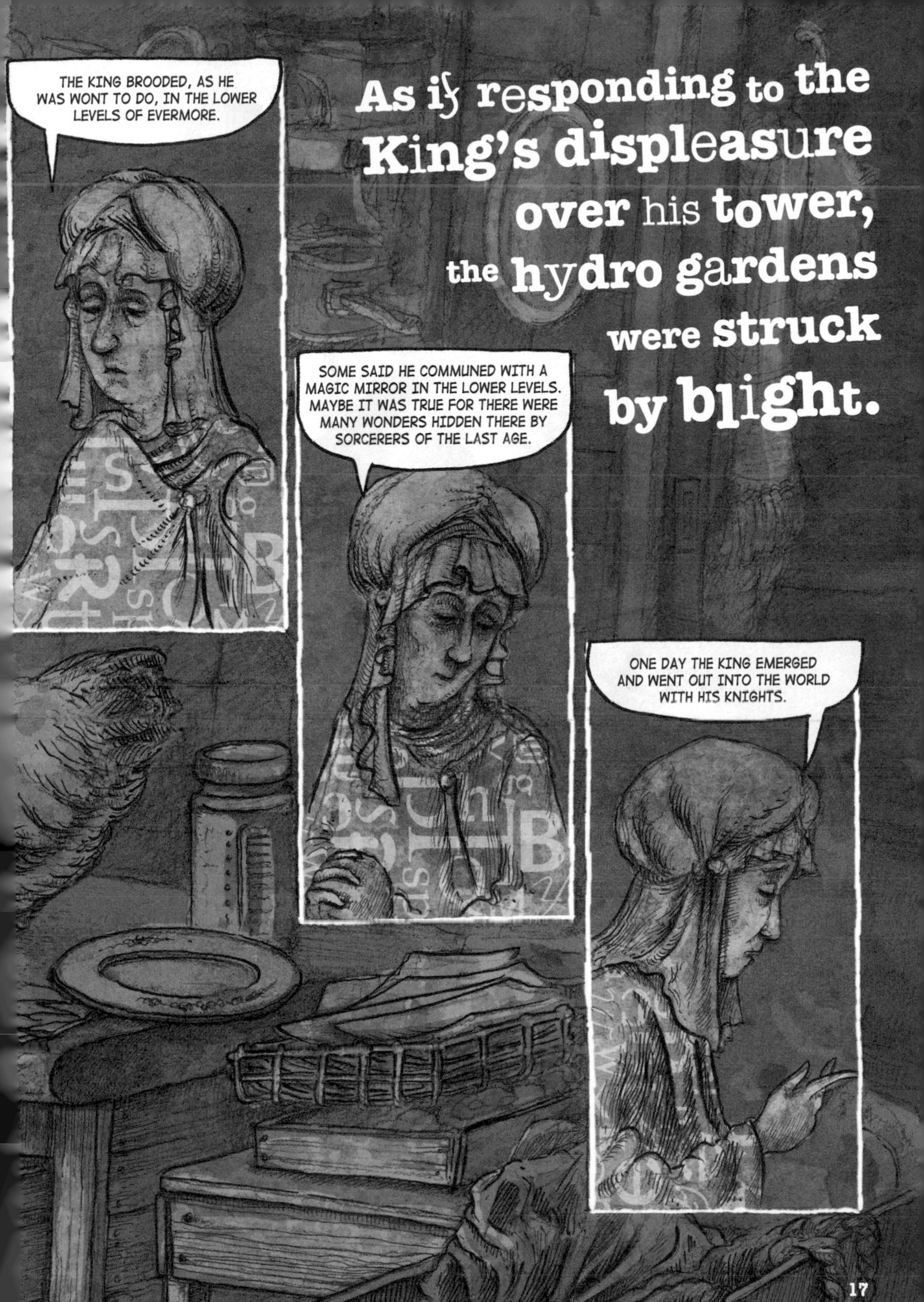

THE KING BROODED, AS HE WAS WONT TO DO, IN THE LOWER LEVELS OF EVERMORE.
As if responding to the King's displeasure over his tower, the hydro gardens were struck by blight.
SOME SAID HE COMMUNED WITH A MAGIC MIRROR IN THE LOWER LEVELS. MAYBE IT WAS TRUE FOR THERE WERE MANY WONDERS HIDDEN THERE BY SORCERERS OF THE LAST AGE.
ONE DAY THE KING EMERGED AND WENT OUT INTO THE WORLD WITH HIS KNIGHTS.

At length

after many long, uneasy days, the King returned to Evermore with another cache of food and the announcement that a third tower would be constructed from the white stone of the ruins where the food cache had been found. Since the fallen from the red ruins had been slain, the knights themselves had to carry back the stone. No one else could go, for the knights alone had armour, brought up from the lower levels of Evermore by the King, to keep them safe from the sicknesses and poisons outside the walls. The poisons had faded as the sleepers slept, but according to the King, the activities of the fallen caused the spilling and releasing of new poisons. The fetching and carrying was hot, hard work, for a great deal of stone was needed for this tower, which was to be half as high again as the Rose Tower.

No one complained or protested, for the King had the power of life and death. Had he not wakened the sleepers and brought them from darkness into the light? And he alone knew how to find the ancient food caches to sustain the kingdom when the hydro-gardens faltered.

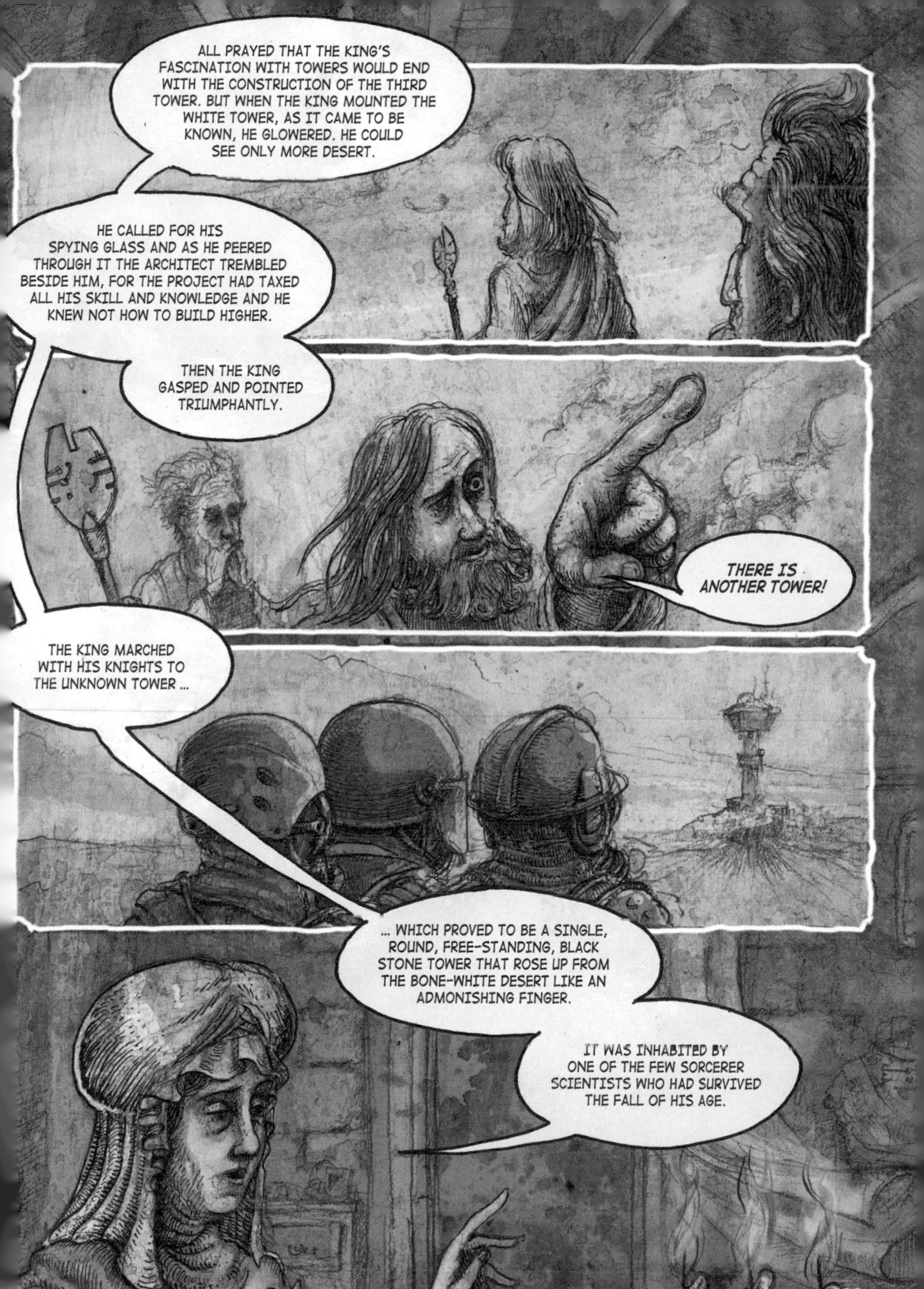
ALL PRAYED THAT THE KING'S FASCINATION WITH TOWERS WOULD END WITH THE CONSTRUCTION OF THE THIRD TOWER. BUT WHEN THE KING MOUNTED THE WHITE TOWER, AS IT CAME TO BE KNOWN, HE GLOWERED. HE COULD SEE ONLY MORE DESERT.
HE CALLED FOR HIS SPYING GLASS AND AS HE PEERED THROUGH IT THE ARCHITECT TREMBLED BESIDE HIM, FOR THE PROJECT HAD TAXED ALL HIS SKILL AND KNOWLEDGE AND HE KNEW NOT HOW TO BUILD HIGHER.
THEN THE KING GASPED AND POINTED TRIUMPHANTLY.
THERE IS ANOTHER TOWER!
THE KING MARCHED WITH HIS KNIGHTS TO THE UNKNOWN TOWER ...
... WHICH PROVED TO BE A SINGLE, ROUND, FREE-STANDING, BLACK STONE TOWER THAT ROSE UP FROM THE BONE-WHITE DESERT LIKE AN ADMONISHING FINGER.
IT WAS INHABITED BY ONE OF THE FEW SORCERER SCIENTISTS WHO HAD SURVIVED THE FALL OF HIS AGE.

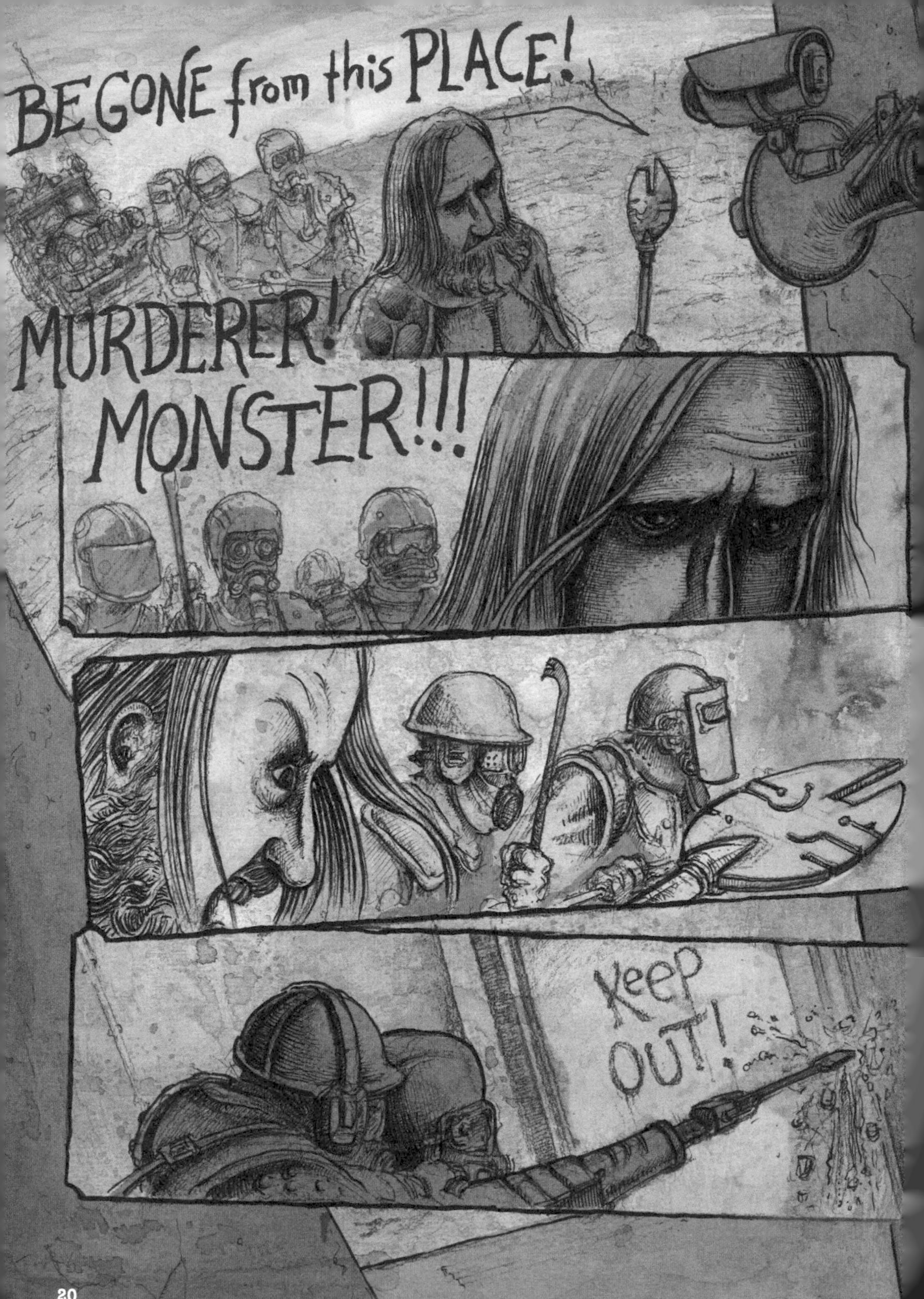
BEGONE from this PLACE!
MURDERER!
MONSTER!!!
Keep OUT!

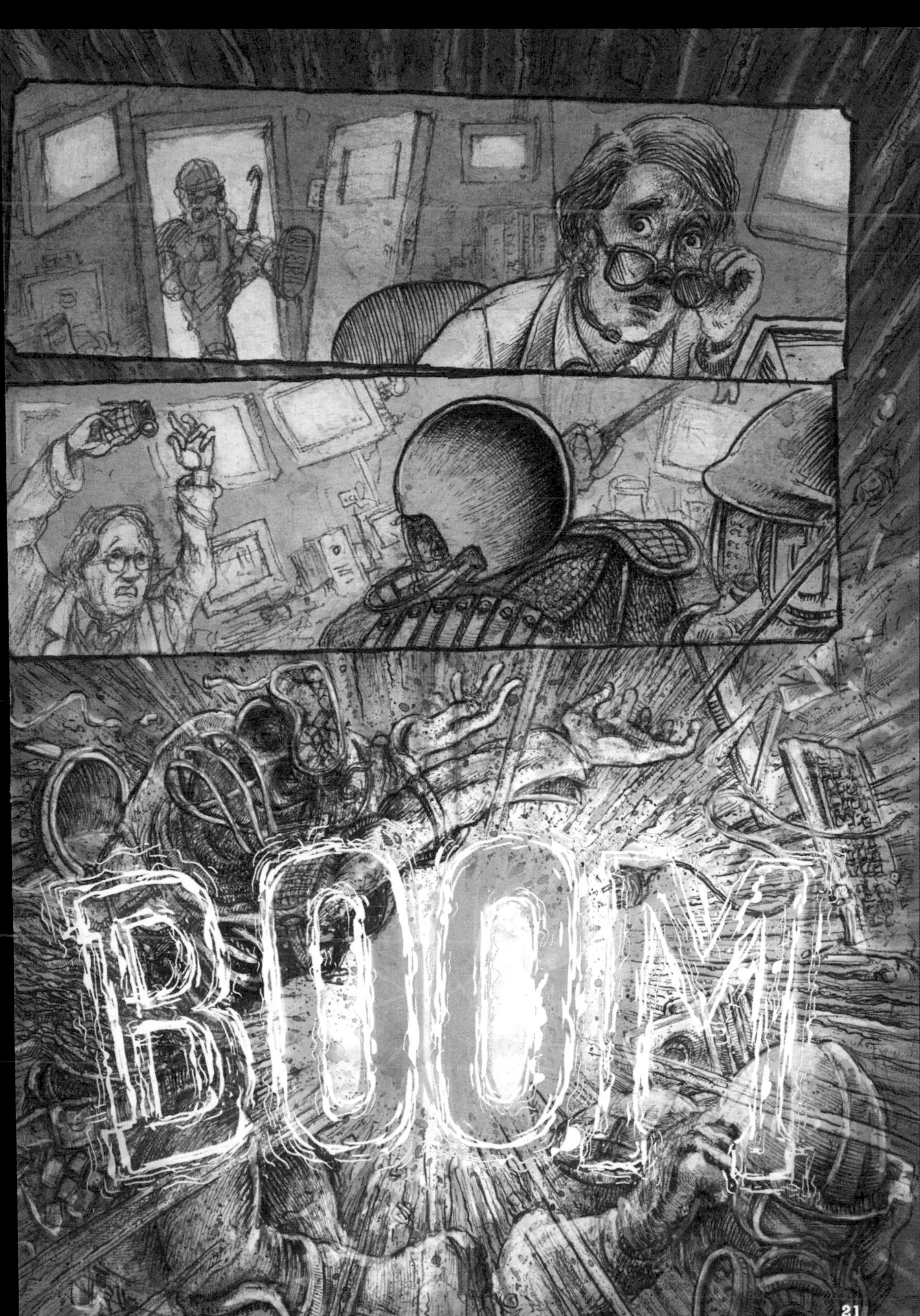
BOOM

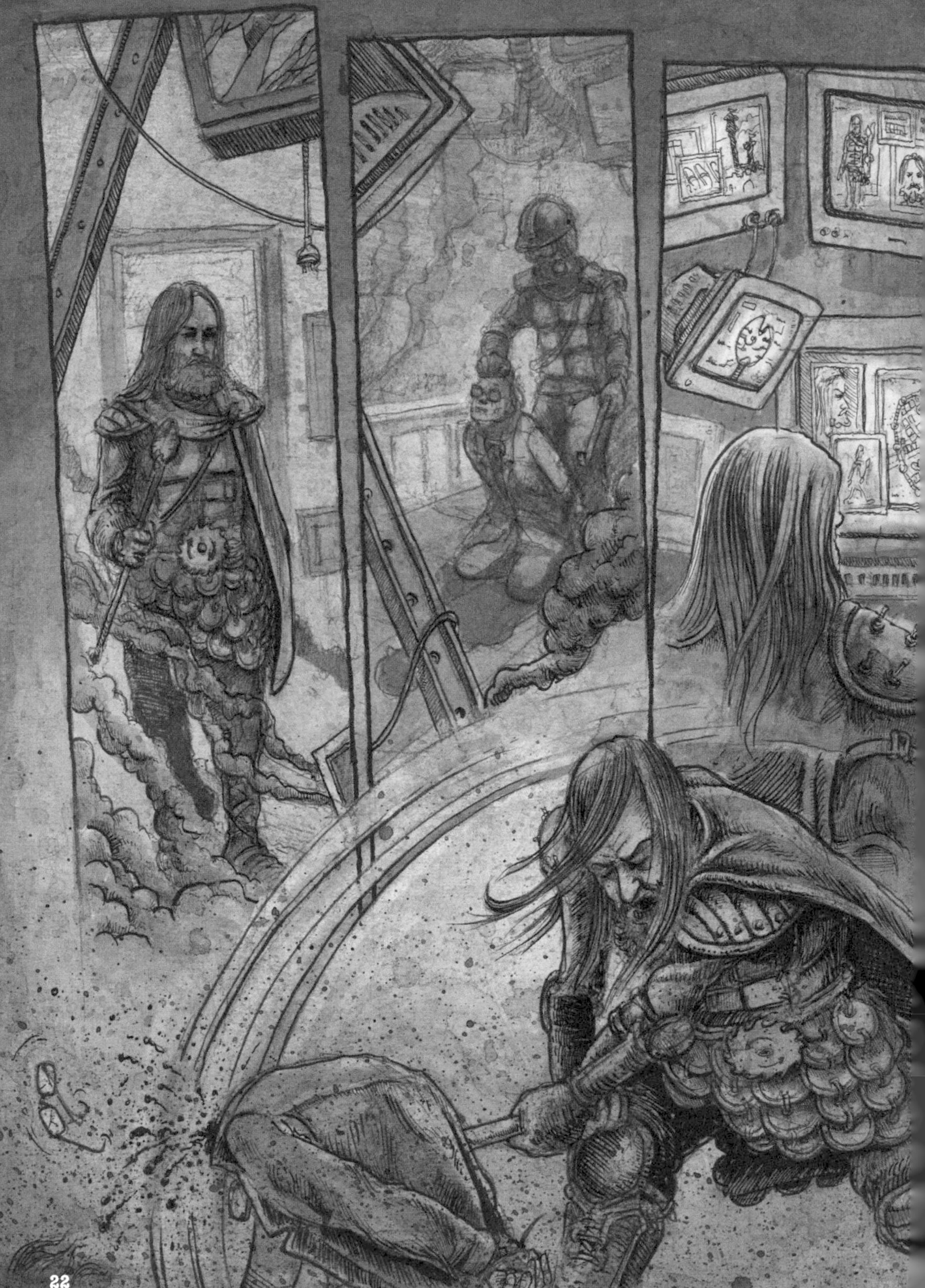

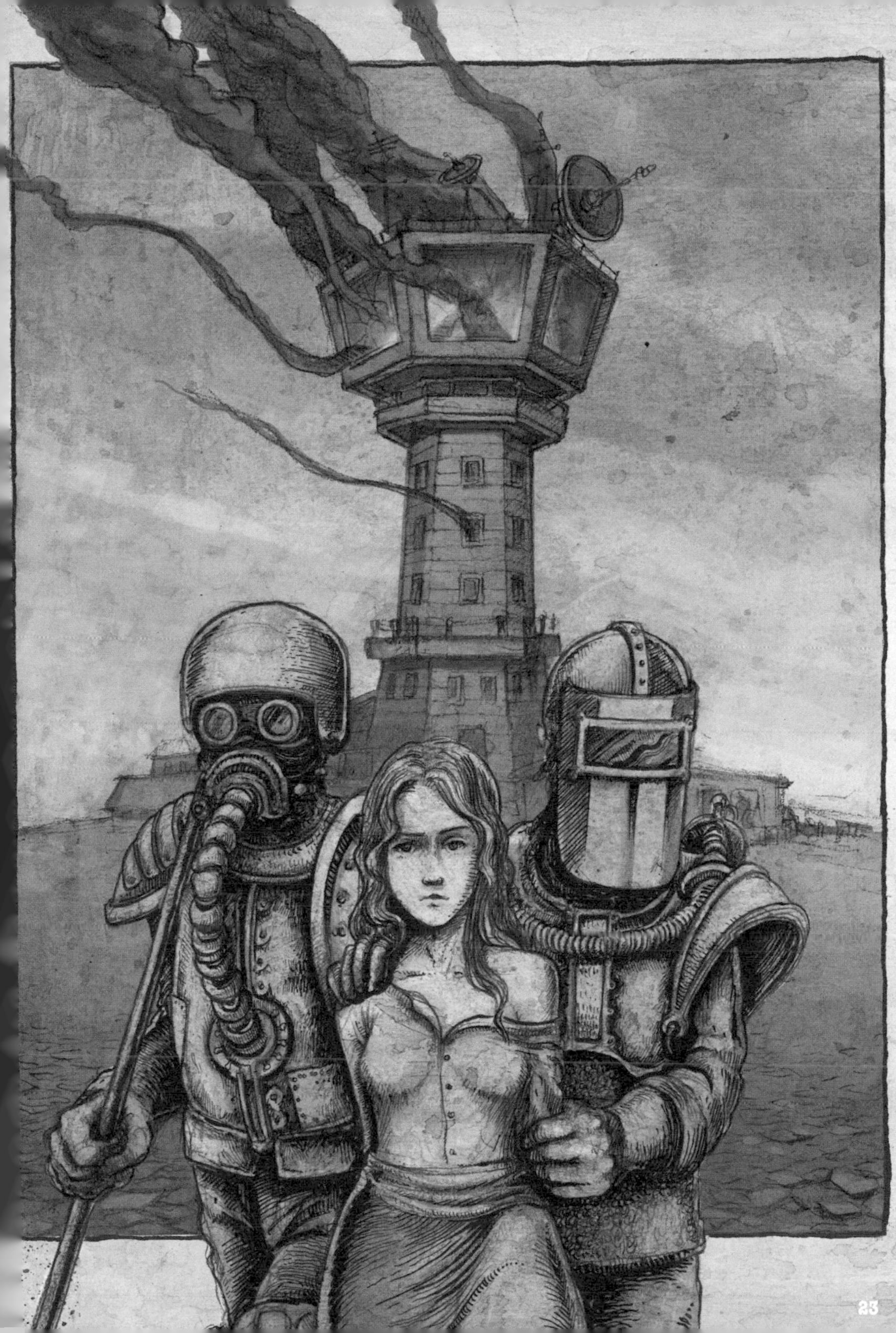

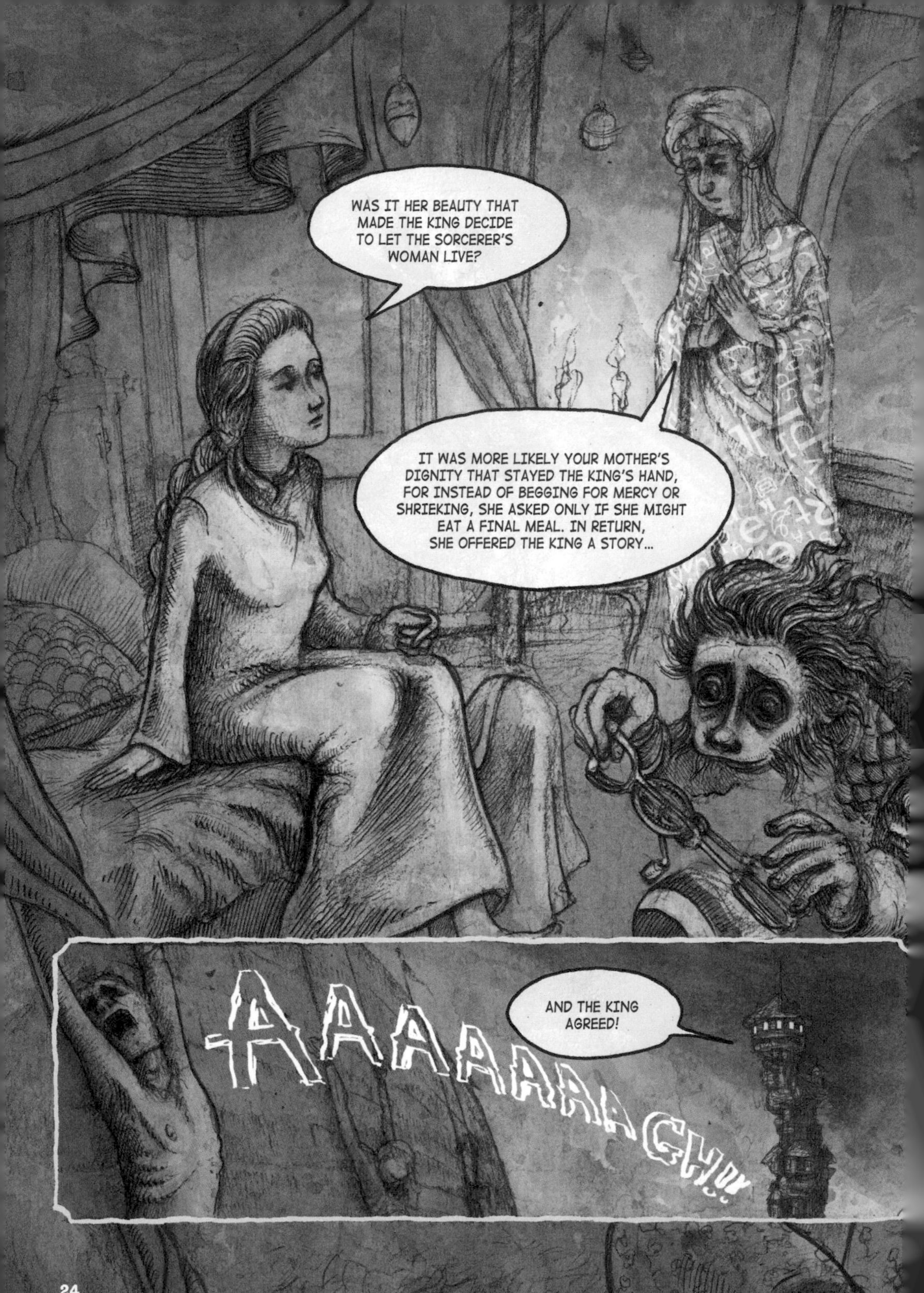
WAS IT HER BEAUTY THAT MADE THE KING DECIDE TO LET THE SORCERER'S WOMAN LIVE?
IT WAS MORE LIKELY YOUR MOTHER'S DIGNITY THAT STAYED THE KING'S HAND, FOR INSTEAD OF BEGGING FOR MERCY OR SHRIEKING, SHE ASKED ONLY IF SHE MIGHT EAT A FINAL MEAL. IN RETURN, SHE OFFERED THE KING A STORY...
AAAAAAAAGH!!
AND THE KING AGREED!

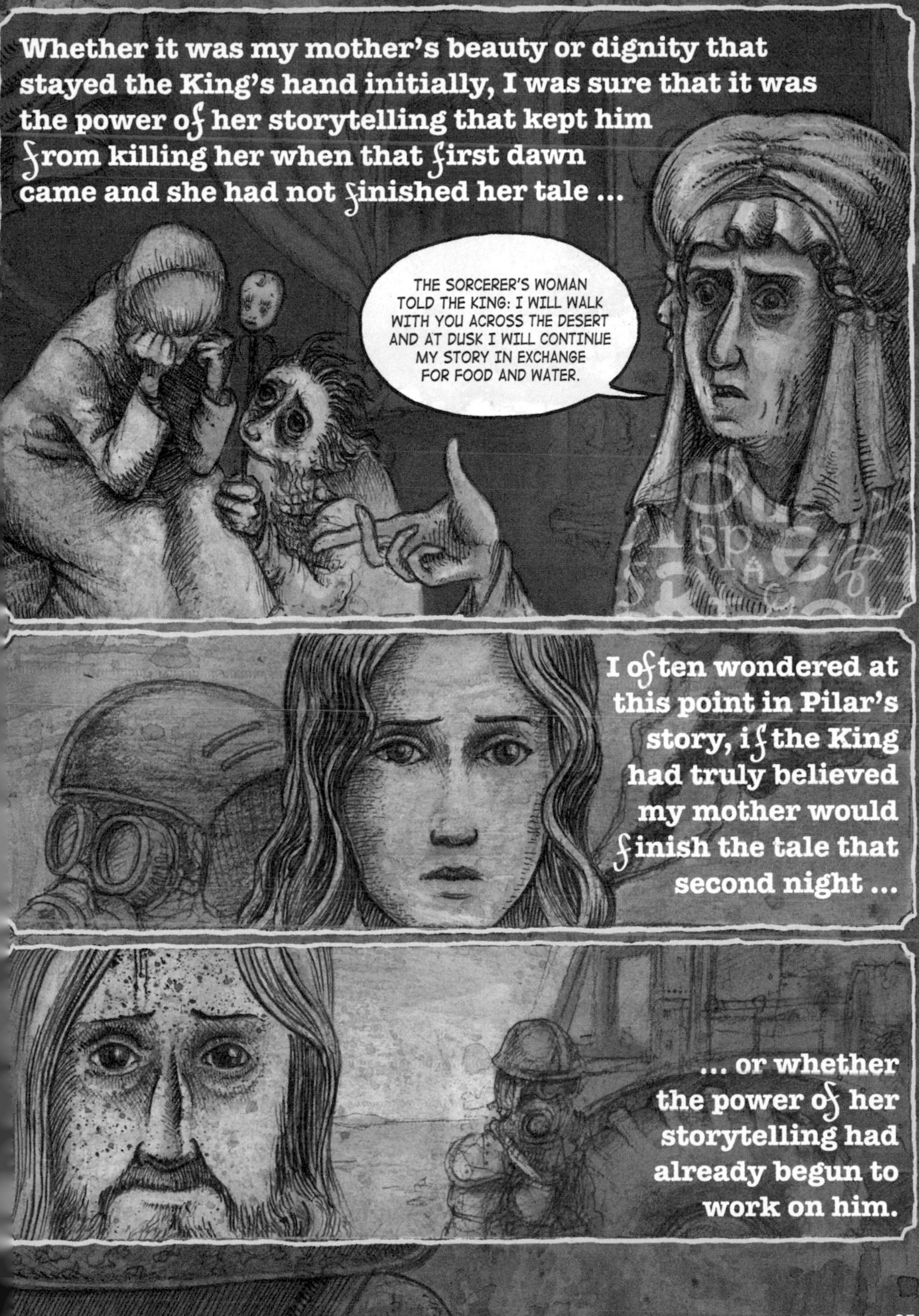
Whether it was my mother's beauty or dignity that stayed the King's hand initially, I was sure that it was the power of her storytelling that kept him from killing her when that first dawn came and she had not finished her tale ...
THE SORCERER'S WOMAN TOLD THE KING: I WILL WALK WITH YOU ACROSS THE DESERT AND AT DUSK I WILL CONTINUE MY STORY IN EXCHANGE FOR FOOD AND WATER.
I often wondered at this point in Pilar's story, if the King had truly believed my mother would finish the tale that second night ...
... or whether the power of her storytelling had already begun to work on him.

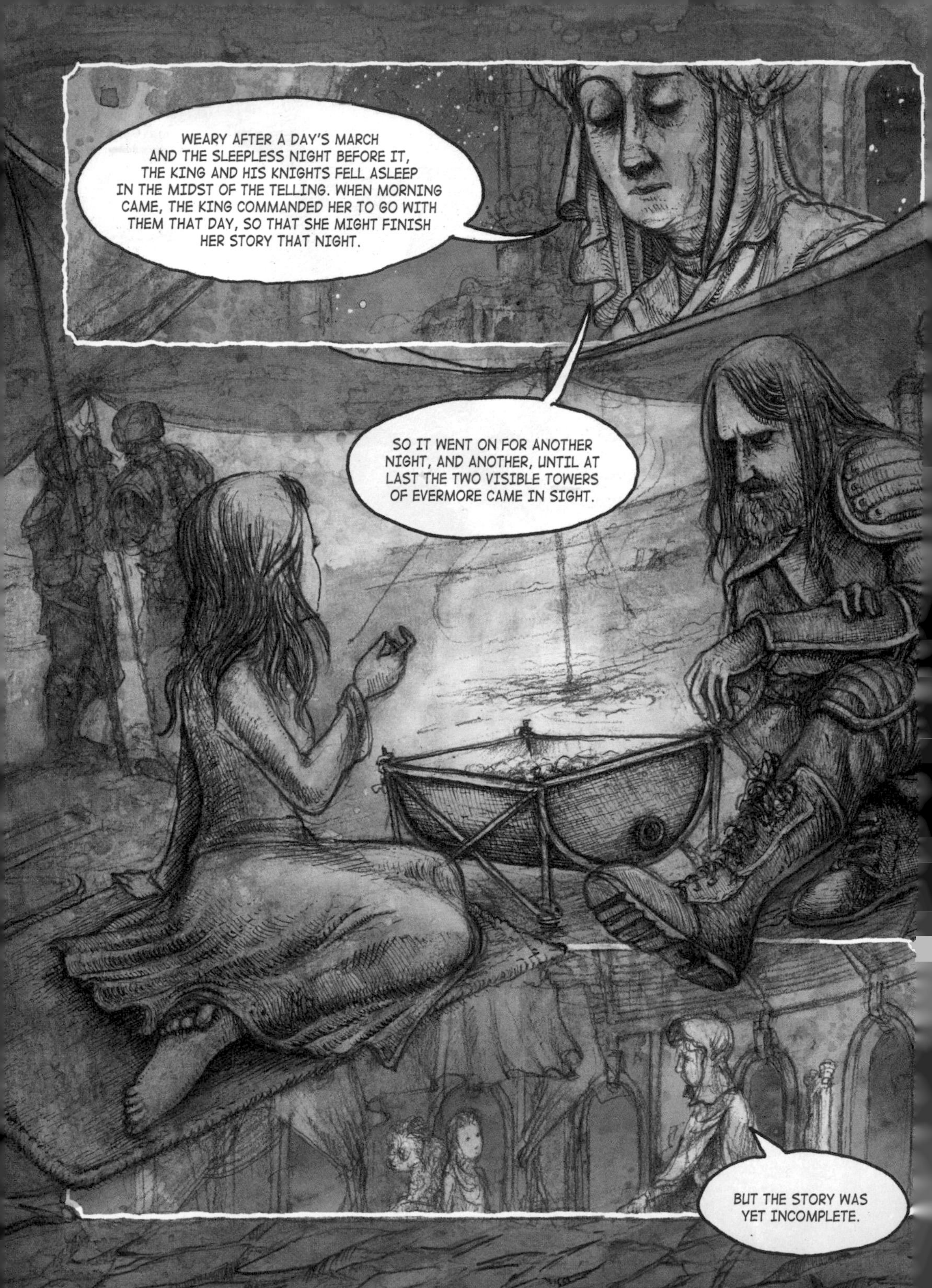
WEARY AFTER A DAY'S MARCH AND THE SLEEPLESS NIGHT BEFORE IT, THE KING AND HIS KNIGHTS FELL ASLEEP IN THE MIDST OF THE TELLING. WHEN MORNING CAME, THE KING COMMANDED HER TO GO WITH THEM THAT DAY, SO THAT SHE MIGHT FINISH HER STORY THAT NIGHT.
SO IT WENT ON FOR ANOTHER NIGHT, AND ANOTHER, UNTIL AT LAST THE TWO VISIBLE TOWERS OF EVERMORE CAME IN SIGHT.
BUT THE STORY WAS YET INCOMPLETE.

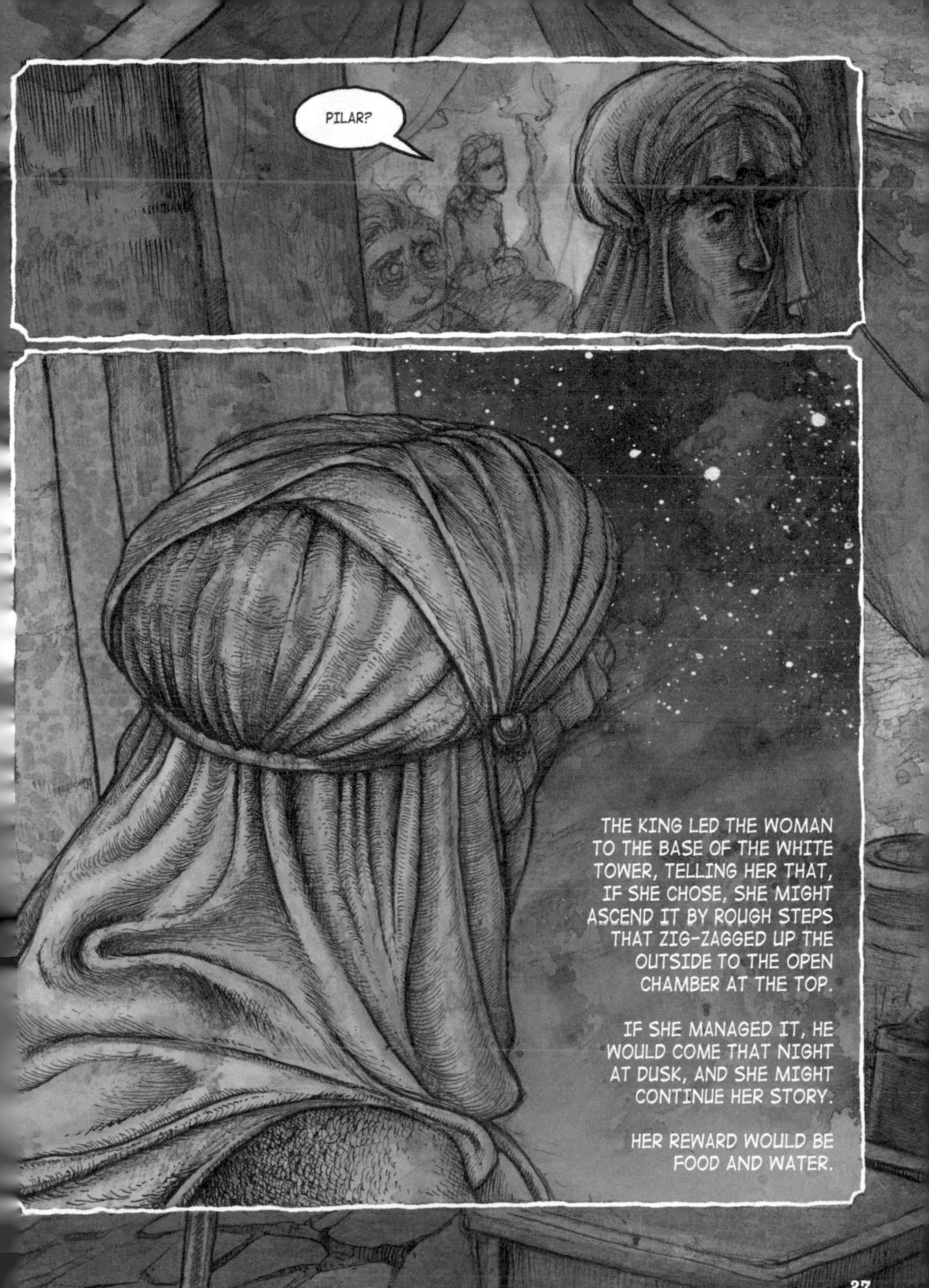
PILAR?
THE KING LED THE WOMAN TO THE BASE OF THE WHITE TOWER, TELLING HER THAT, IF SHE CHOSE, SHE MIGHT ASCEND IT BY ROUGH STEPS THAT ZIG-ZAGGED UP THE OUTSIDE TO THE OPEN CHAMBER AT THE TOP.
IF SHE MANAGED IT, HE WOULD COME THAT NIGHT AT DUSK, AND SHE MIGHT CONTINUE HER STORY.
HER REWARD WOULD BE FOOD AND WATER.

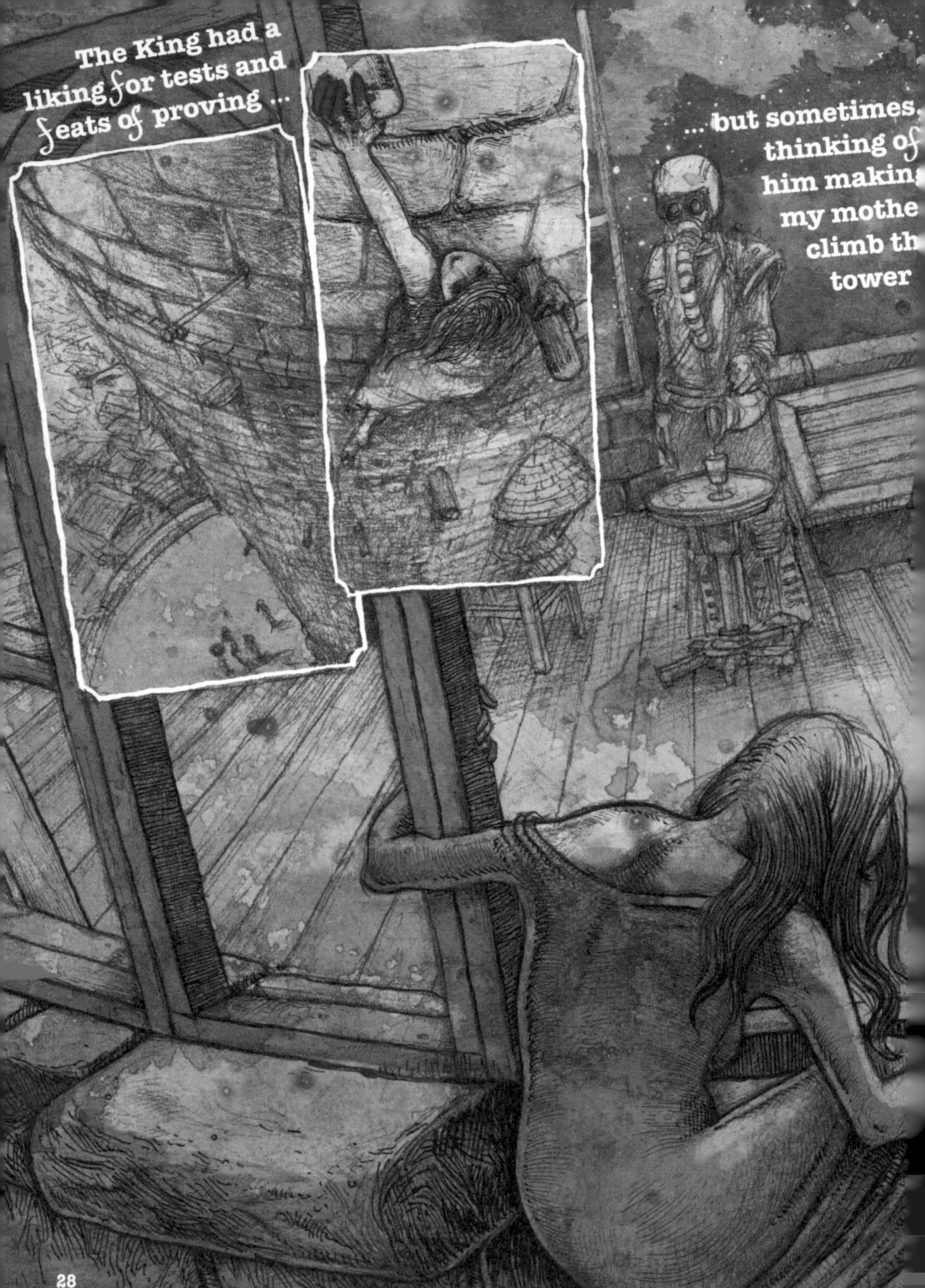
The King had a liking for tests and feats of proving ...
... but sometimes, thinking of him making my mothe climb th tower

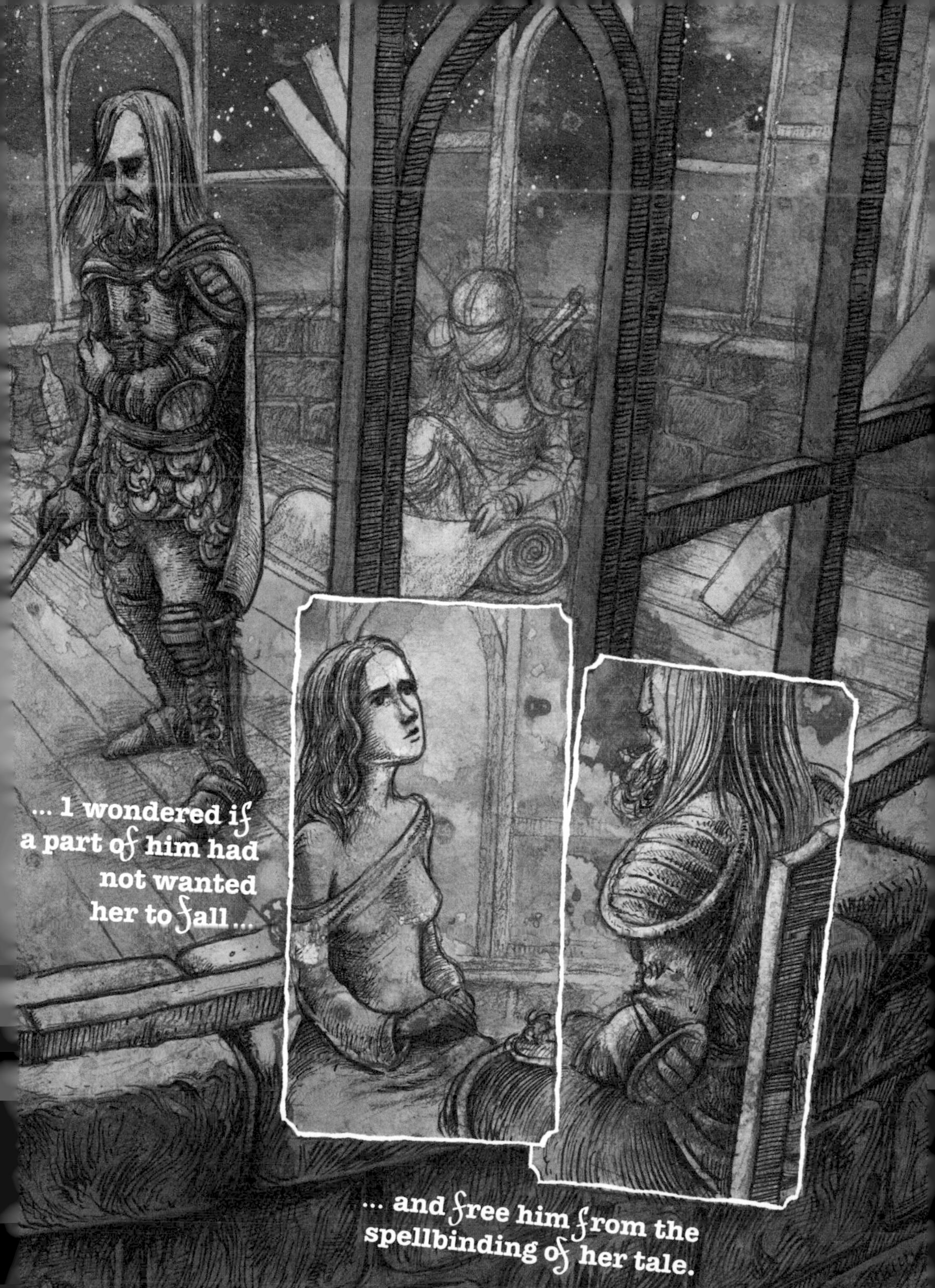
... I wondered if a part of him had not wanted her to fall ...
... and free him from the spellbinding of her tale.

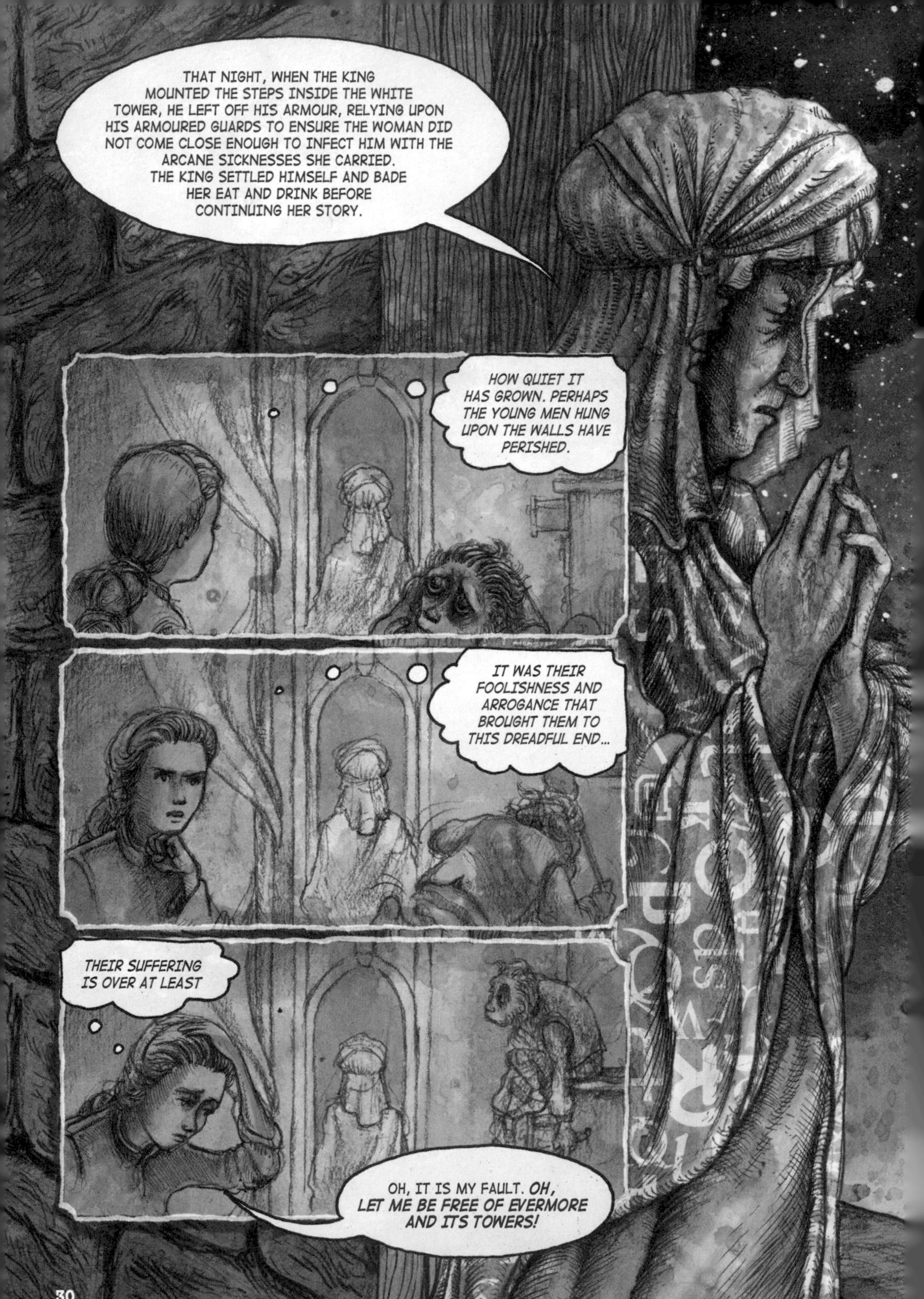
THAT NIGHT, WHEN THE KING MOUNTED THE STEPS INSIDE THE WHITE TOWER, HE LEFT OFF HIS ARMOUR, RELYING UPON HIS ARMOURED GUARDS TO ENSURE THE WOMAN DID NOT COME CLOSE ENOUGH TO INFECT HIM WITH THE ARCANE SICKNESSES SHE CARRIED. THE KING SETTLED HIMSELF AND BADE HER EAT AND DRINK BEFORE CONTINUING HER STORY.
HOW QUIET IT HAS GROWN. PERHAPS THE YOUNG MEN HUNG UPON THE WALLS HAVE PERISHED.
IT WAS THEIR FOOLISHNESS AND ARROGANCE THAT BROUGHT THEM TO THIS DREADFUL END...
THEIR SUFFERING IS OVER AT LEAST
OH, IT IS MY FAULT. OH, LET ME BE FREE OF EVERMORE AND ITS TOWERS!

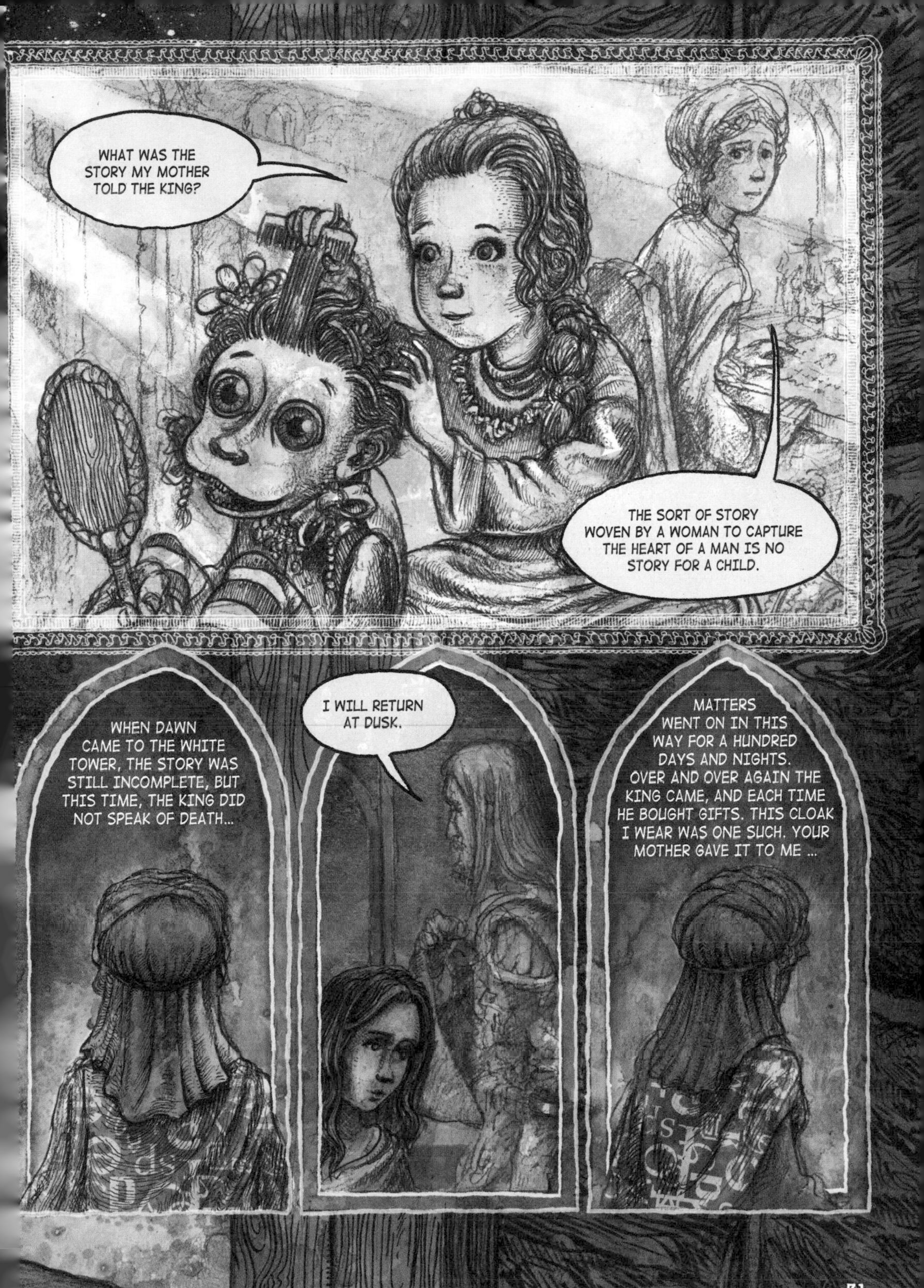
WHAT WAS THE STORY MY MOTHER TOLD THE KING?
THE SORT OF STORY WOVEN BY A WOMAN TO CAPTURE THE HEART OF A MAN IS NO STORY FOR A CHILD.
WHEN DAWN CAME TO THE WHITE TOWER, THE STORY WAS STILL INCOMPLETE, BUT THIS TIME, THE KING DID NOT SPEAK OF DEATH...
I WILL RETURN AT DUSK.
MATTERS WENT ON IN THIS WAY FOR A HUNDRED DAYS AND NIGHTS. OVER AND OVER AGAIN THE KING CAME, AND EACH TIME HE BOUGHT GIFTS. THIS CLOAK I WEAR WAS ONE SUCH. YOUR MOTHER GAVE IT TO ME ...

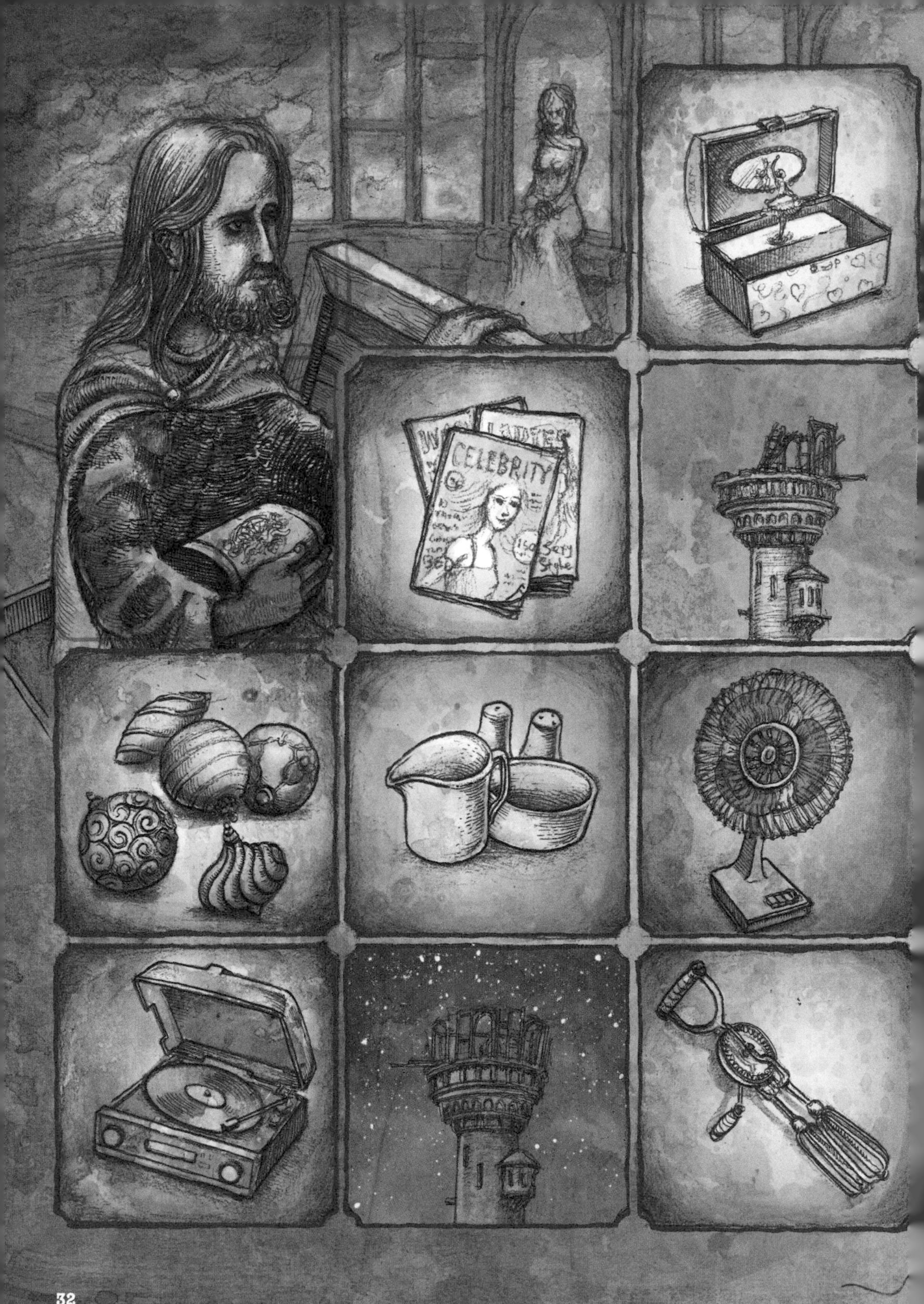
CELEBRITY
150
Sexy Style

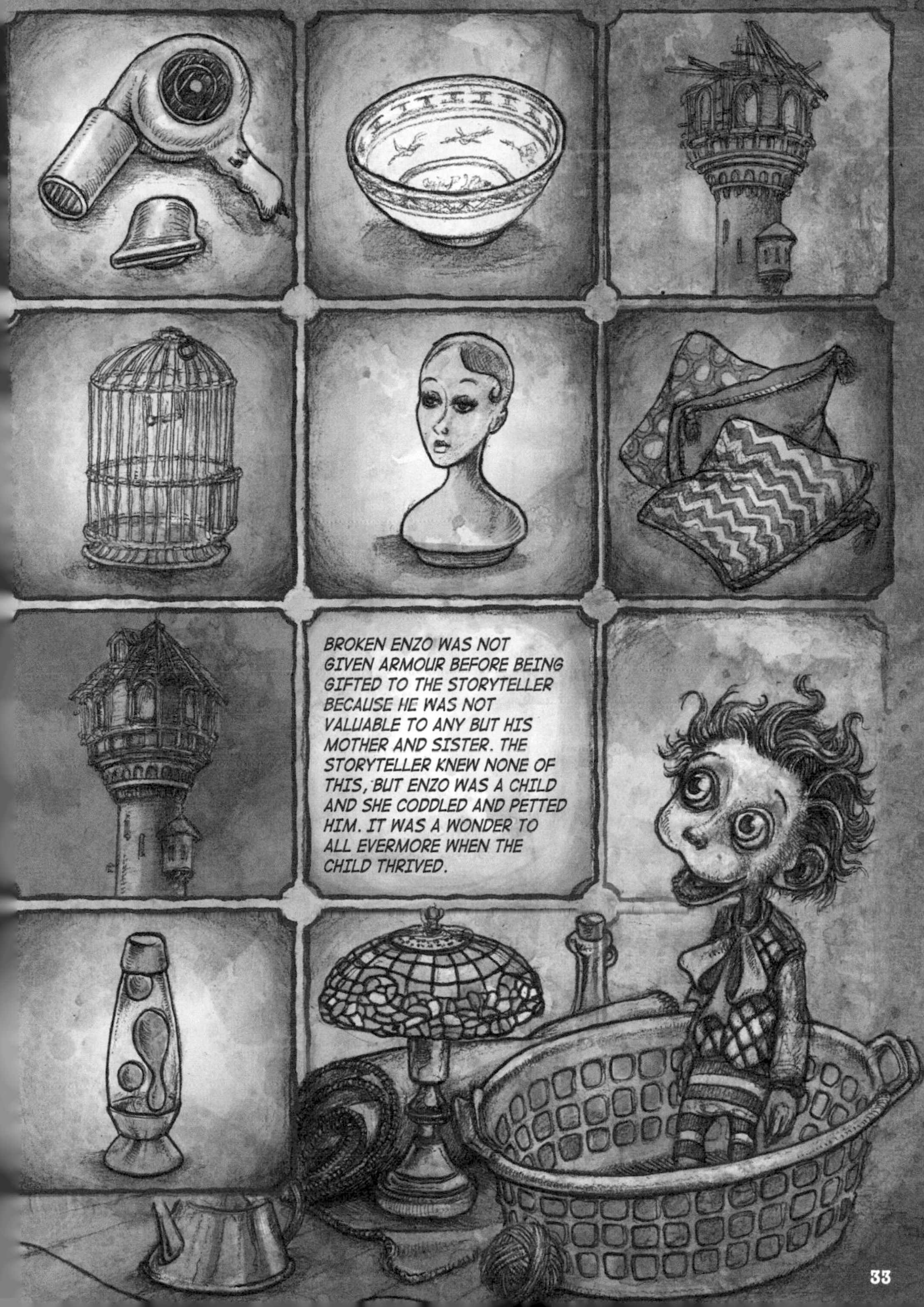
BROKEN ENZO WAS NOT GIVEN ARMOUR BEFORE BEING GIFTED TO THE STORYTELLER BECAUSE HE WAS NOT VALUABLE TO ANY BUT HIS MOTHER AND SISTER. THE STORYTELLER KNEW NONE OF THIS, BUT ENZO WAS A CHILD AND SHE CODDLED AND PETTED HIM. IT WAS A WONDER TO ALL EVERMORE WHEN THE CHILD THRIVED.

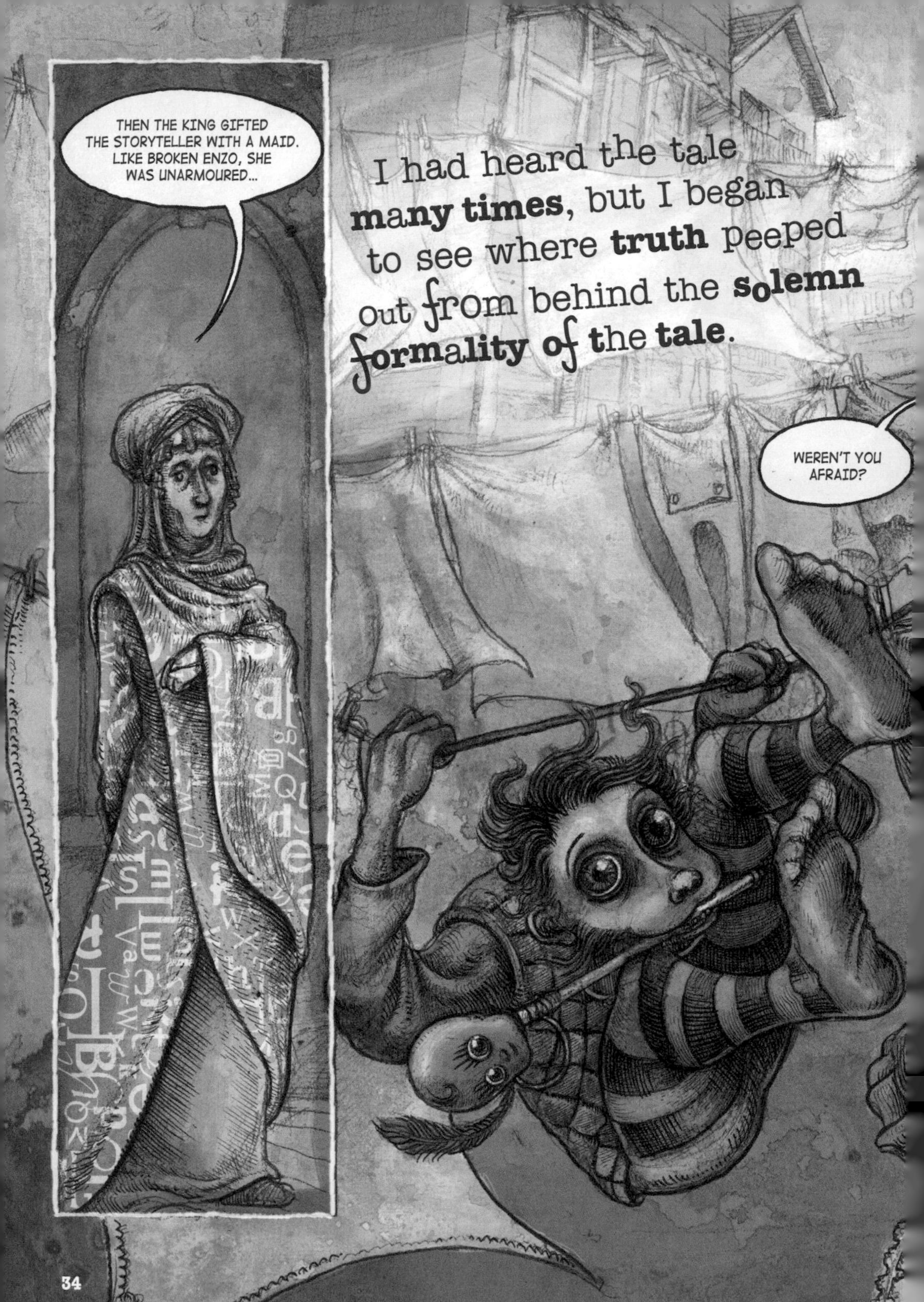
THEN THE KING GIFTED THE STORYTELLER WITH A MAID. LIKE BROKEN ENZO, SHE WAS UNARMOURED...
I had heard the tale **many times**, but I began to see where **truth** peeped out from behind the **solemn formality of the tale**.
WEREN'T YOU AFRAID?

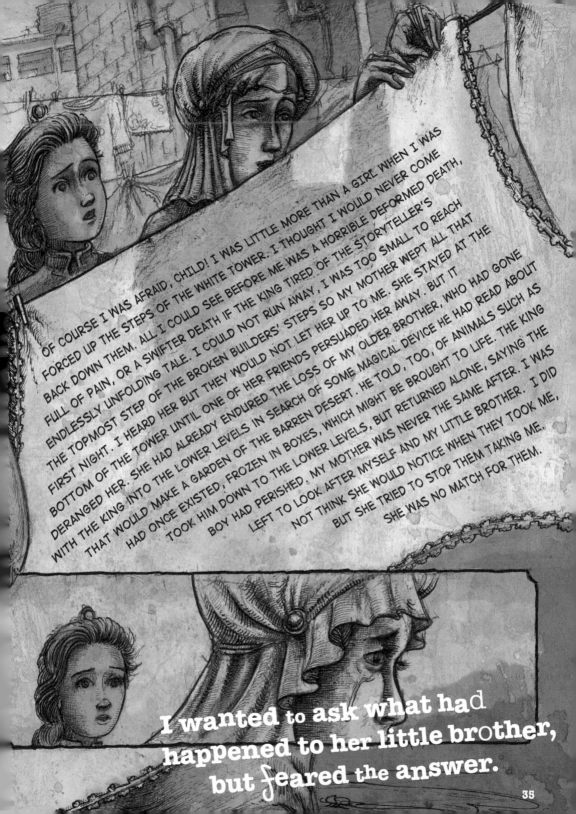

OF COURSE I WAS AFRAID, CHILD! I WAS LITTLE MORE THAN A GIRL WHEN I WAS FORCED UP THE STEPS OF THE WHITE TOWER. I THOUGHT I WOULD NEVER COME BACK DOWN THEM. ALL I COULD SEE BEFORE ME WAS A HORRIBLE DEFORMED DEATH, FULL OF PAIN, OR A SWIFTER DEATH IF THE KING TIRED OF THE STORYTELLER'S ENDLESSLY UNFOLDING TALE. I COULD NOT RUN AWAY, I WAS TOO SMALL TO REACH THE TOPMOST STEP OF THE BROKEN BUILDERS' STEPS SO MY MOTHER WEPT ALL THAT FIRST NIGHT. I HEARD HER BUT THEY WOULD NOT LET HER UP TO ME. SHE STAYED AT THE BOTTOM OF THE TOWER UNTIL ONE OF HER FRIENDS PERSUADED HER AWAY. BUT IT DERANGED HER. SHE HAD ALREADY ENDURED THE LOSS OF MY OLDER BROTHER, WHO HAD GONE WITH THE KING INTO THE LOWER LEVELS IN SEARCH OF SOME MAGICAL DEVICE HE HAD READ ABOUT THAT WOULD MAKE A GARDEN OF THE BARREN DESERT. HE TOLD, TOO, OF ANIMALS SUCH AS HAD ONCE EXISTED, FROZEN IN BOXES, WHICH MIGHT BE BROUGHT TO LIFE. THE KING TOOK HIM DOWN TO THE LOWER LEVELS, BUT RETURNED ALONE, SAYING THE BOY HAD PERISHED. MY MOTHER WAS NEVER THE SAME AFTER. I WAS LEFT TO LOOK AFTER MYSELF AND MY LITTLE BROTHER. I DID NOT THINK SHE WOULD NOTICE WHEN THEY TOOK ME, BUT SHE TRIED TO STOP THEM TAKING ME. SHE WAS NO MATCH FOR THEM.

I wanted to ask what had happened to her little brother, but feared the answer.

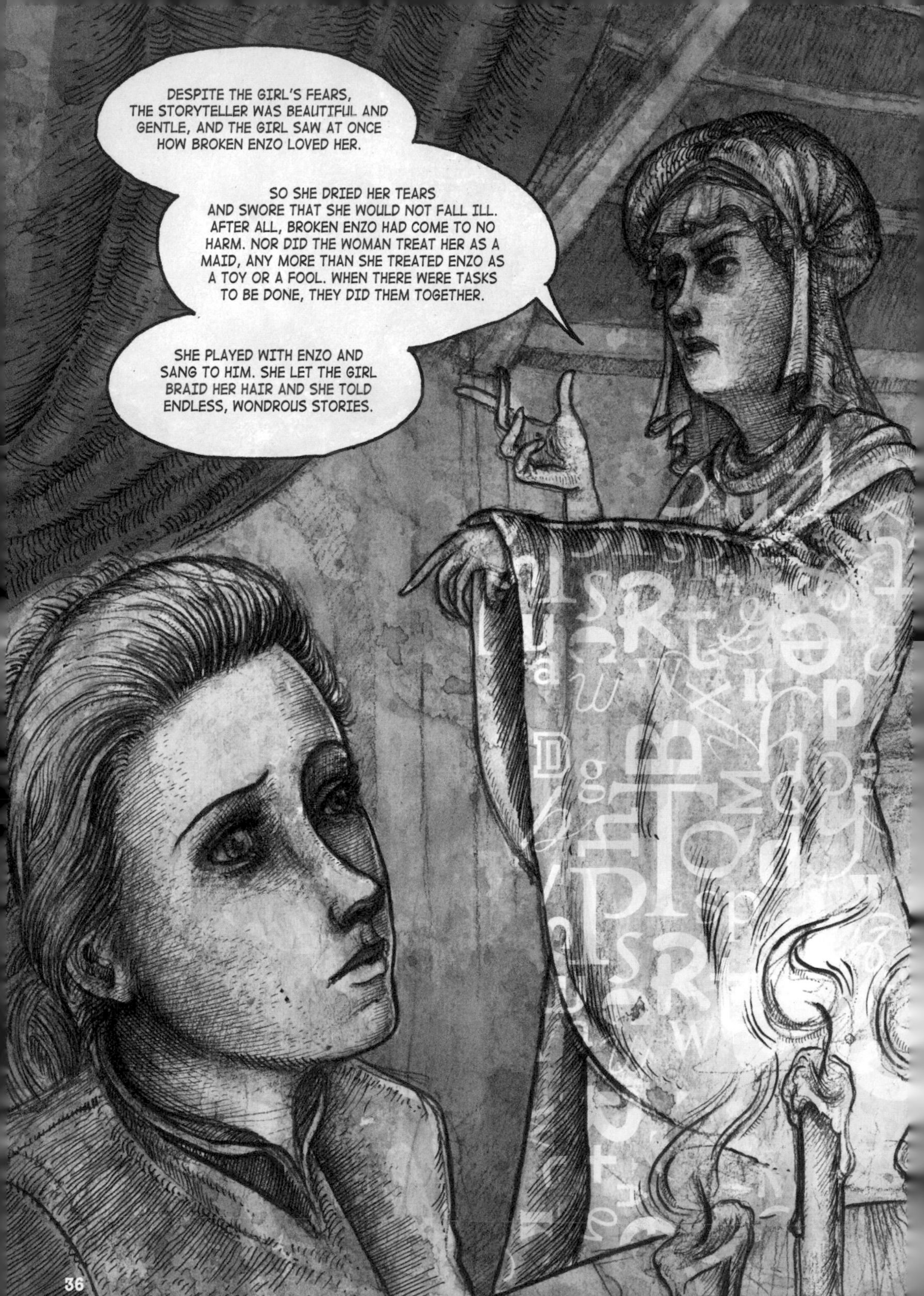
DESPITE THE GIRL'S FEARS, THE STORYTELLER WAS BEAUTIFUL AND GENTLE, AND THE GIRL SAW AT ONCE HOW BROKEN ENZO LOVED HER.
SO SHE DRIED HER TEARS AND SWORE THAT SHE WOULD NOT FALL ILL. AFTER ALL, BROKEN ENZO HAD COME TO NO HARM. NOR DID THE WOMAN TREAT HER AS A MAID, ANY MORE THAN SHE TREATED ENZO AS A TOY OR A FOOL. WHEN THERE WERE TASKS TO BE DONE, THEY DID THEM TOGETHER.
SHE PLAYED WITH ENZO AND SANG TO HIM. SHE LET THE GIRL BRAID HER HAIR AND SHE TOLD ENDLESS, WONDROUS STORIES.

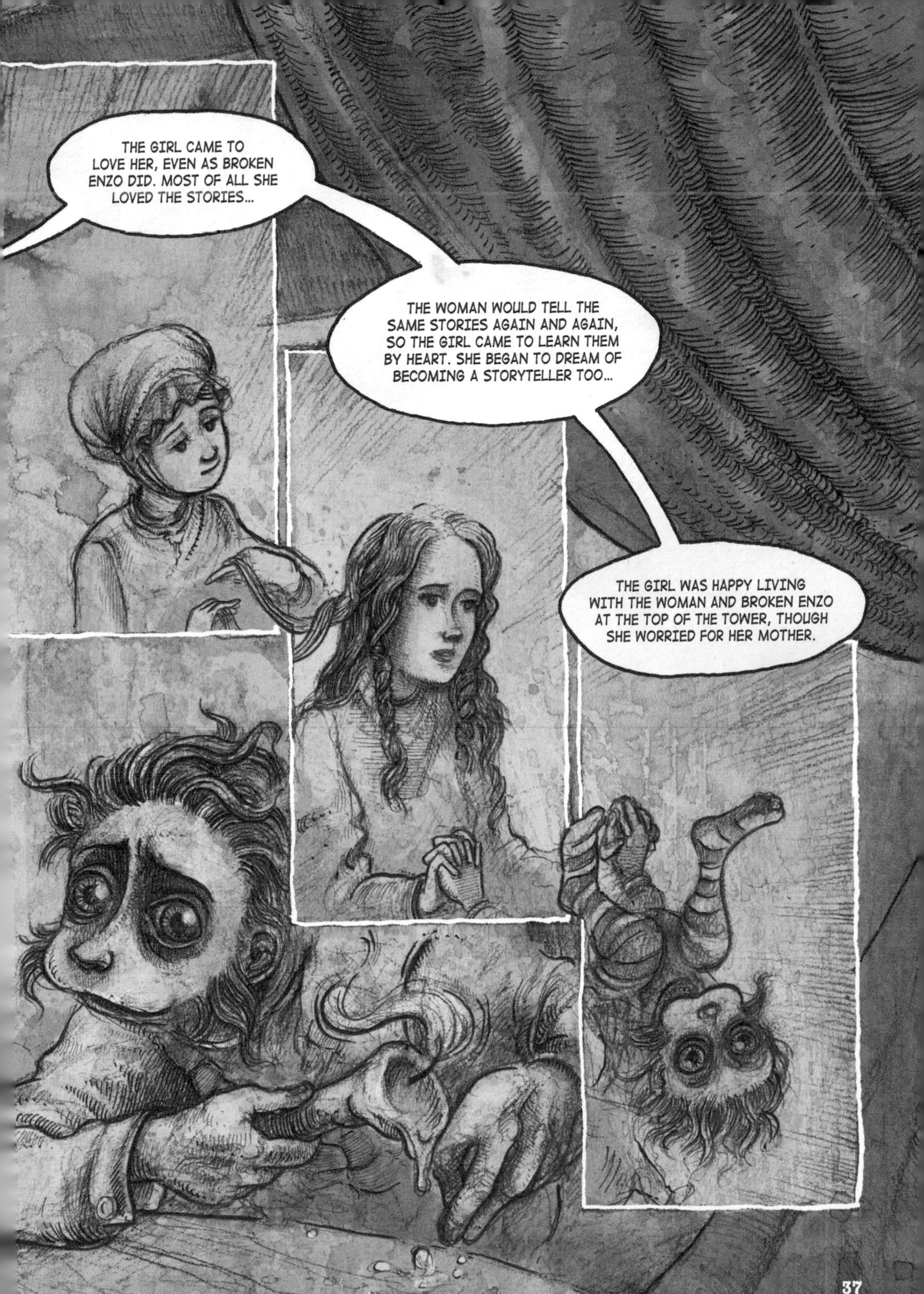
THE GIRL CAME TO LOVE HER, EVEN AS BROKEN ENZO DID. MOST OF ALL SHE LOVED THE STORIES...
THE WOMAN WOULD TELL THE SAME STORIES AGAIN AND AGAIN, SO THE GIRL CAME TO LEARN THEM BY HEART. SHE BEGAN TO DREAM OF BECOMING A STORYTELLER TOO...
THE GIRL WAS HAPPY LIVING WITH THE WOMAN AND BROKEN ENZO AT THE TOP OF THE TOWER, THOUGH SHE WORRIED FOR HER MOTHER.

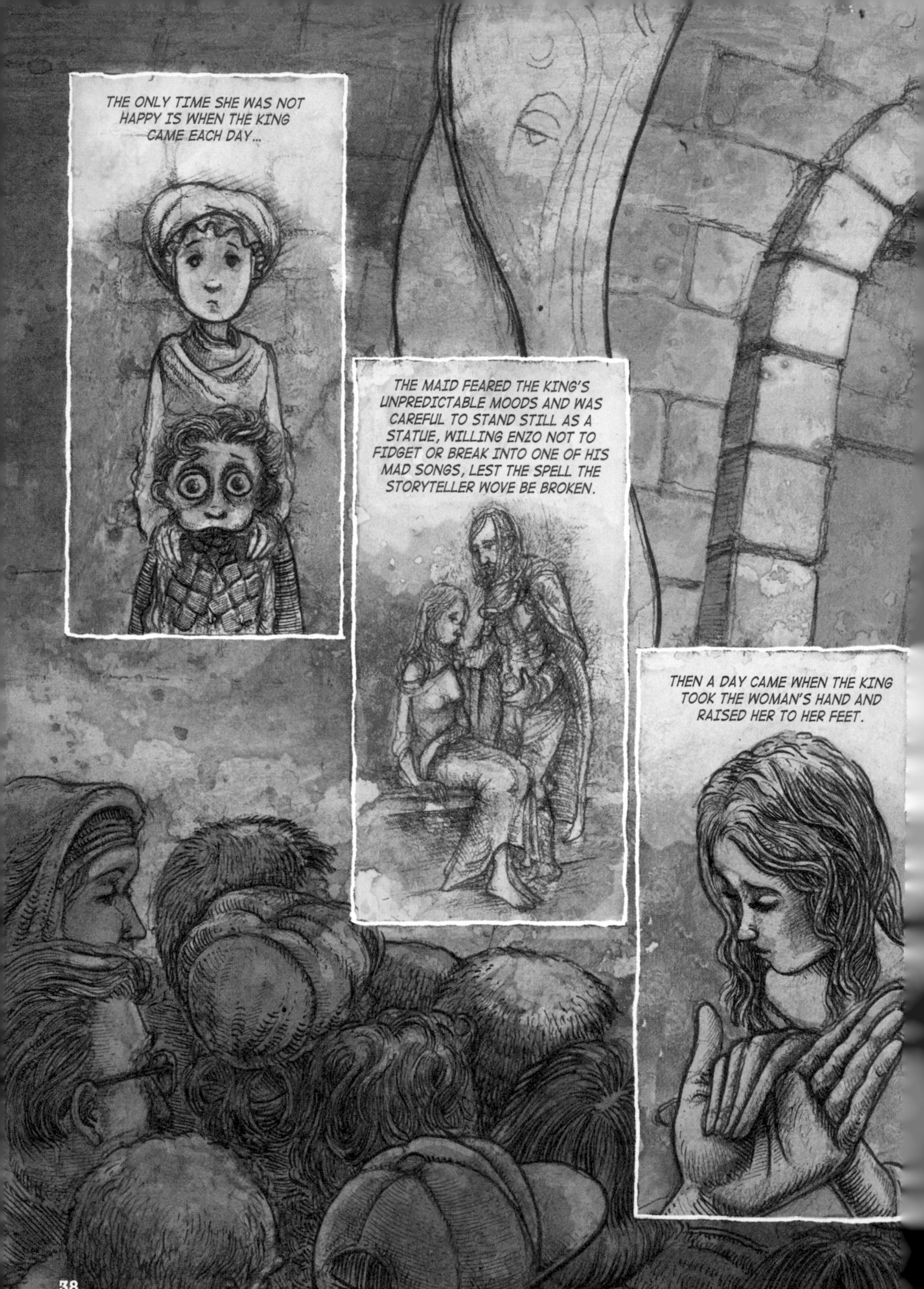
THE ONLY TIME SHE WAS NOT HAPPY IS WHEN THE KING CAME EACH DAY...
THE MAID FEARED THE KING'S UNPREDICTABLE MOODS AND WAS CAREFUL TO STAND STILL AS A STATUE, WILLING ENZO NOT TO FIDGET OR BREAK INTO ONE OF HIS MAD SONGS, LEST THE SPELL THE STORYTELLER WOVE BE BROKEN.
THEN A DAY CAME WHEN THE KING TOOK THE WOMAN'S HAND AND RAISED HER TO HER FEET.

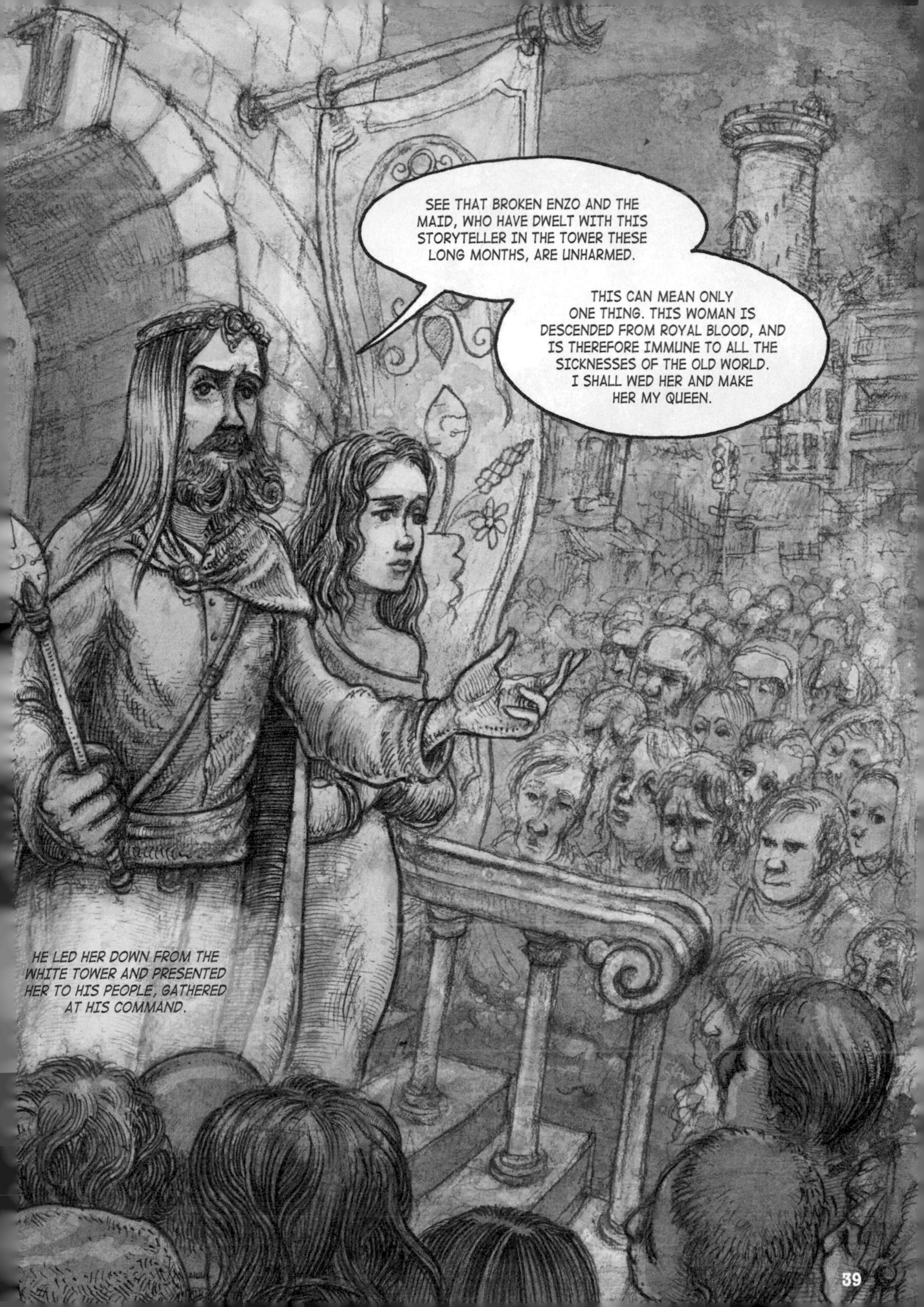
SEE THAT BROKEN ENZO AND THE MAID, WHO HAVE DWELT WITH THIS STORYTELLER IN THE TOWER THESE LONG MONTHS, ARE UNHARMED.
THIS CAN MEAN ONLY ONE THING. THIS WOMAN IS DESCENDED FROM ROYAL BLOOD, AND IS THEREFORE IMMUNE TO ALL THE SICKNESSES OF THE OLD WORLD. I SHALL WED HER AND MAKE HER MY QUEEN.
HE LED HER DOWN FROM THE WHITE TOWER AND PRESENTED HER TO HIS PEOPLE, GATHERED AT HIS COMMAND.

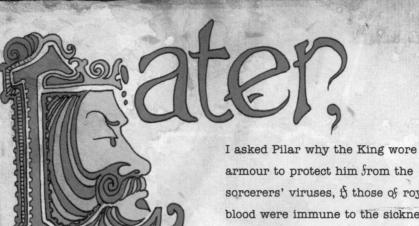

Later,

I asked Pilar why the King wore armour to protect him from the sorcerers' viruses, if those of royal blood were immune to the sicknesses of the old world. I do not remember her answer, but I decided it was because the King was a man who made himself a king. It was not until I was older that I came to wonder how the King knew a true princess born was immune to the sicknesses of the fallen. Perhaps, being King, he knew everything. But if so, why build the Rose Tower and the Invisible Tower before raising up the White Tower that had shown him where to find the woman he would make his Queen? Surely if he saw all things, he would make no mistakes.

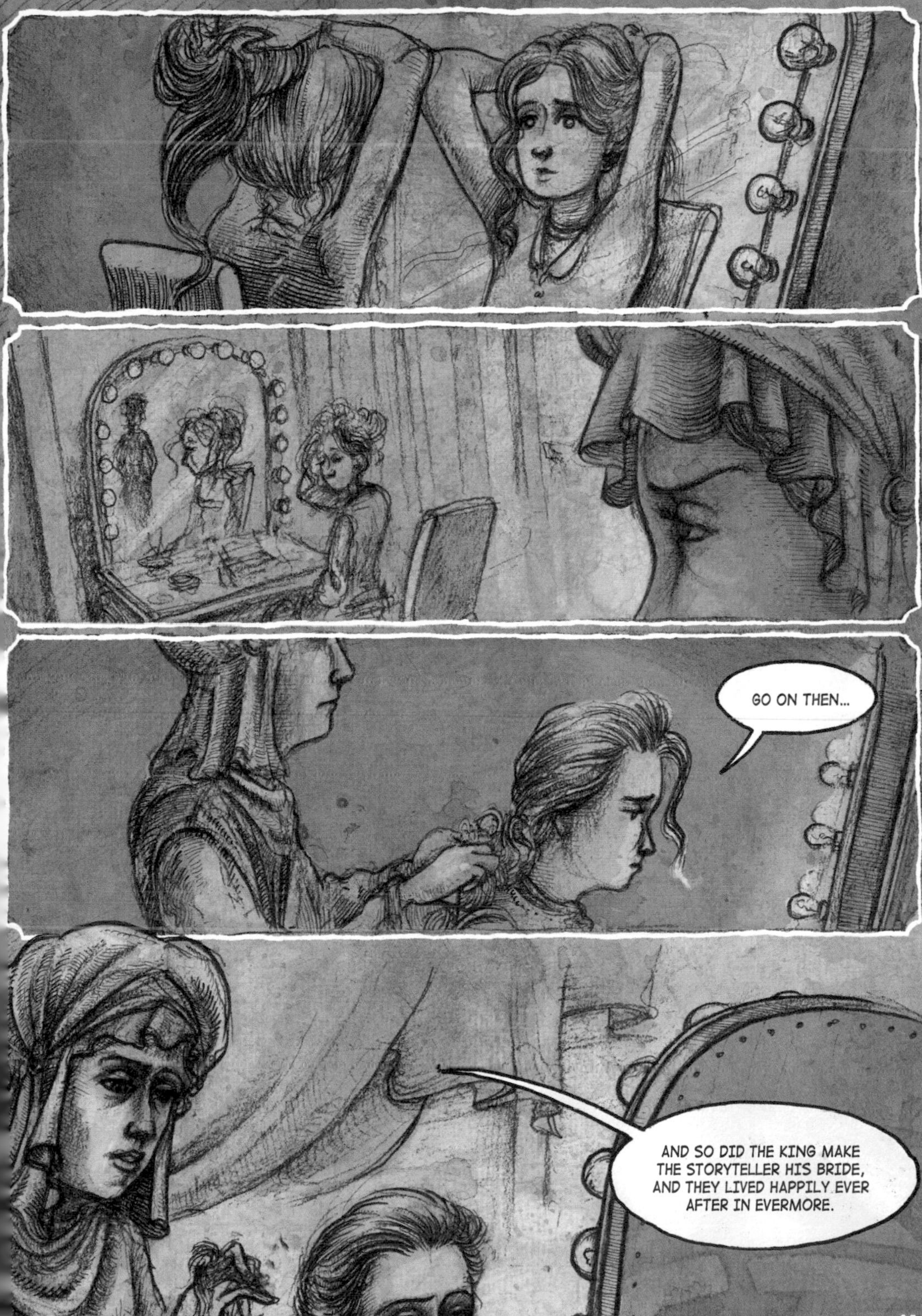
GO ON THEN...
AND SO DID THE KING MAKE THE STORYTELLER HIS BRIDE, AND THEY LIVED HAPPILY EVER AFTER IN EVERMORE.

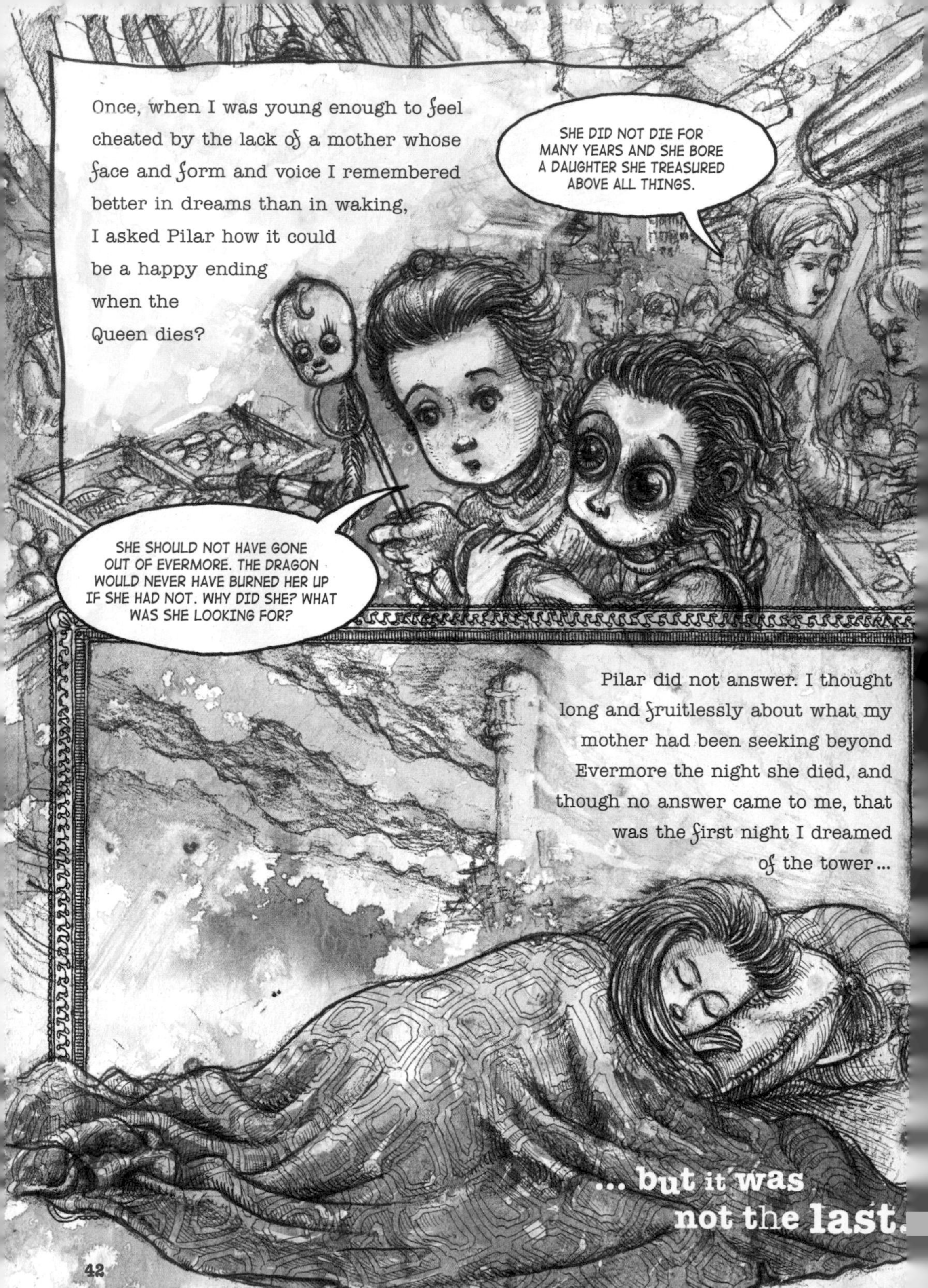
Once, when I was young enough to feel cheated by the lack of a mother whose face and form and voice I remembered better in dreams than in waking, I asked Pilar how it could be a happy ending when the Queen dies?
SHE DID NOT DIE FOR MANY YEARS AND SHE BORE A DAUGHTER SHE TREASURED ABOVE ALL THINGS.
SHE SHOULD NOT HAVE GONE OUT OF EVERMORE. THE DRAGON WOULD NEVER HAVE BURNED HER UP IF SHE HAD NOT. WHY DID SHE? WHAT WAS SHE LOOKING FOR?
Pilar did not answer. I thought long and fruitlessly about what my mother had been seeking beyond Evermore the night she died, and though no answer came to me, that was the first night I dreamed of the tower...
... but it was not the last.

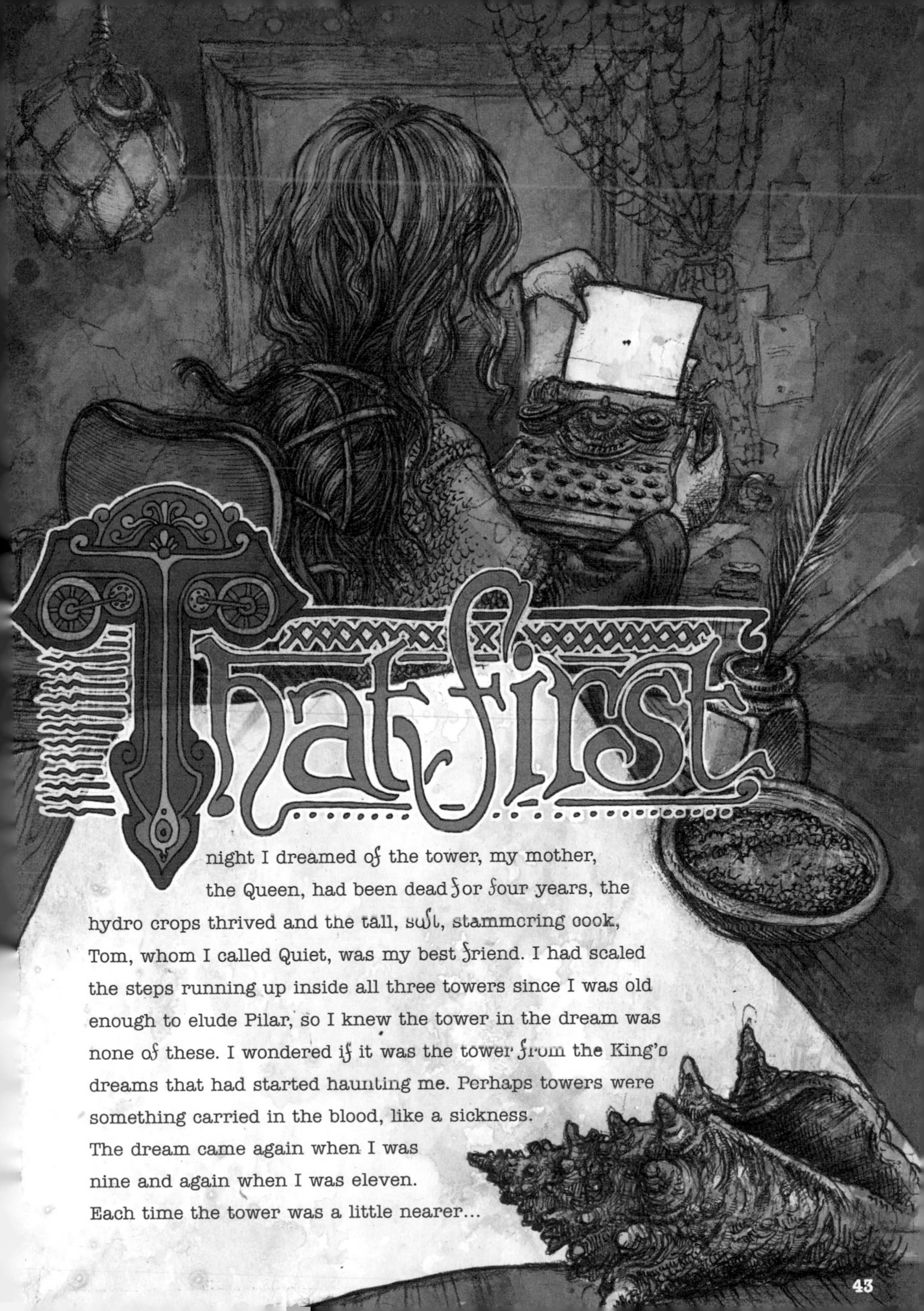

That first

night I dreamed of the tower, my mother, the Queen, had been dead for four years, the hydro crops thrived and the tall, soft, stammering cook, Tom, whom I called Quiet, was my best friend. I had scaled the steps running up inside all three towers since I was old enough to elude Pilar, so I knew the tower in the dream was none of these. I wondered if it was the tower from the King's dreams that had started haunting me. Perhaps towers were something carried in the blood, like a sickness.

The dream came again when I was nine and again when I was eleven. Each time the tower was a little nearer...

...OR PERHAPS THE TOWER IN MY DREAMS IS THE BLACK TOWER WHERE THE KING FOUND MY MOTHER.

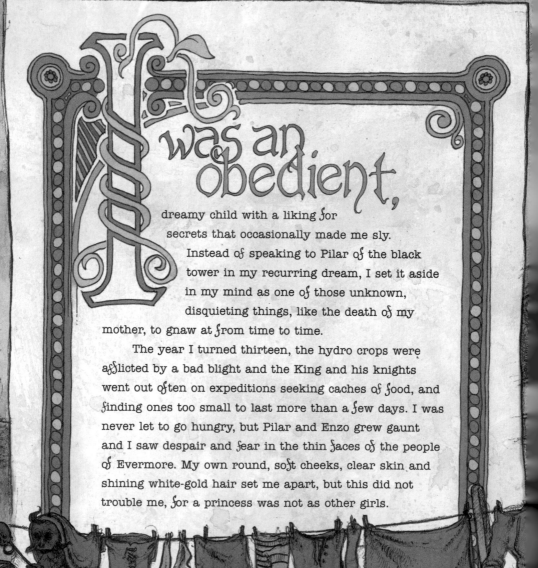

I was an obedient,

dreamy child with a liking for secrets that occasionally made me sly.

Instead of speaking to Pilar of the black tower in my recurring dream, I set it aside in my mind as one of those unknown, disquieting things, like the death of my mother, to gnaw at from time to time.

The year I turned thirteen, the hydro crops were afflicted by a bad blight and the King and his knights went out often on expeditions seeking caches of food, and finding ones too small to last more than a few days. I was never let to go hungry, but Pilar and Enzo grew gaunt and I saw despair and fear in the thin faces of the people of Evermore. My own round, soft cheeks, clear skin and shining white-gold hair set me apart, but this did not trouble me, for a princess was not as other girls.

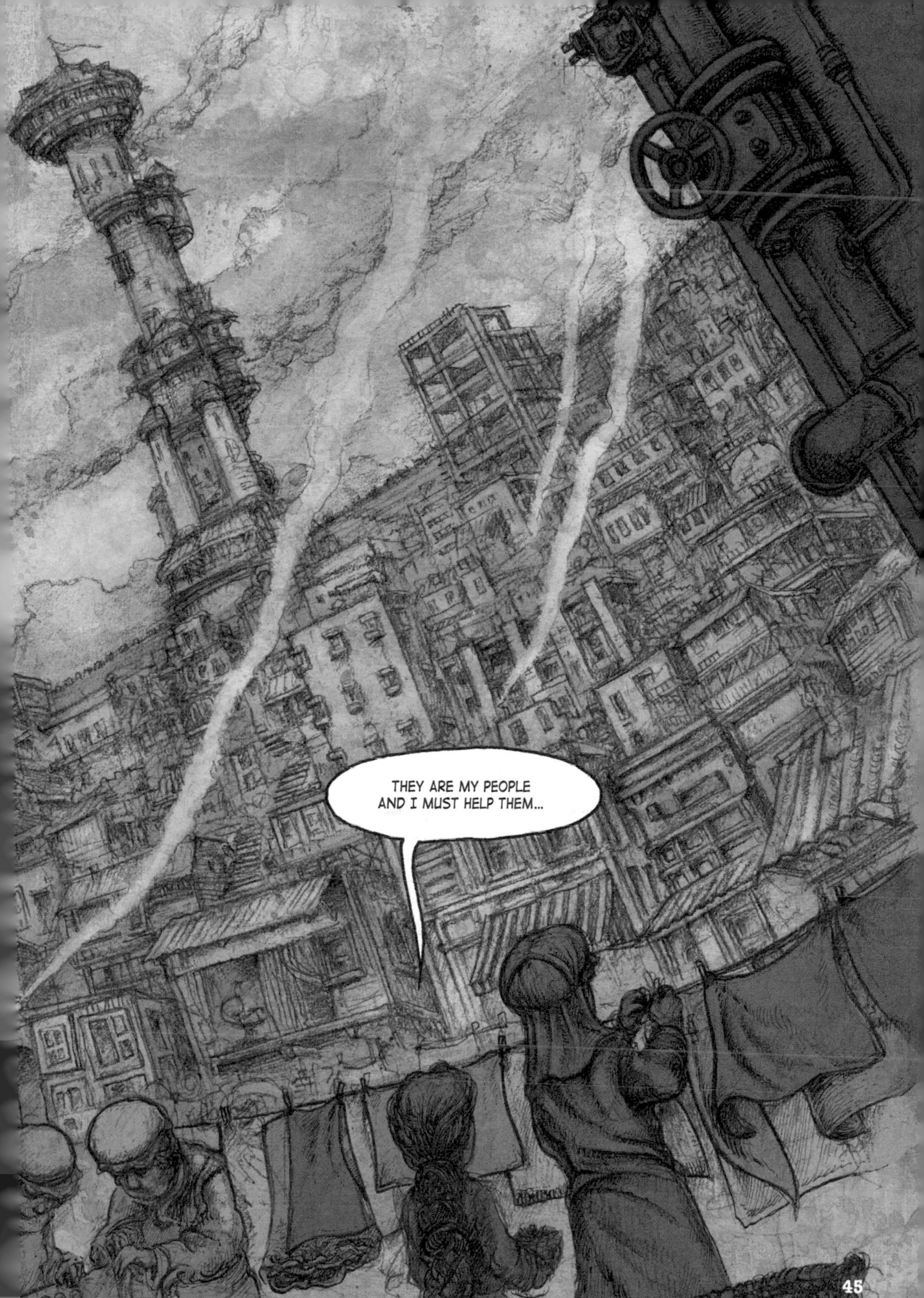
THEY ARE MY PEOPLE AND I MUST HELP THEM...

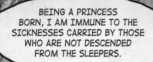

BEING A PRINCESS BORN, I AM IMMUNE TO THE SICKNESSES CARRIED BY THOSE WHO ARE NOT DESCENDED FROM THE SLEEPERS.

I WILL ASK THE KING IF I CAN GO WITH HIM NEXT TIME HE AND HIS KNIGHTS SEEK FOR FOOD. IT MAY BE THAT I CAN GO INTO PLACES THAT THE KNIGHTS CANNOT GO IN THEIR ARMOUR.

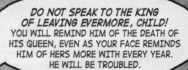

DO NOT SPEAK TO THE KING OF LEAVING EVERMORE, CHILD! YOU WILL REMIND HIM OF THE DEATH OF HIS QUEEN, EVEN AS YOUR FACE REMINDS HIM OF HERS MORE WITH EVERY YEAR. HE WILL BE TROUBLED.

It was not the unusual seriousness of her tone that dried the spit in my mouth, for although perhaps overly accepting, I did not lack courage. It was the suggestion that the King might be troubled. He had a tendency to command the lopping off of heads or hands, or bloody and painful executions, when his mood grew dark. He had always been gentle, if distant, with me, so that if I could not love him, I had never thought to fear him. But lately, for the first time, his hectic black gaze had sometimes rested upon me in a way that made the hairs on my neck and arms prickle. Even so, I did not imagine he would ever do me harm.

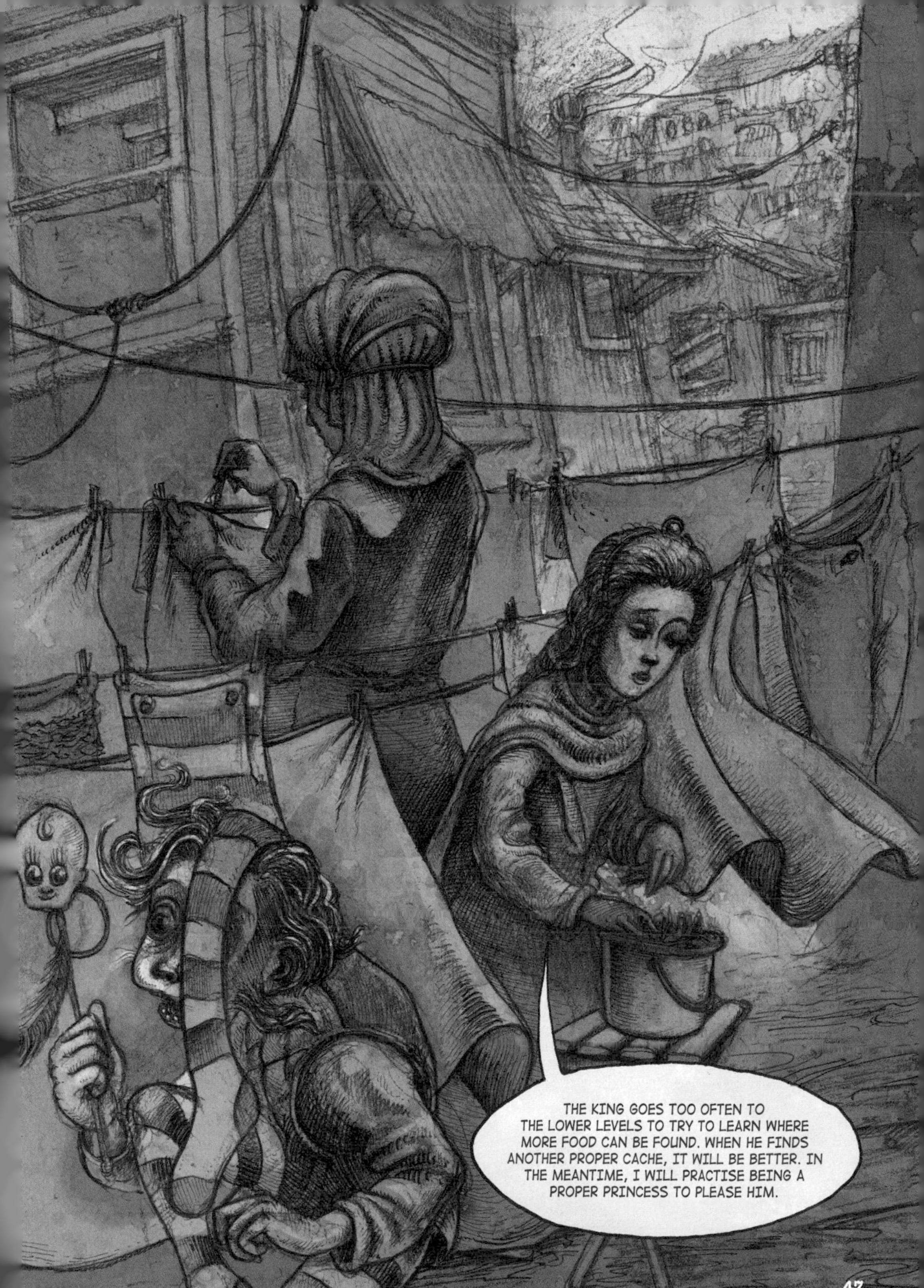
THE KING GOES TOO OFTEN TO THE LOWER LEVELS TO TRY TO LEARN WHERE MORE FOOD CAN BE FOUND. WHEN HE FINDS ANOTHER PROPER CACHE, IT WILL BE BETTER. IN THE MEANTIME, I WILL PRACTISE BEING A PROPER PRINCESS TO PLEASE HIM.

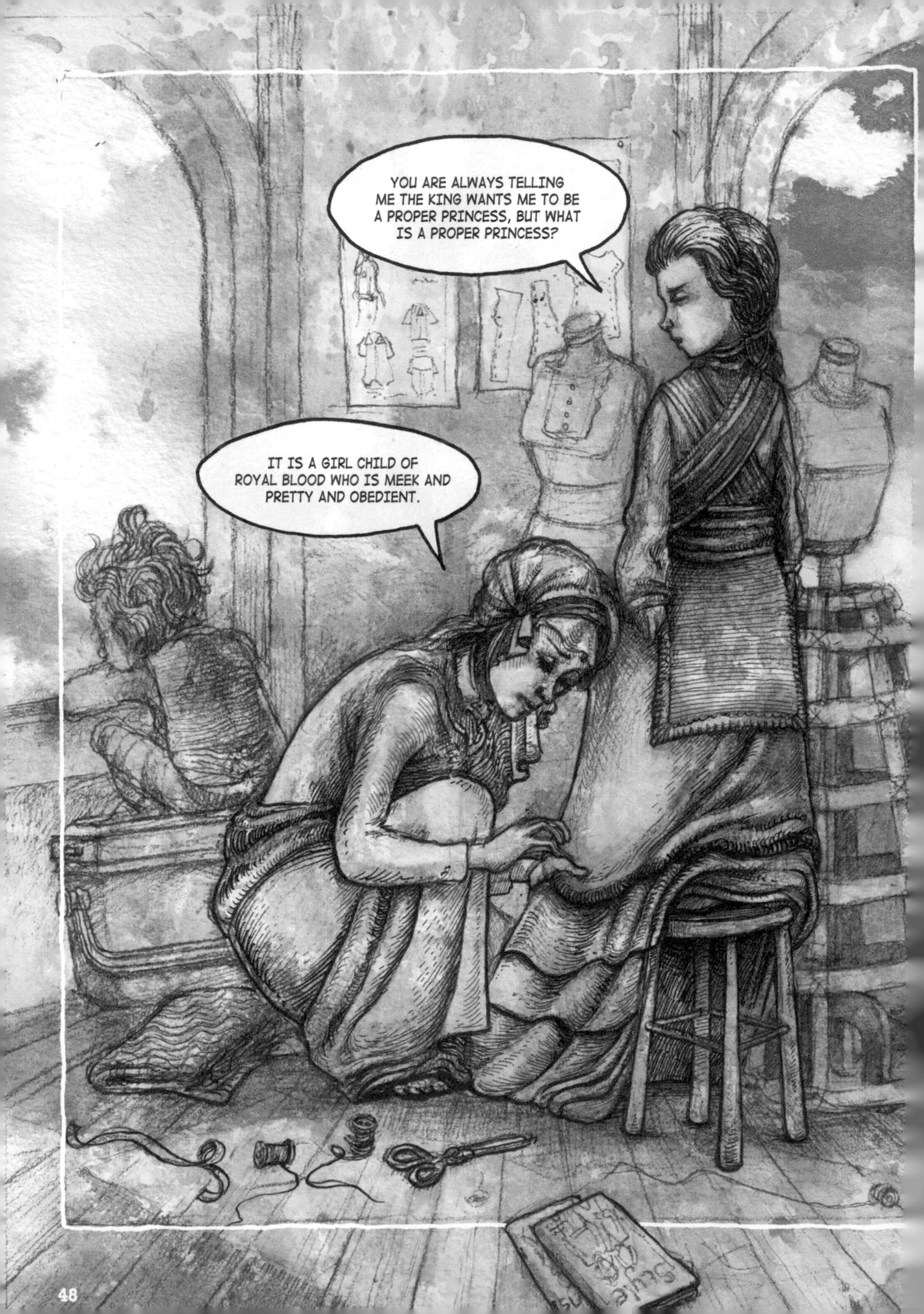
YOU ARE ALWAYS TELLING ME THE KING WANTS ME TO BE A PROPER PRINCESS, BUT WHAT IS A PROPER PRINCESS?
IT IS A GIRL CHILD OF ROYAL BLOOD WHO IS MEEK AND PRETTY AND OBEDIENT.

Writing of the Dificulty

I had in setting aside my plans to help my people and ease the burden of the King, it occurs to me that I make myself sound more virtuous than I truly was.

Of surety I pitied the common folk, but part of my desire to venture out arose because of how dull it was in Evermore during the famine. People stayed in their homes when there were no hydro crops to tend, husbanding their strength and what food they had. There was none of the gay, busy work that comes from harvesting and storing food. Not that I had ever been permitted to help in the work, for a proper princess did not soil her hands with manual labour. But at least I might walk about among the people and smile when someone asked me to bless their child or a sack of new seed. One day, thinking again of going out of Evermore, it struck me that stories were full of proper princesses who were bored. Might I not confess my boredom prettily to the King and suggest accompanying him on a foraging journey as an antidote?

Despite Pilar's strenuous opposition, I did speak of my boredom to the King. I meant to use it as a stepping stone to a request to accompany him next time he went in search of food. But he smiled his distant, cold, indulgent smile and said he would ease my boredom. The next day, a goldon ball was brought to me to play with.

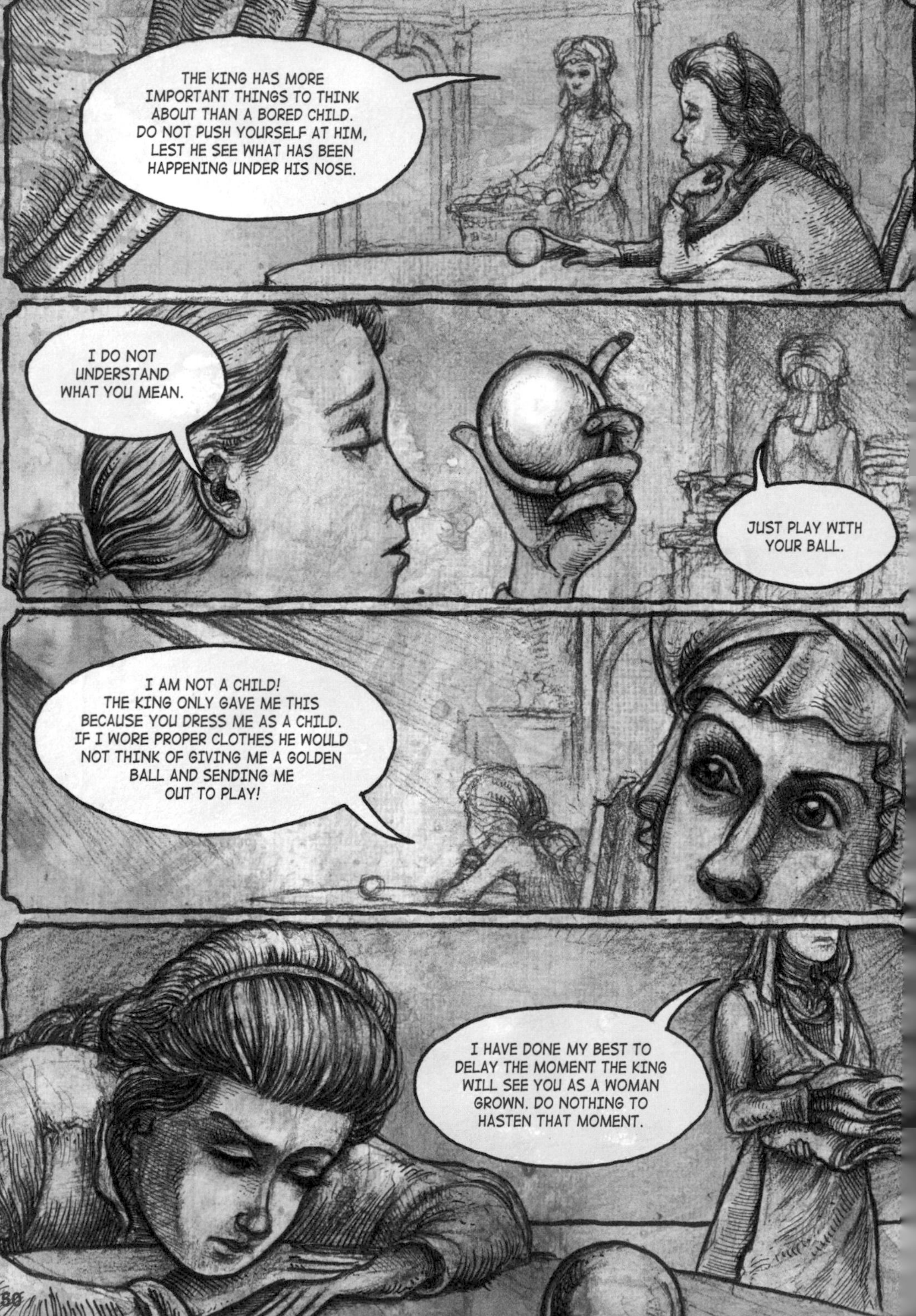
THE KING HAS MORE IMPORTANT THINGS TO THINK ABOUT THAN A BORED CHILD. DO NOT PUSH YOURSELF AT HIM, LEST HE SEE WHAT HAS BEEN HAPPENING UNDER HIS NOSE.
I DO NOT UNDERSTAND WHAT YOU MEAN.
JUST PLAY WITH YOUR BALL.
I AM NOT A CHILD! THE KING ONLY GAVE ME THIS BECAUSE YOU DRESS ME AS A CHILD. IF I WORE PROPER CLOTHES HE WOULD NOT THINK OF GIVING ME A GOLDEN BALL AND SENDING ME OUT TO PLAY!
I HAVE DONE MY BEST TO DELAY THE MOMENT THE KING WILL SEE YOU AS A WOMAN GROWN. DO NOTHING TO HASTEN THAT MOMENT.

The hungry time dragged on and on, and it occurred to me to wonder if this was why my mother had left Evermore the night the dragon had taken her. Perhaps the hydro crops had failed then as well, for they had always done so from time to time. She might have longed to help, even as I did.

She could not have known she would be taken by a dragon, for they were so rare that I had never seen one, even from afar. In truth, I was troubled by the mystery of the dragon that had savaged my mother so horribly that she had died of her injuries. Pilar told me the King slew the dragon, but I did not see how he had managed it, if dragons were as horridsome as the ones in her stories.

Occasionally I had nightmares in which I would see my mother's face half-burned away, her lovely gown scorched and sodden with blood. Where could that image have come from? Had I caught a glimpse of her destroyed face when the King brought her back? I do not remember. But I never ceased plaguing Pilar for answers. Nor of trying to think of reasons and schemes to get outside Evermore ...

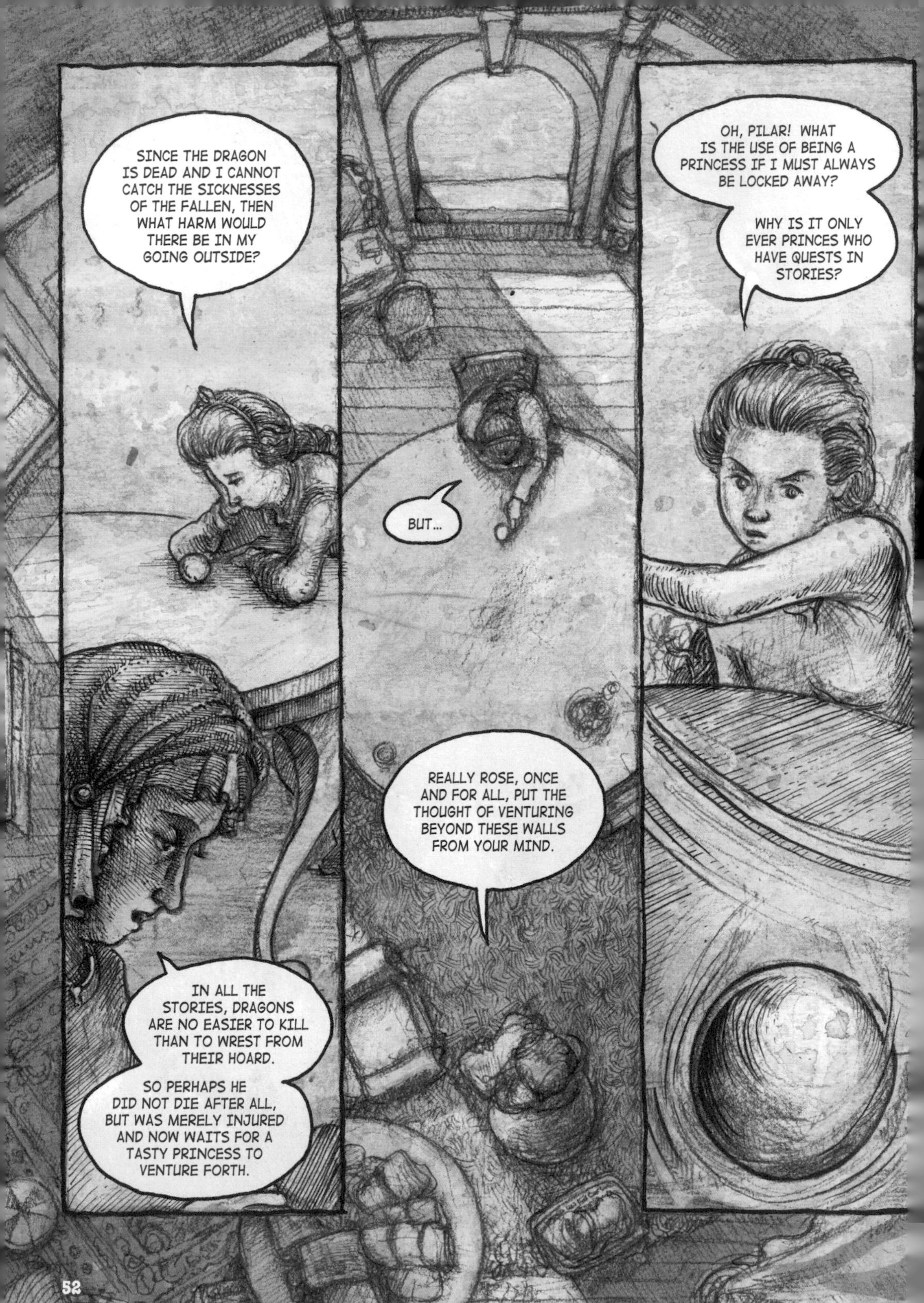
SINCE THE DRAGON IS DEAD AND I CANNOT CATCH THE SICKNESSES OF THE FALLEN, THEN WHAT HARM WOULD THERE BE IN MY GOING OUTSIDE?
IN ALL THE STORIES, DRAGONS ARE NO EASIER TO KILL THAN TO WREST FROM THEIR HOARD.
SO PERHAPS HE DID NOT DIE AFTER ALL, BUT WAS MERELY INJURED AND NOW WAITS FOR A TASTY PRINCESS TO VENTURE FORTH.
BUT...
REALLY ROSE, ONCE AND FOR ALL, PUT THE THOUGHT OF VENTURING BEYOND THESE WALLS FROM YOUR MIND.
OH, PILAR! WHAT IS THE USE OF BEING A PRINCESS IF I MUST ALWAYS BE LOCKED AWAY?
WHY IS IT ONLY EVER PRINCES WHO HAVE QUESTS IN STORIES?

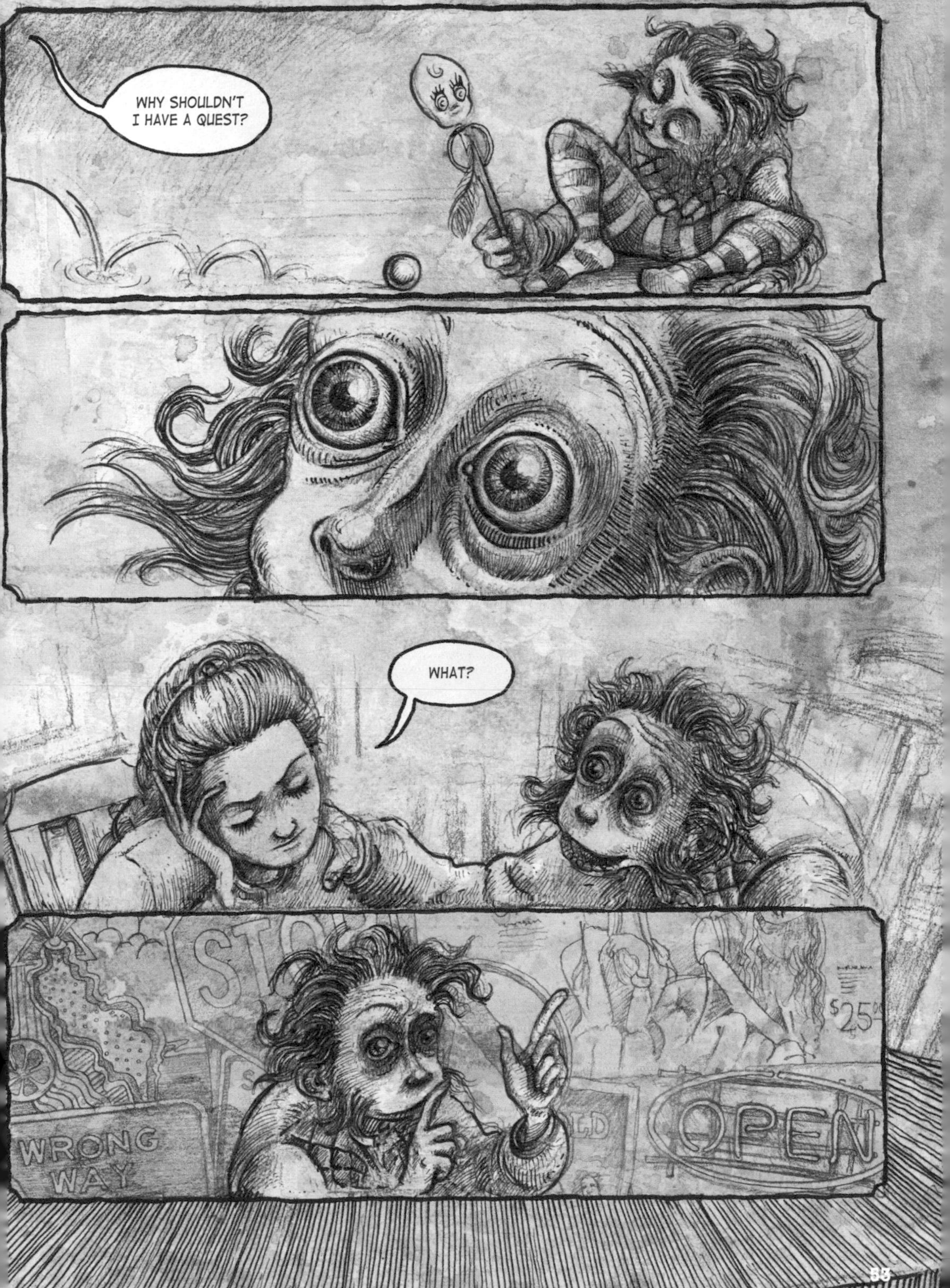
WHY SHOULDN'T I HAVE A QUEST?
WHAT?
WRONG WAY
OPEN
$25

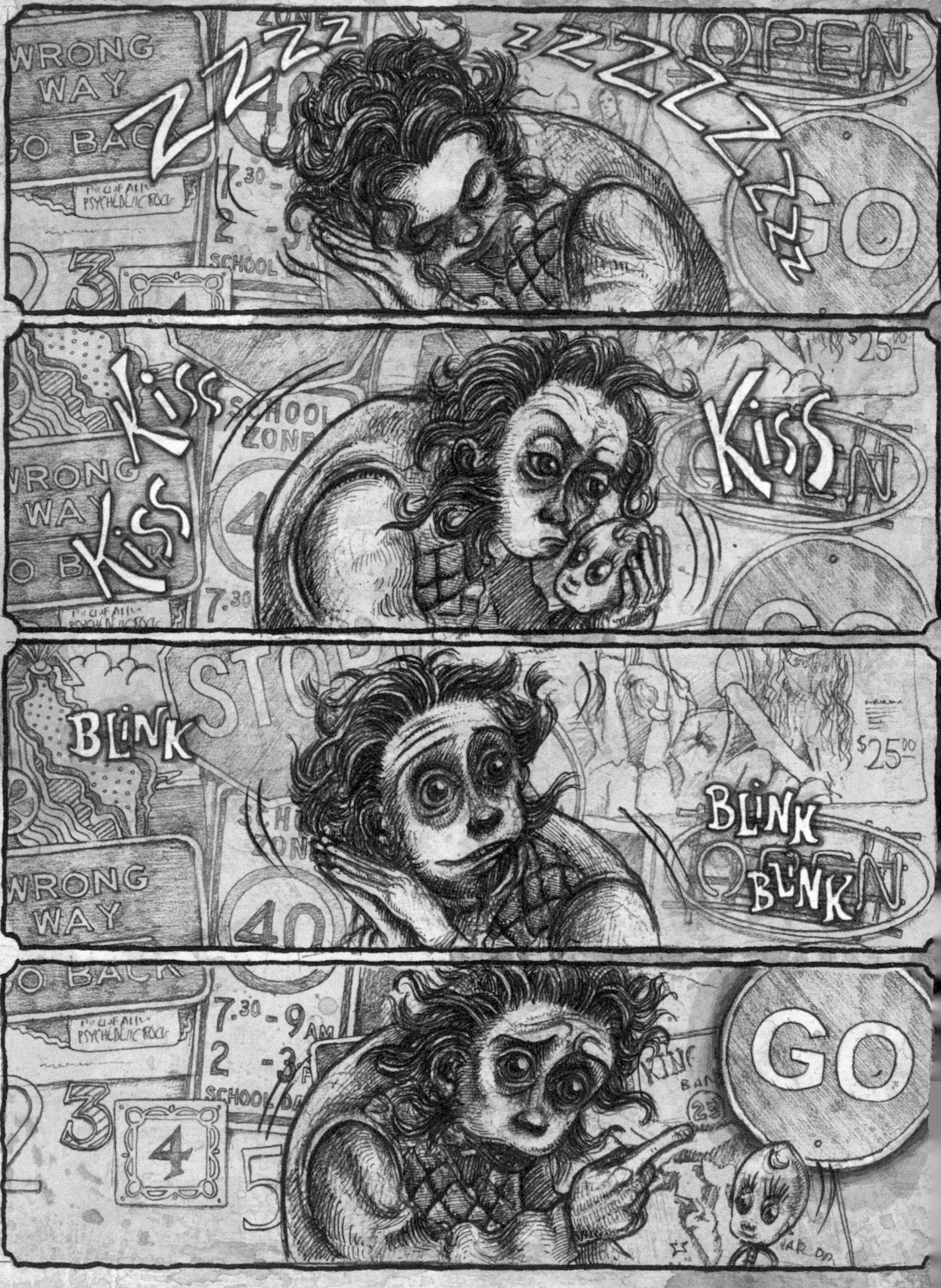
ZZZZZ
ZZZZZZZZZ
KISS
KISS
KISS
BLINK
BLINK
BLINK
GO

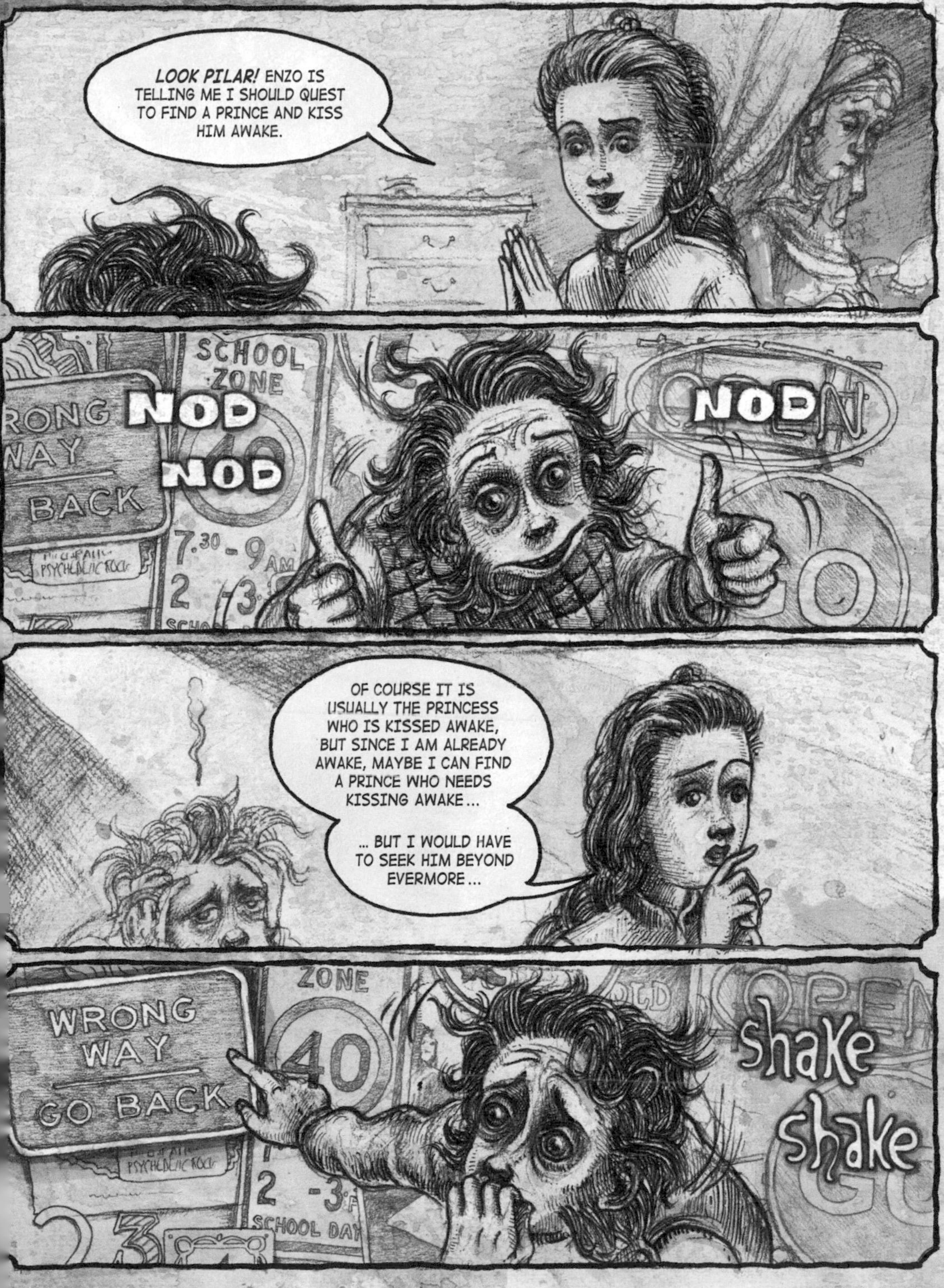
LOOK PILAR! ENZO IS TELLING ME I SHOULD QUEST TO FIND A PRINCE AND KISS HIM AWAKE.
SCHOOL ZONE
WRONG WAY BACK
NOD
NOD
NOD
PSYCHEDELIC ROCK
OF COURSE IT IS USUALLY THE PRINCESS WHO IS KISSED AWAKE, BUT SINCE I AM ALREADY AWAKE, MAYBE I CAN FIND A PRINCE WHO NEEDS KISSING AWAKE…
… BUT I WOULD HAVE TO SEEK HIM BEYOND EVERMORE…
ZONE
WRONG WAY GO BACK
40
PSYCHEDELIC ROCK
SCHOOL DAY
shake
shake

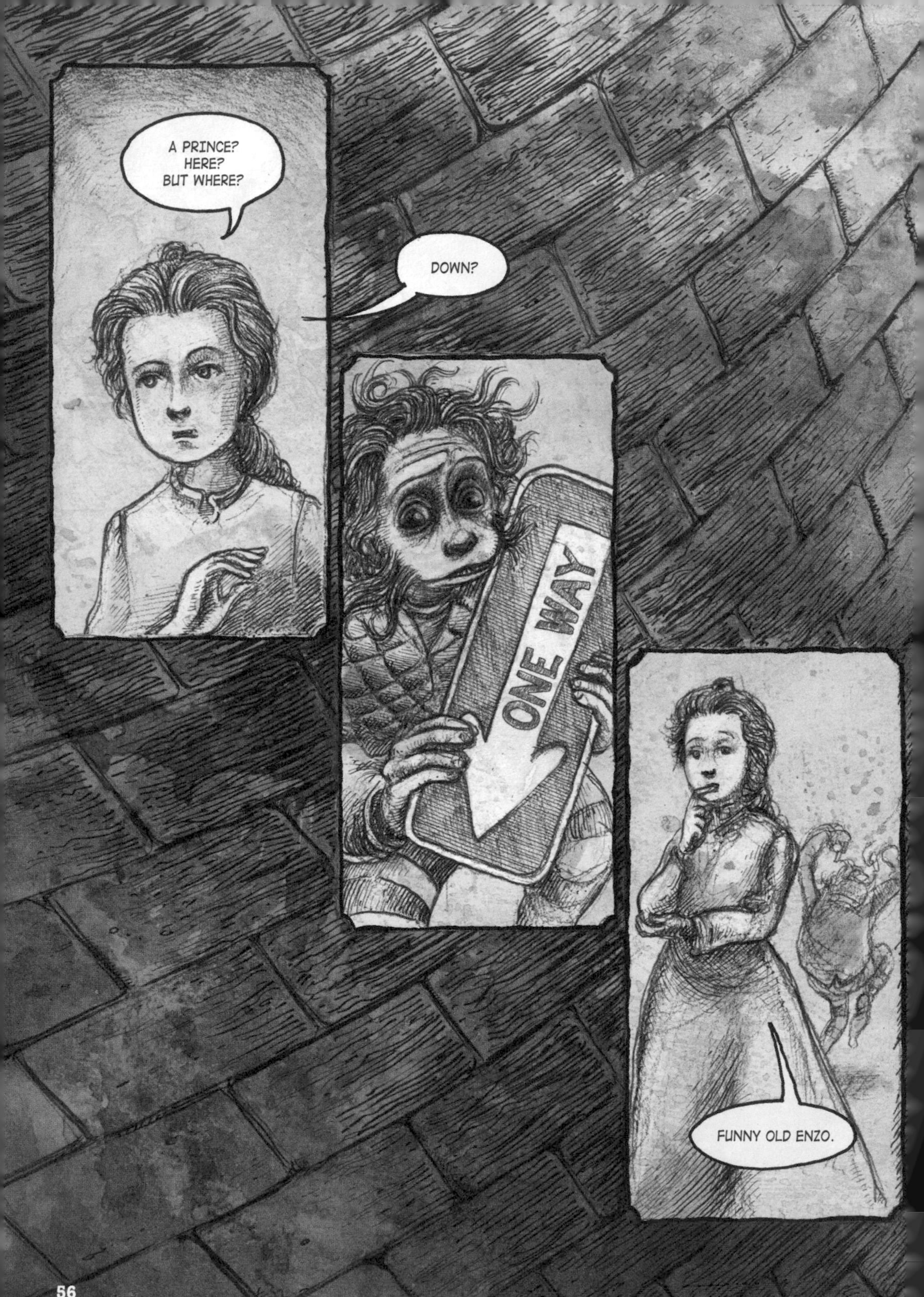
A PRINCE?
HERE?
BUT WHERE?
DOWN?
ONE WAY
FUNNY OLD ENZO.

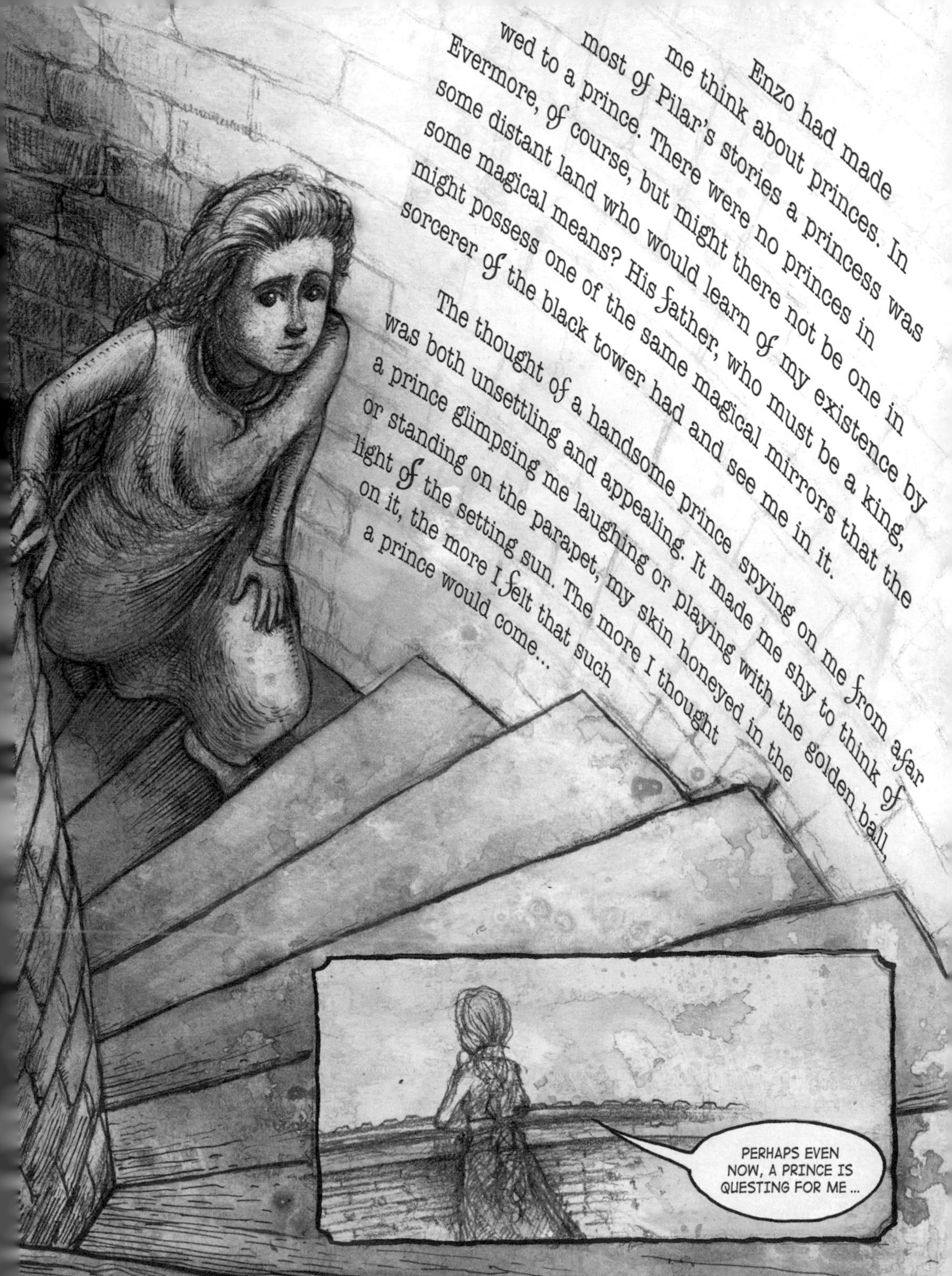
Enzo had made
me think about princes. In
most of Pilar's stories a princess was
wed to a prince. There were no princes in
Evermore, of course, but might there not be one in
some distant land who would learn of my existence by
some magical means? His father, who must be a king,
might possess one of the same magical mirrors that the
sorcerer of the black tower had and see me in it.
The thought of a handsome prince spying on me from afar
was both unsettling and appealing. It made me shy to think of
a prince glimpsing me laughing or playing with the golden ball,
or standing on the parapet, my skin honeyed in the
light of the setting sun. The more I thought
on it, the more I felt that such
a prince would come...
PERHAPS EVEN NOW, A PRINCE IS QUESTING FOR ME ...

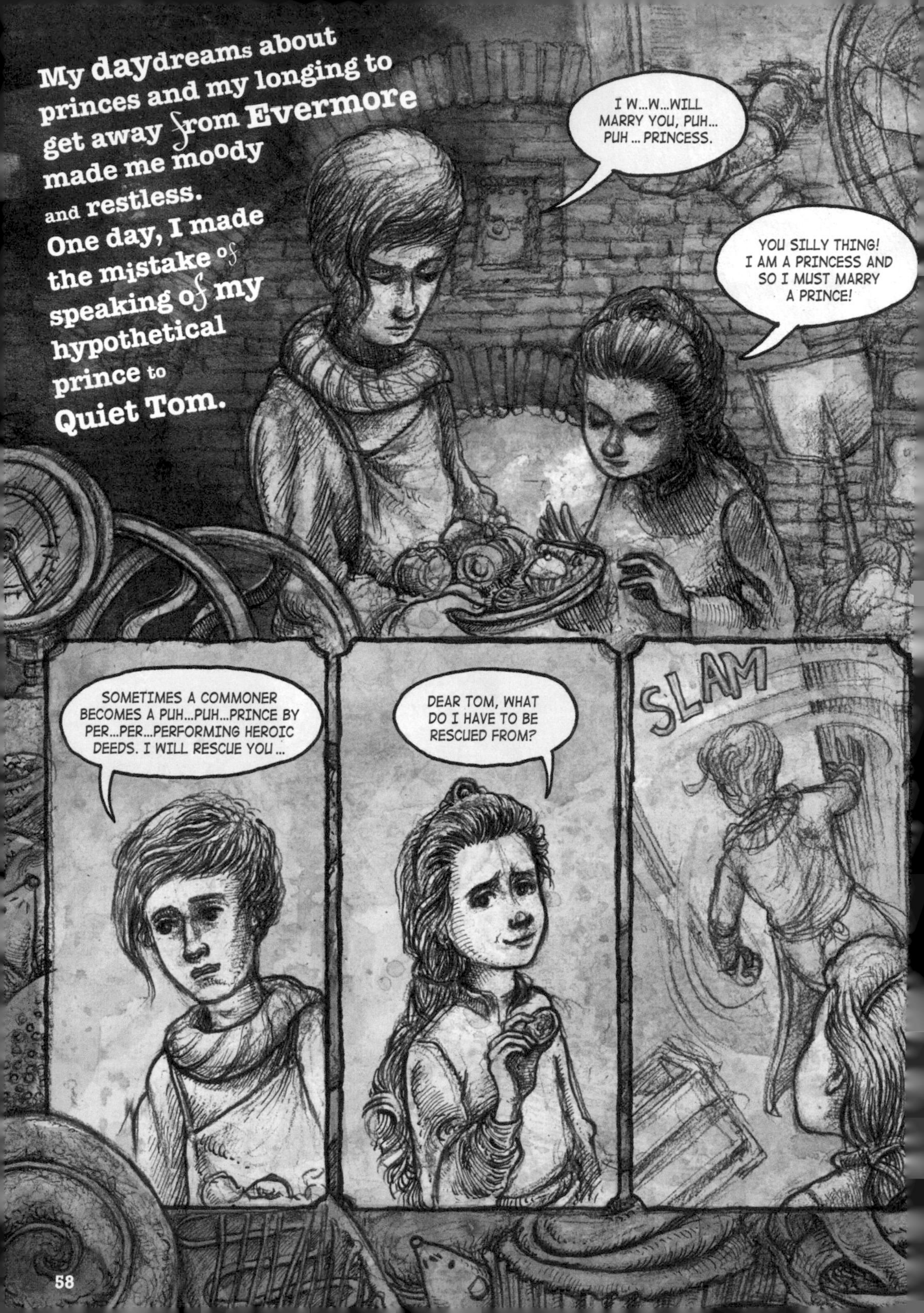
My daydreams about princes and my longing to get away from Evermore made me moody and restless. One day, I made the mistake of speaking of my hypothetical prince to Quiet Tom.
I W...W...WILL MARRY YOU, PUH... PUH ... PRINCESS.
YOU SILLY THING! I AM A PRINCESS AND SO I MUST MARRY A PRINCE!
SOMETIMES A COMMONER BECOMES A PUH...PUH...PRINCE BY PER...PER...PERFORMING HEROIC DEEDS. I WILL RESCUE YOU ...
DEAR TOM, WHAT DO I HAVE TO BE RESCUED FROM?
SLAM

**QuietTom** was sweet-natured and kind, generous and far cleverer than anyone guessed. He was my dearest friend and I loved him, but he bore no resemblance to the handsome, haughty, dashing, young princes of Pilar's stories. Yet I suddenly understood that he loved me, and not merely as a friend. It frightened me for, ignorant as I was of many things, I knew the King would never entertain the thought of marrying his daughter to a commoner.

A chill of fear ran through me at the thought of Quiet Tom going to the King to blush and stammer out his request for a task to prove himself worthy of a princess. The King was a hard, voluble, arrogant man and Tom's gentle awkwardness would incite his disdain and make him merciless.

I resolved to find Tom and beg him not to trouble the King. I did not want him to come to any harm. At the same time I was irritated by his suggestion that I needed rescuing.

A baker's lad! And that he should rescue me! As far as I knew he had never held anything more lethal than a kitchen knife in his hand.

I found him and forbade him to speak to the King, but the stubborn set of his chin did not reassure me.

There was nothing for me to do but pray he would forget. However, just before my sixteenth birthday Tom told me he had begun to train and strengthen himself so that he could apply to be a squire.

I guessed at once

that Quiet Tom only wanted to be a squire so that he might some day challenge one of the knights for his armour. That was how a knight was made – a man won or fought a knight for his or her armour. It was not the knighthood Tom wanted, of course. It was the armour, for no quest beyond the walls of Evermore could be undertaken without it. This told me that he still meant to approach the King for a quest. My blood froze at the thought of the sort of quest the King might set Tom ...

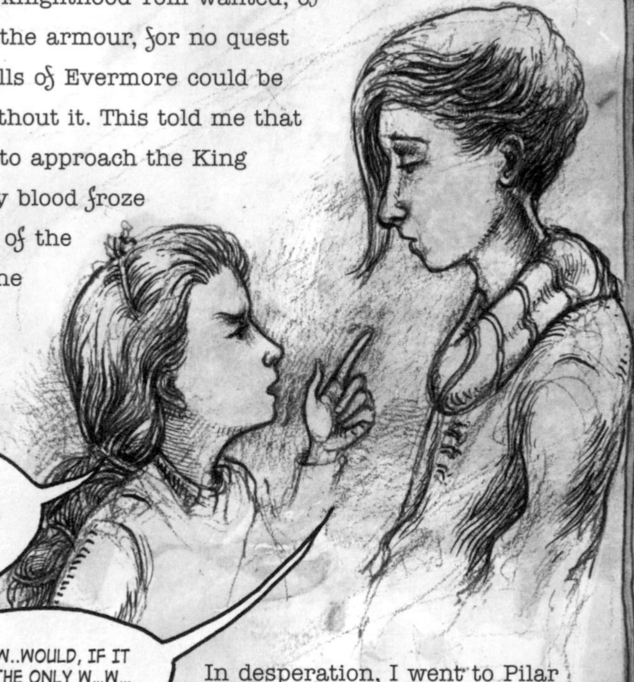

> I KNOW WHAT YOU INTEND, TOM. BUT TO WIN THE ARMOUR OF A KNIGHT, YOU WILL HAVE TO KILL THE MAN WHO WEARS IT. COULD YOU KILL, QUIET?

> I W...W..WOULD, IF IT WAS THE ONLY W...W... WAY TO SAVE YOU.

> I DO NOT NEED SAVING!

In desperation, I went to Pilar and told her all of it, begging her to talk sense into Quiet. She was angrier than I had ever seen her.

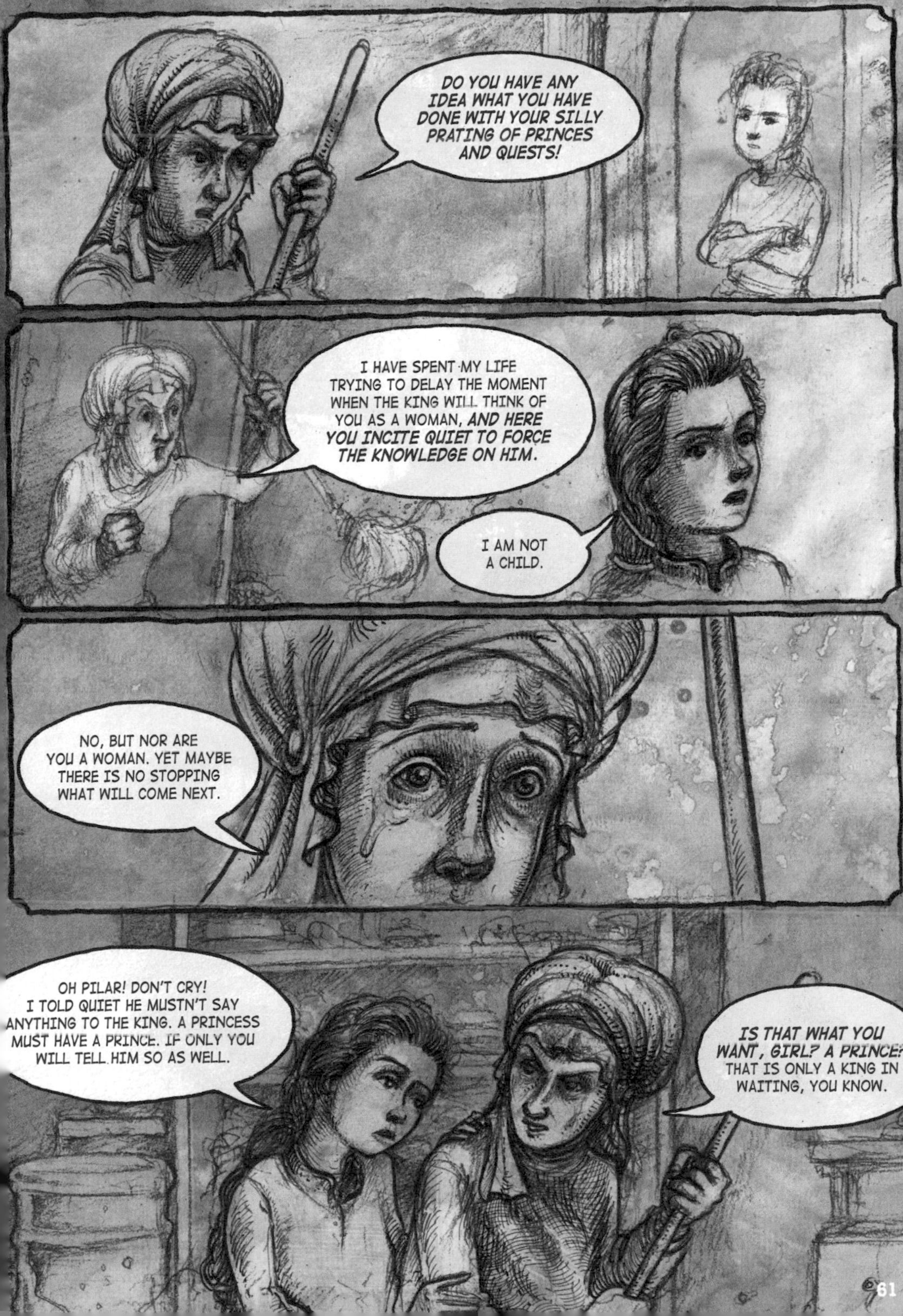

DO YOU HAVE ANY IDEA WHAT YOU HAVE DONE WITH YOUR SILLY PRATING OF PRINCES AND QUESTS!
I HAVE SPENT MY LIFE TRYING TO DELAY THE MOMENT WHEN THE KING WILL THINK OF YOU AS A WOMAN, AND HERE YOU INCITE QUIET TO FORCE THE KNOWLEDGE ON HIM.
I AM NOT A CHILD.
NO, BUT NOR ARE YOU A WOMAN. YET MAYBE THERE IS NO STOPPING WHAT WILL COME NEXT.
OH PILAR! DON'T CRY! I TOLD QUIET HE MUSTN'T SAY ANYTHING TO THE KING. A PRINCESS MUST HAVE A PRINCE. IF ONLY YOU WILL TELL HIM SO AS WELL.
IS THAT WHAT YOU WANT, GIRL? A PRINCE? THAT IS ONLY A KING IN WAITING, YOU KNOW.

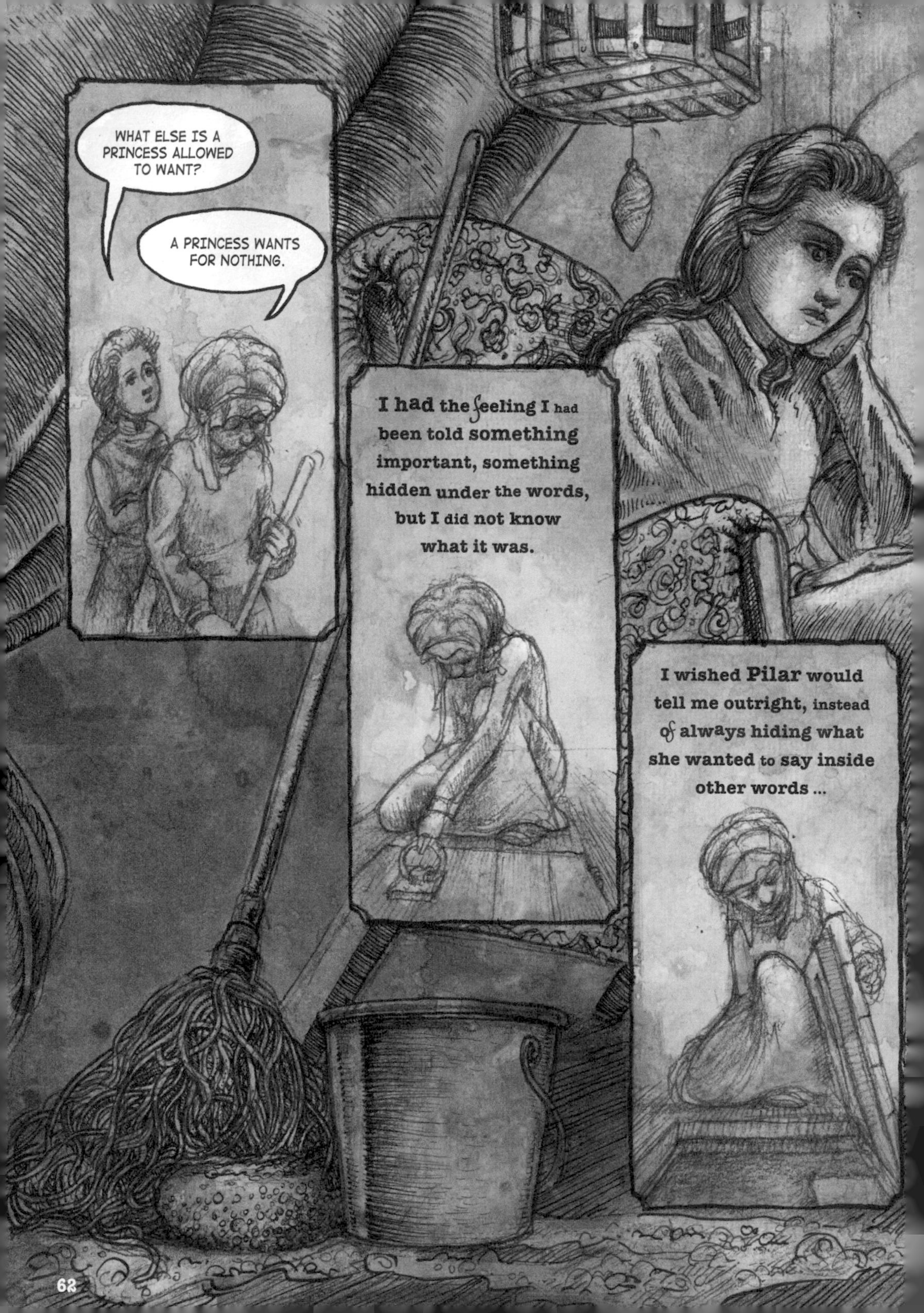
WHAT ELSE IS A PRINCESS ALLOWED TO WANT?
A PRINCESS WANTS FOR NOTHING.
I had the feeling I had been told something important, something hidden under the words, but I did not know what it was.
I wished Pilar would tell me outright, instead of always hiding what she wanted to say inside other words ...

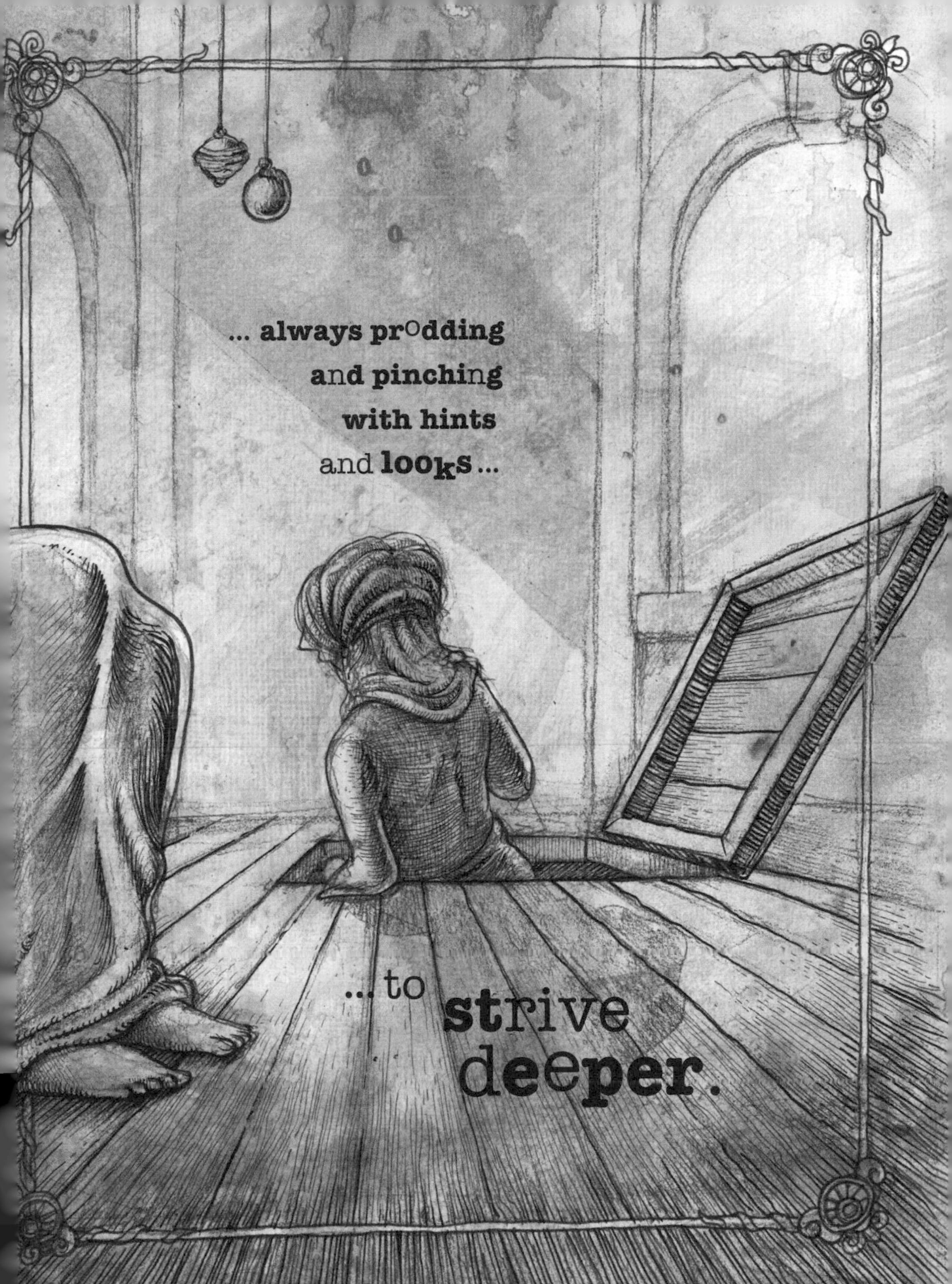
... always prodding
and pinching
with hints
and looks ...
... to strive deeper.

At last

the King went out with his knights from Evermore, and after a time, he returned with another cache of food and also devices and tools to repair the hydrofarm equipment. The hungry time was over. When the harvest came, the crops were so bountiful that a feast of thanksgiving was held.

Quiet Tom learned how to make pastries and elaborate sweet confections. Sometimes he hid pink sugar mice in the platters of fruit and cake sent to my chamber. Despite the fact that he was growing in strength and in height, and training himself with a wooden stave and sword, he spoke no more of quests or rescuing, to my relief. I knew Pilar had spoken to him, though she never told me what she said. The only thing she did tell me was that he had sworn not to raise the matter of my hand with the King.

The whole incident had shown me that much of my thinking about marriage and princes came from stories. Reality was more frightening and ambiguous, even dangerous. I still disliked the too-young, fussy, frilly clothes Pilar sewed for me, but I was content to go on being a child for a little longer.

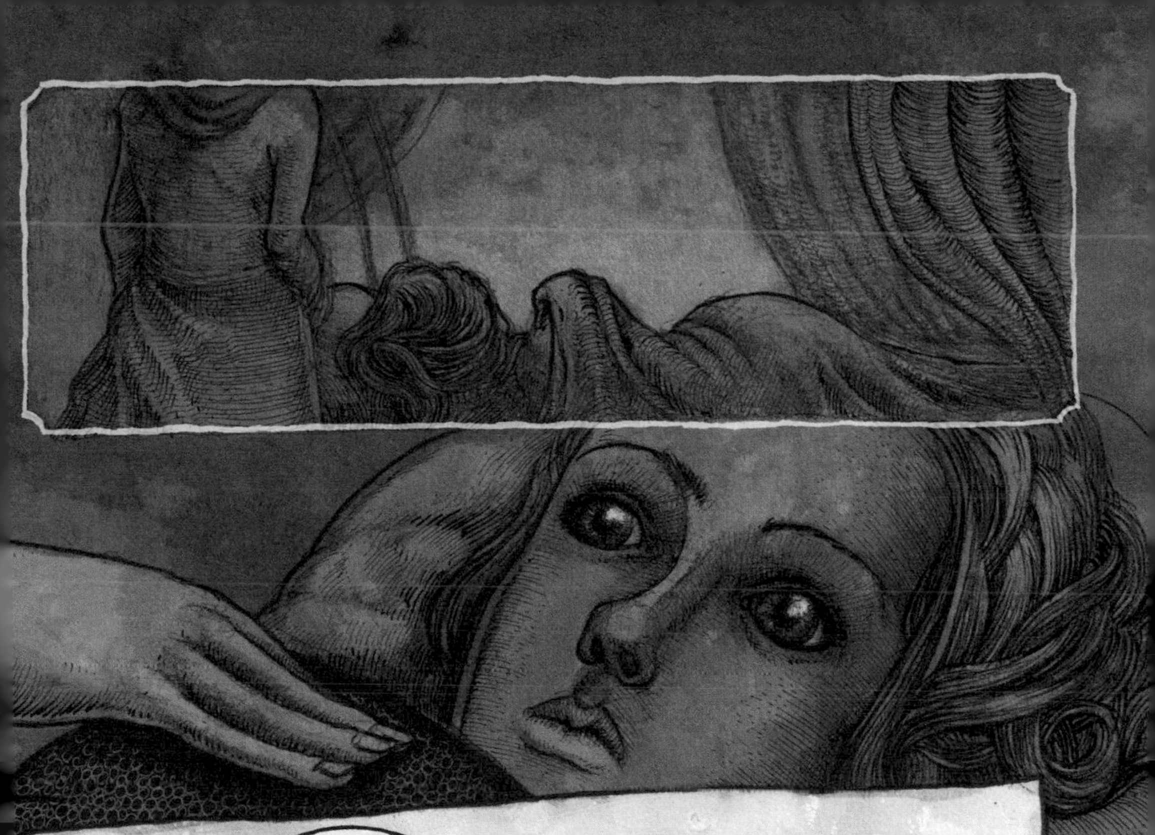

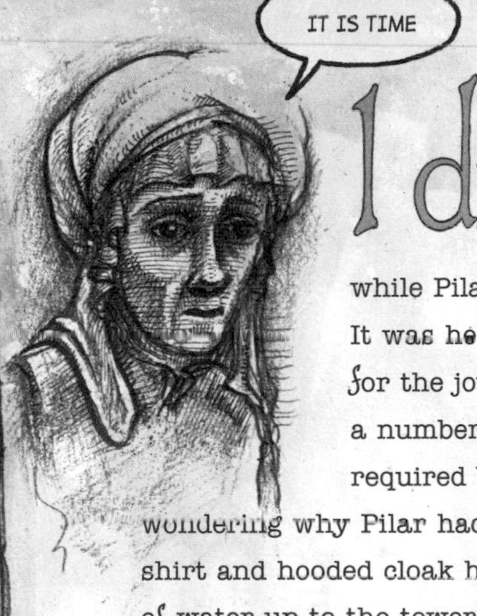
IT IS TIME

I dressed swiftly

while Pilar readied the pack she had prepared. It was heavy, for it contained boots made especially for the journey ahead. Pilar had ordered them through a number of intermediaries, for only knights and squires required boots. It would not have done to have the King wondering why Pilar had ordered boots. She had sewn my trews and shirt and hooded cloak herself, smuggling them and a screw-top bottle of water up to the tower. Despite the heat, there would be high mountains to cross, and ice winds to contend with, before the journey was done. Food had been saved up from meals and hidden in Enzo's little rat's nest of treasures.

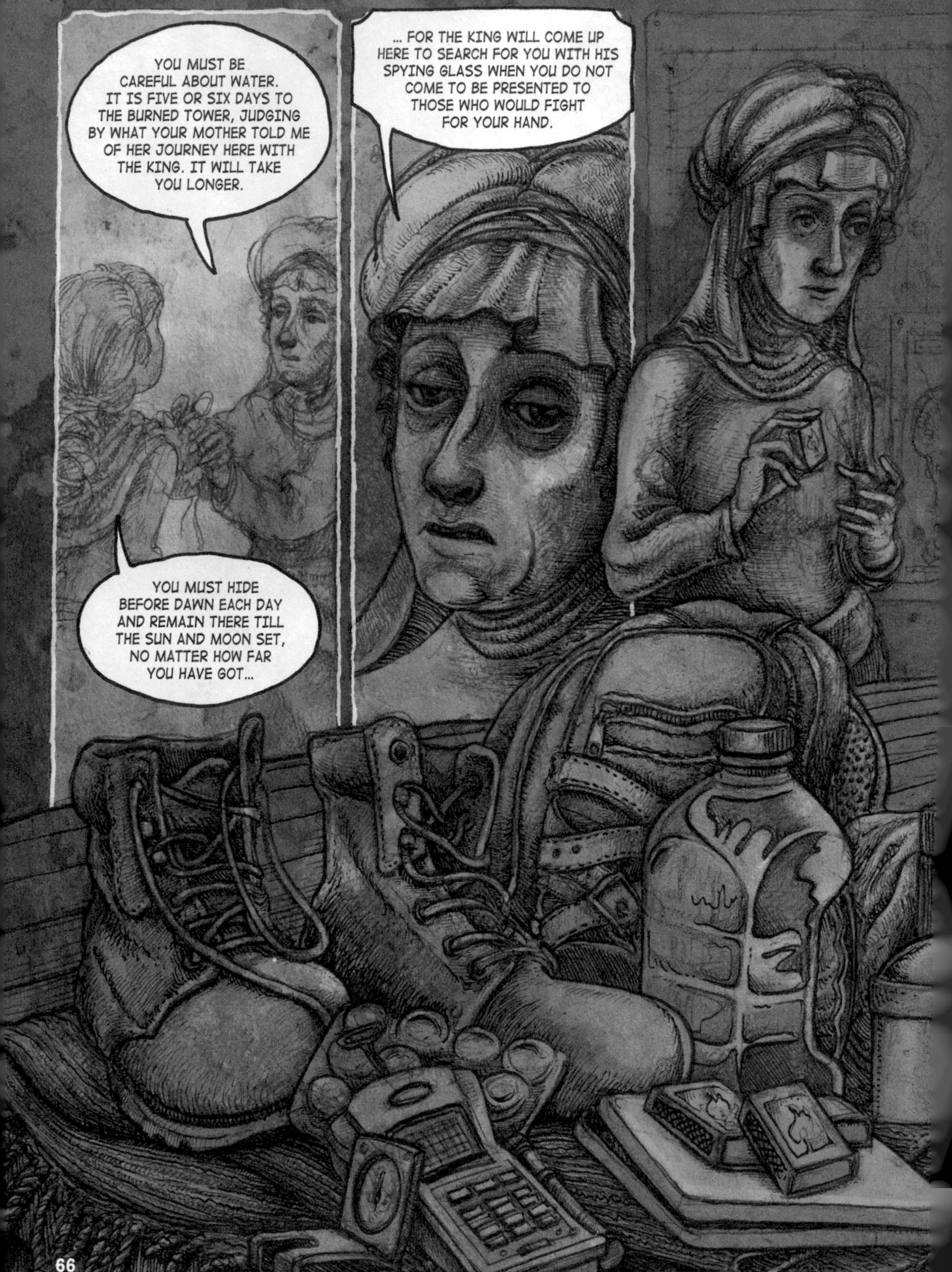
YOU MUST BE CAREFUL ABOUT WATER. IT IS FIVE OR SIX DAYS TO THE BURNED TOWER, JUDGING BY WHAT YOUR MOTHER TOLD ME OF HER JOURNEY HERE WITH THE KING. IT WILL TAKE YOU LONGER.
YOU MUST HIDE BEFORE DAWN EACH DAY AND REMAIN THERE TILL THE SUN AND MOON SET, NO MATTER HOW FAR YOU HAVE GOT...
... FOR THE KING WILL COME UP HERE TO SEARCH FOR YOU WITH HIS SPYING GLASS WHEN YOU DO NOT COME TO BE PRESENTED TO THOSE WHO WOULD FIGHT FOR YOUR HAND.

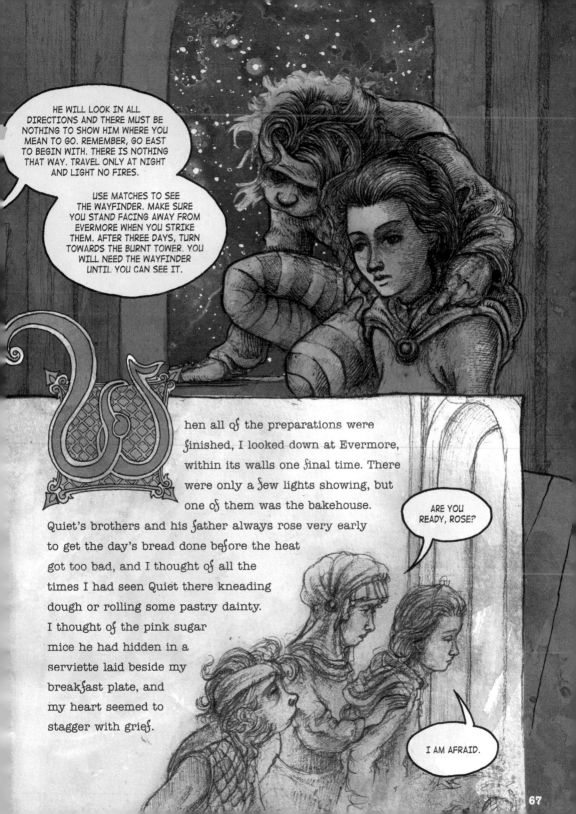

HE WILL LOOK IN ALL DIRECTIONS AND THERE MUST BE NOTHING TO SHOW HIM WHERE YOU MEAN TO GO. REMEMBER, GO EAST TO BEGIN WITH. THERE IS NOTHING THAT WAY. TRAVEL ONLY AT NIGHT AND LIGHT NO FIRES.

USE MATCHES TO SEE THE WAYFINDER. MAKE SURE YOU STAND FACING AWAY FROM EVERMORE WHEN YOU STRIKE THEM. AFTER THREE DAYS, TURN TOWARDS THE BURNT TOWER. YOU WILL NEED THE WAYFINDER UNTIL YOU CAN SEE IT.

When all of the preparations were finished, I looked down at Evermore, within its walls one final time. There were only a few lights showing, but one of them was the bakehouse. Quiet's brothers and his father always rose very early to get the day's bread done before the heat got too bad, and I thought of all the times I had seen Quiet there kneading dough or rolling some pastry dainty. I thought of the pink sugar mice he had hidden in a serviette laid beside my breakfast plate, and my heart seemed to stagger with grief.

ARE YOU READY, ROSE?

I AM AFRAID.

ONLY A FOOL WOULD NOT BE AFRAID. THERE HAVE BEEN TIMES I WANTED TO SHAKE YOU AND BOX YOUR EARS TO MAKE YOU SEE THE DANGERS, BUT YOU WERE NEVER A FOOL. ONLY IGNORANT. SOME OF THAT WAS MY DOING. BUT FEAR OR NOT, YOU MUST FIND THE COURAGE TO ACT, OR PERISH.

... ARE PERILOUS, AYE. IF THEY HAD BEEN STRONGER THE KING WOULD HAVE HAD THEM HAMMERED AWAY.

IT IS THEIR WEAKNESS THAT KEPT THEM SAFE, EVEN AS YOUR WEAKNESS HAS KEPT YOU SAFE UNTIL NOW.

THE STEPS ...

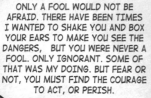

Pilar stiffened and we **both listened to** the **distant grinding sound** of **the gate being opened.** **The thing we had been waiting** for **all** the **long night.**

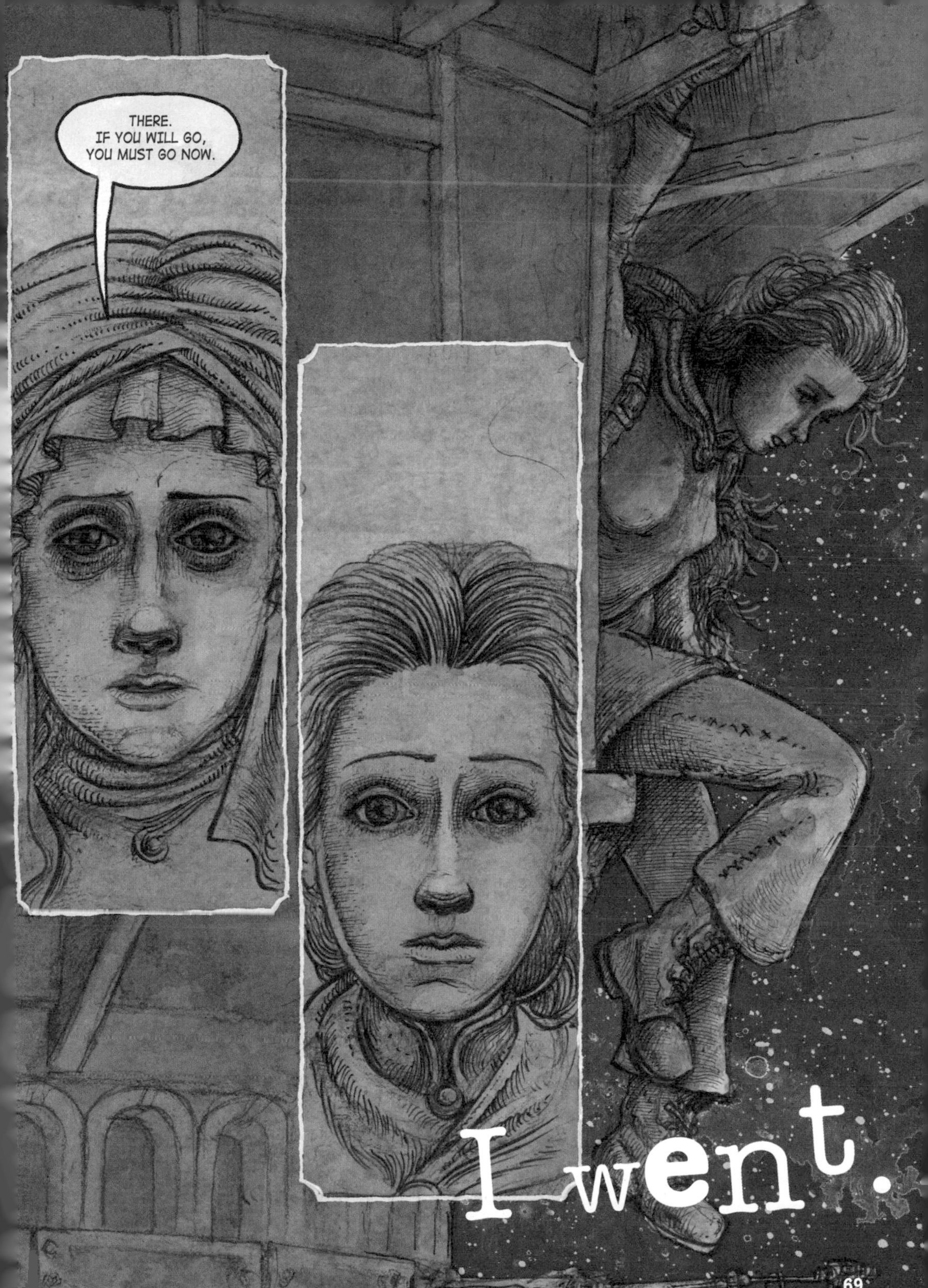
THERE.
IF YOU WILL GO,
YOU MUST GO NOW.
I went.

I do not know where I found the courage to descend those endless, crumbling, steps in the darkness. I slipped time and time again.

I tore my nails and grazed my knees and wept and swore words I had not even known I knew. I was amazed at the capacity my body and mind had for terror. I thought I should faint or die or my heart would burst a dozen times, but I endured. I climbed and clawed ever downward, too frightened of falling to worry about being seen, and then, at last, my foot touched the ground.

For a moment I thought my senses had tricked me, but when I looked about I saw that I had truly reached the ground. I had to will my fingers to let go of the stone. I swayed and thought I would faint. But then I noticed a thin red seam of light along the eastern horizon and realised it had taken much longer than we had calculated. Very soon, more men who would vie for my hand by trying to kill one another would rise and be feasted by the King.

Then I would be summoned to receive their compliments and declarations, before they fought from dawn to dusk. To save them and myself, I had to get as far away as I could from the walled city before I was called for. I did not waste any time in getting out the boots and putting them on.

The sand was cool yet and I ran, praying that Pilar had managed to set the fire that would distract the knights who guarded the gates, to give me time to get around the eastern side of Evermore before they emerged. Then I would be hidden from them. There were guards in the Rose Tower, of course, but that was on the western side of the gate, so that its eastern view was blocked by the White Tower.

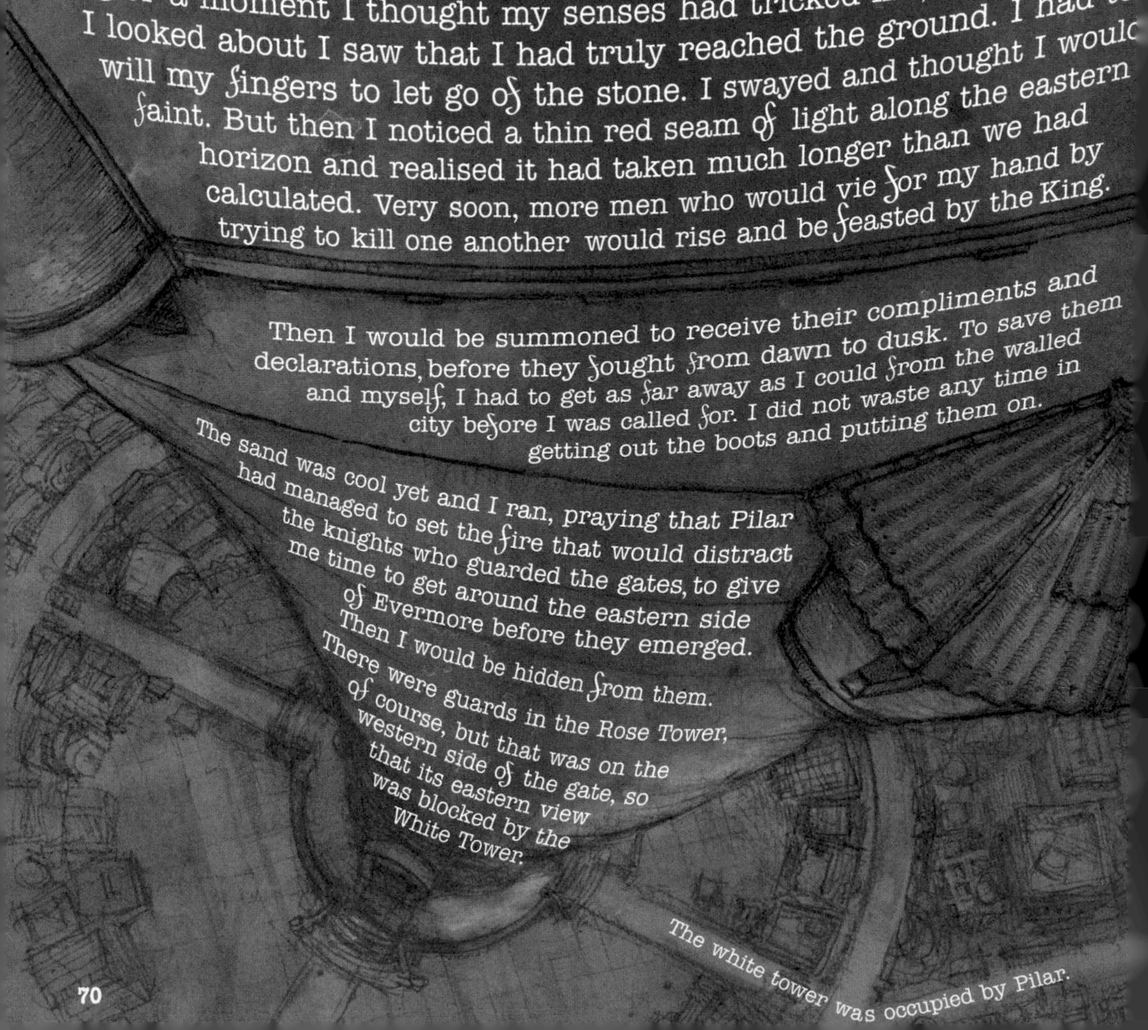

The white tower was occupied by Pilar.

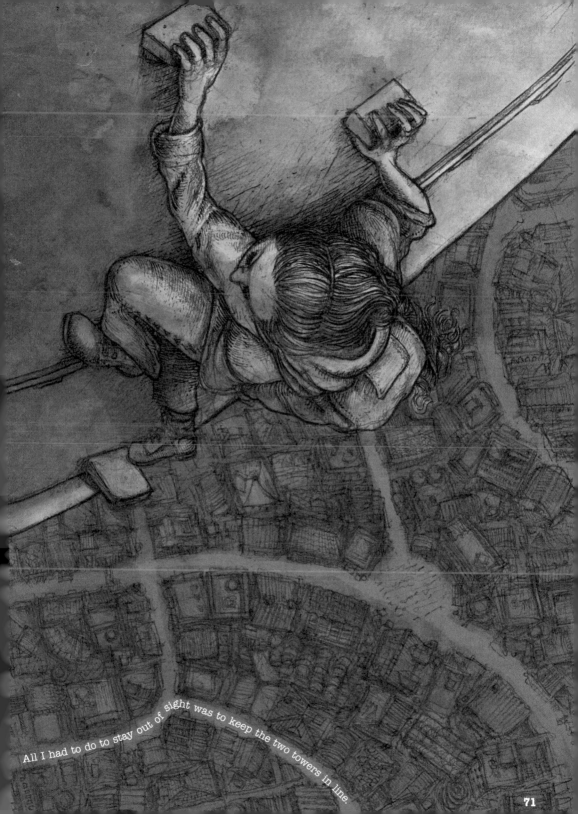

All I had to do to stay out of sight was to keep the two towers in line.

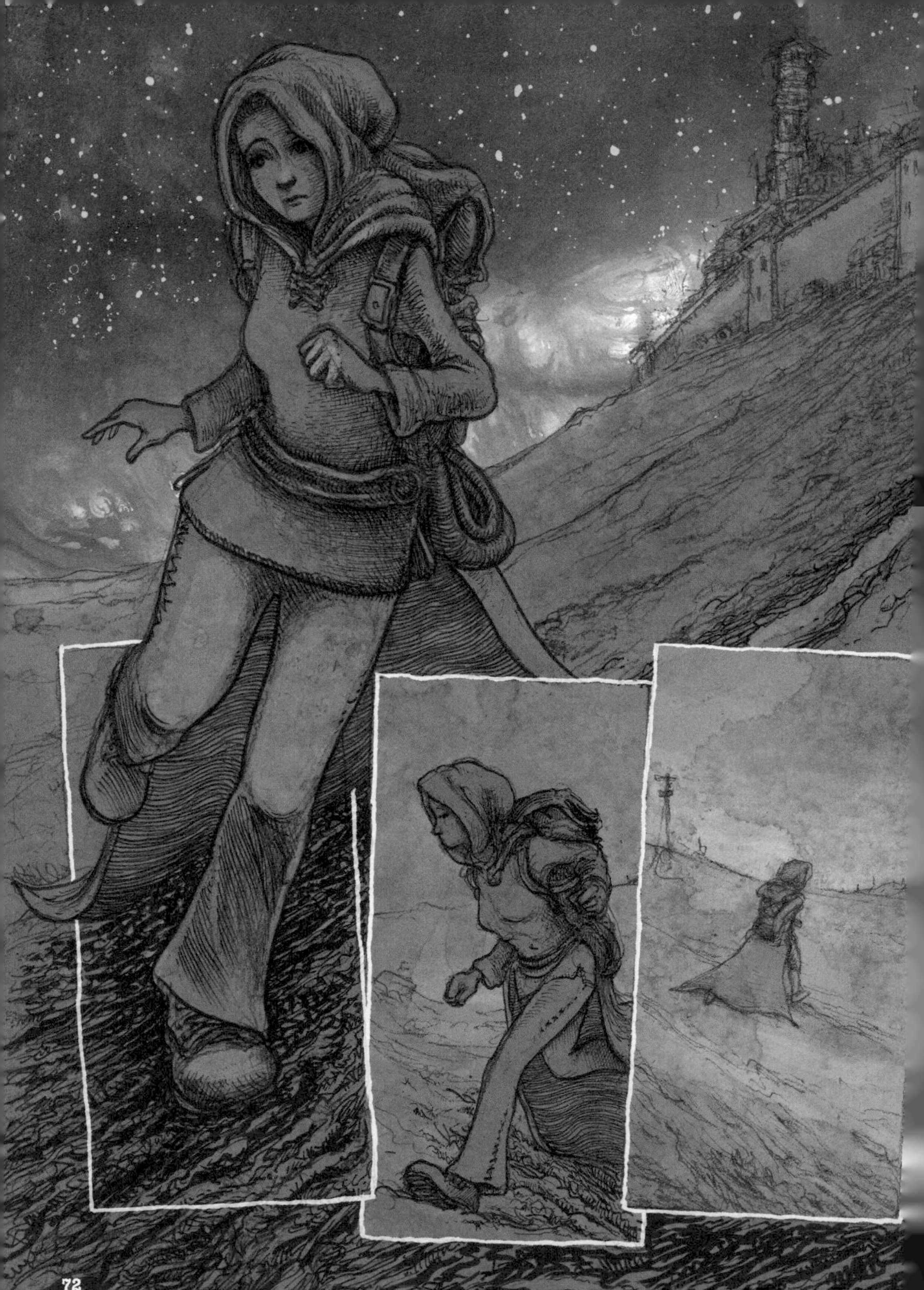

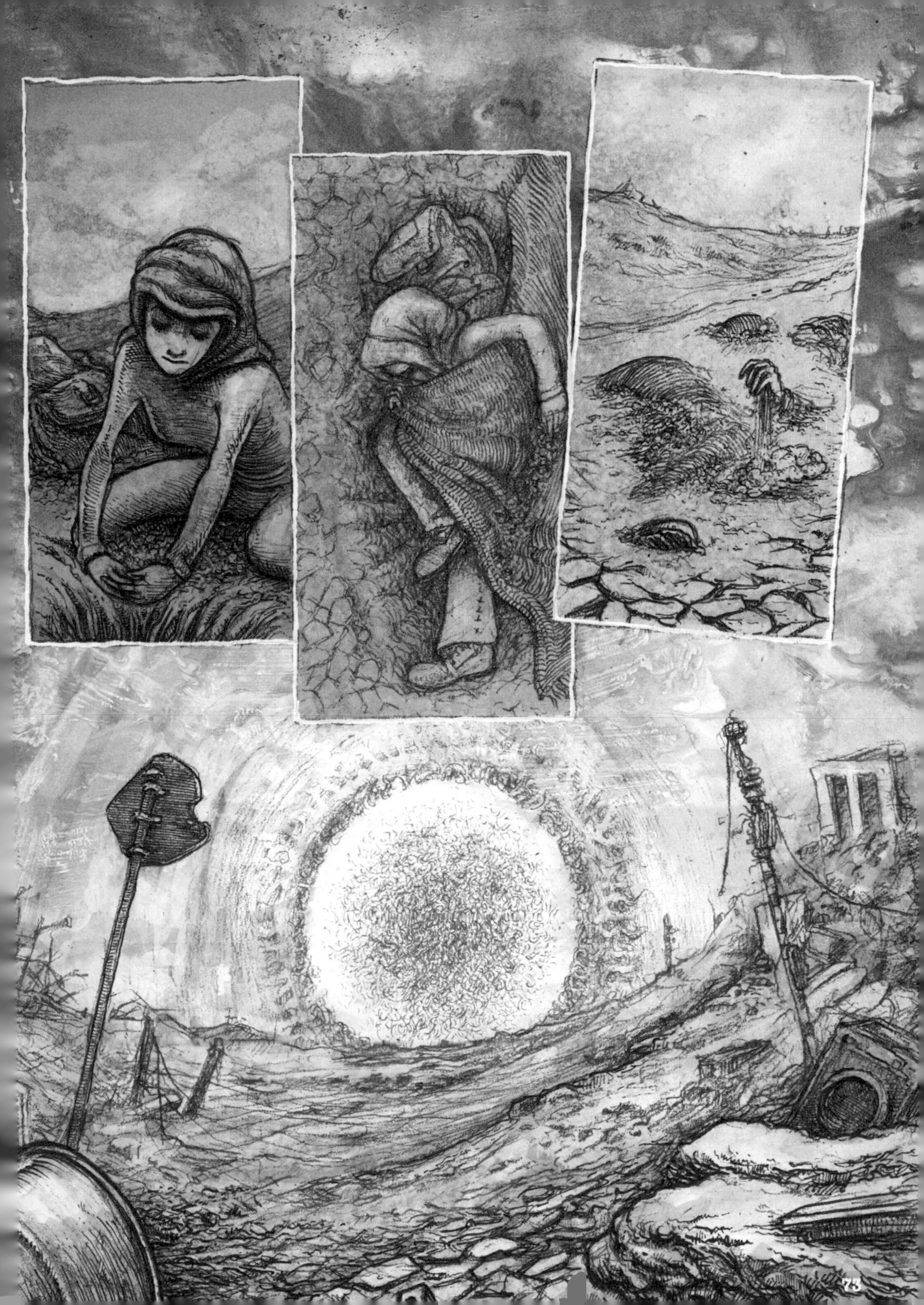

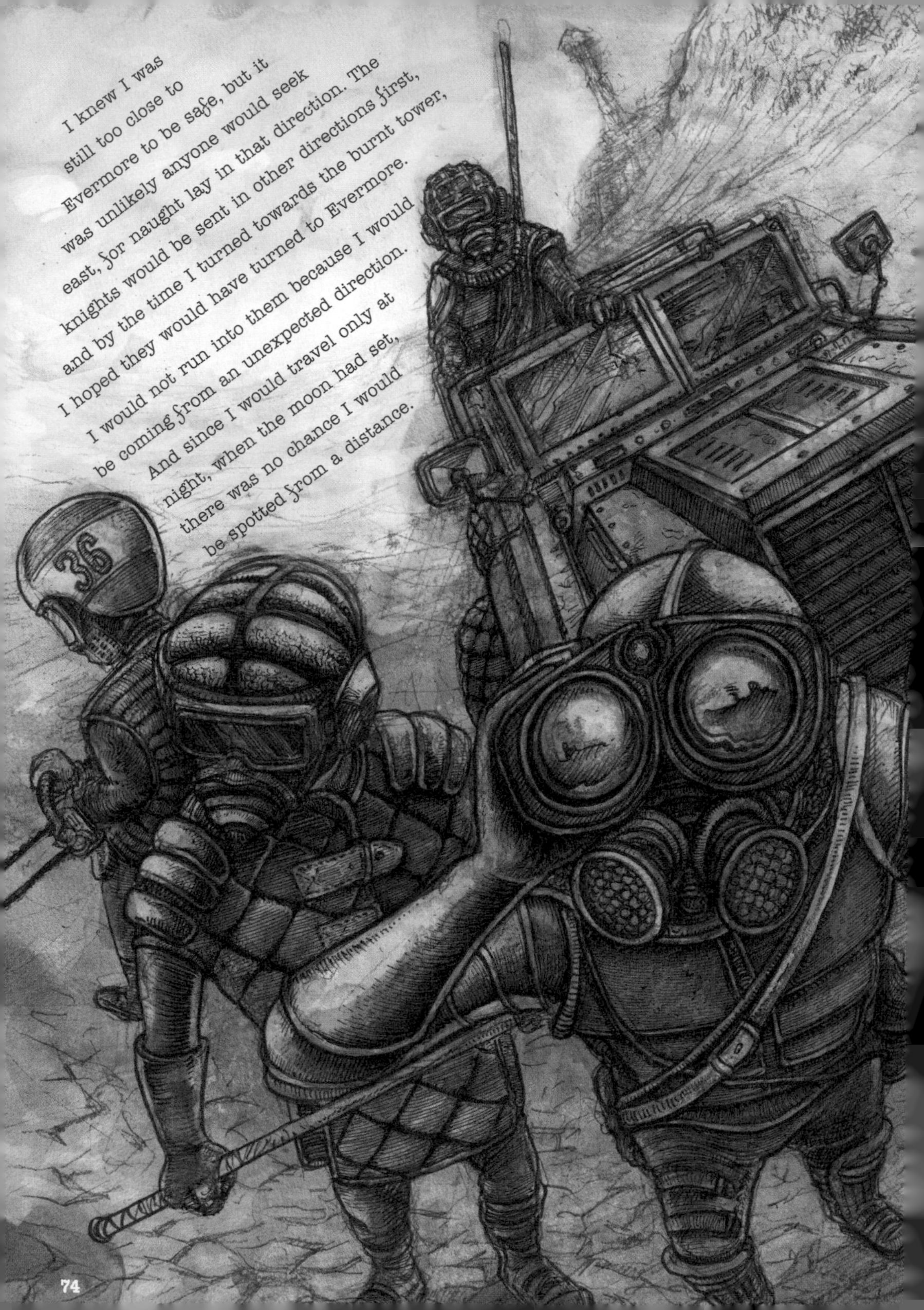

I knew I was still too close to Evermore to be safe, but it was unlikely anyone would seek east, for naught lay in that direction. The knights would be sent in other directions first, and by the time I turned towards the burnt tower, I hoped they would have turned to Evermore. I would not run into them because I would be coming from an unexpected direction. And since I would travel only at night, when the moon had set, there was no chance I would be spotted from a distance.

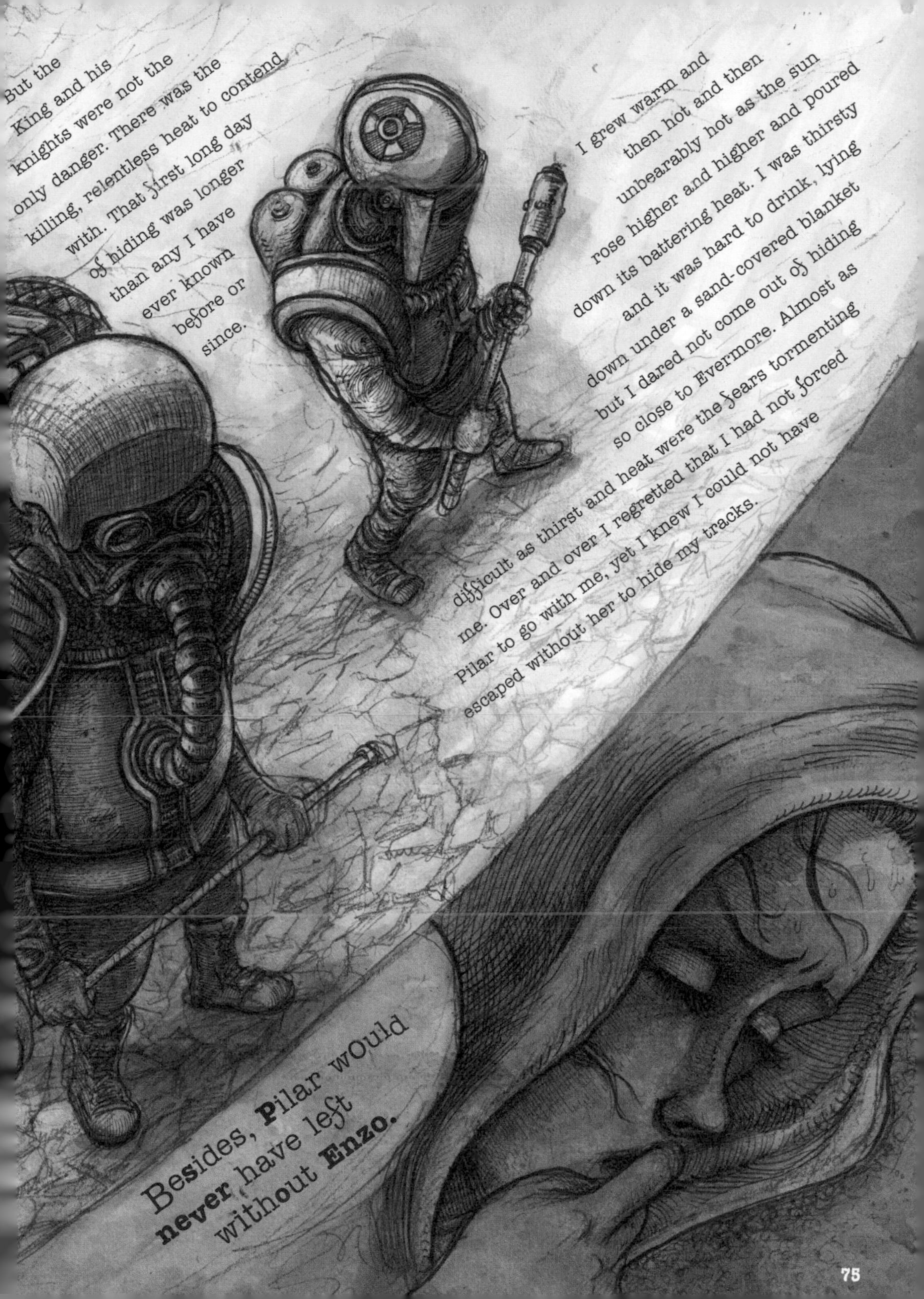

But the King and his knights were not the only danger. There was the killing, relentless heat to contend with. That first long day of hiding was longer than any I have ever known before or since.

I grew warm and then hot and then unbearably hot as the sun rose higher and higher and poured down its battering heat. I was thirsty and it was hard to drink, lying down under a sand-covered blanket but I dared not come out of hiding so close to Evermore. Almost as difficult as thirst and heat were the fears tormenting me. Over and over I regretted that I had not forced Pilar to go with me, yet I knew I could not have escaped without her to hide my tracks.

Besides, **P**ilar would **never** have left without **Enzo.**

By the end of that first day, I had managed to drink so little that there was not moisture enough in me for a tear. Even now I recall the thirst as a dreadful torment. Nor had it been possible to eat, so I was ravenous. I had not prepared myself well enough and I could not make that mistake again.

A thousand times during that endless day, I thought it must be nearing dusk, but it grew ever hotter and, in the end, there was nothing but the merciless heat that obliterated thought.

I slept again, or maybe I swooned. When I woke, I was cool and it was dark. I sat up, relishing the faint breeze on my overheated, itching skin. Cursing my stupidity in wasting a moment of the precious, concealing dark, I set off, knowing the King would be in the White Tower, waiting for the moon to rise.

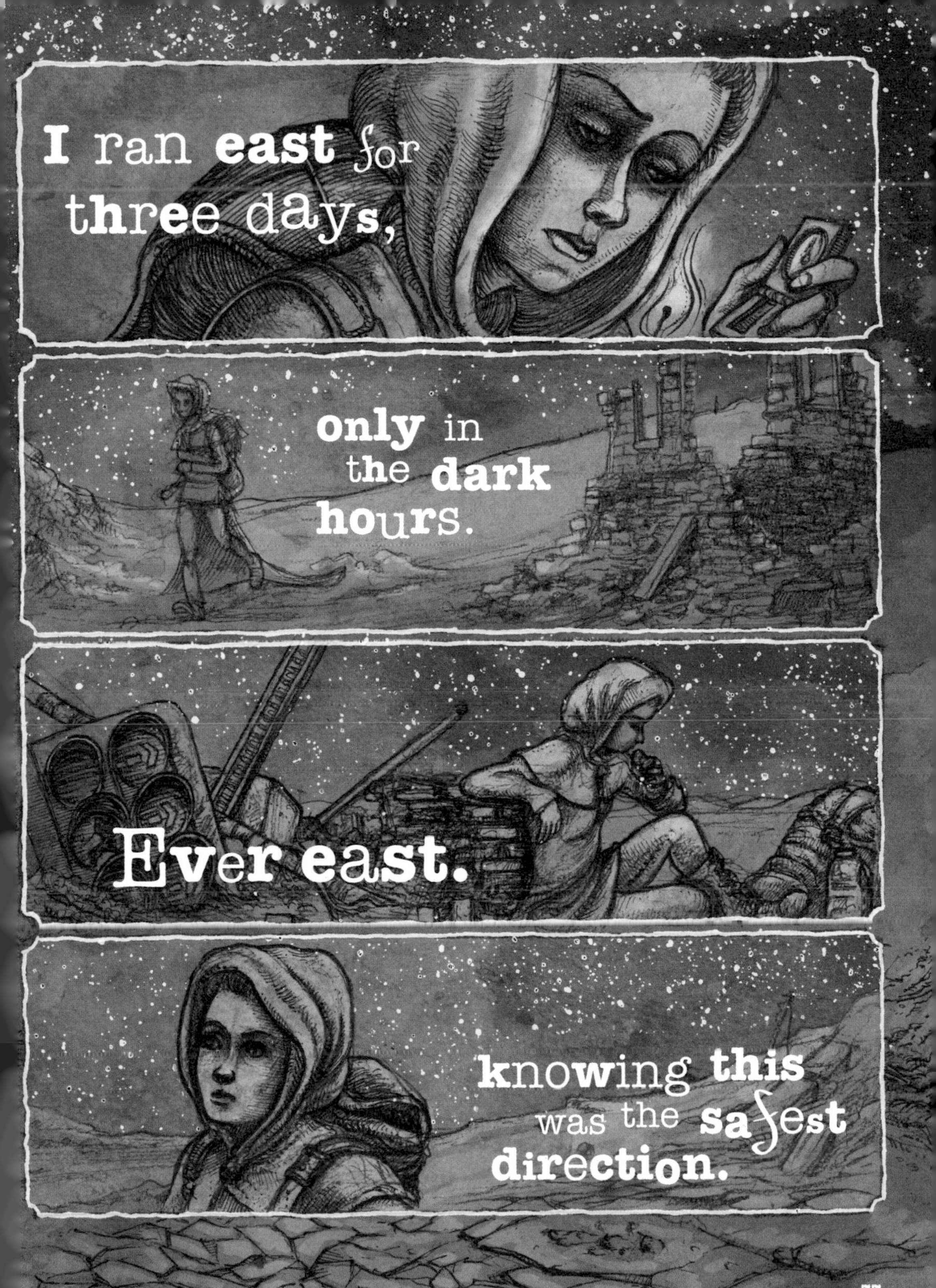
I ran east for three days,
only in the dark hours.
Ever east.
knowing this was the safest direction.

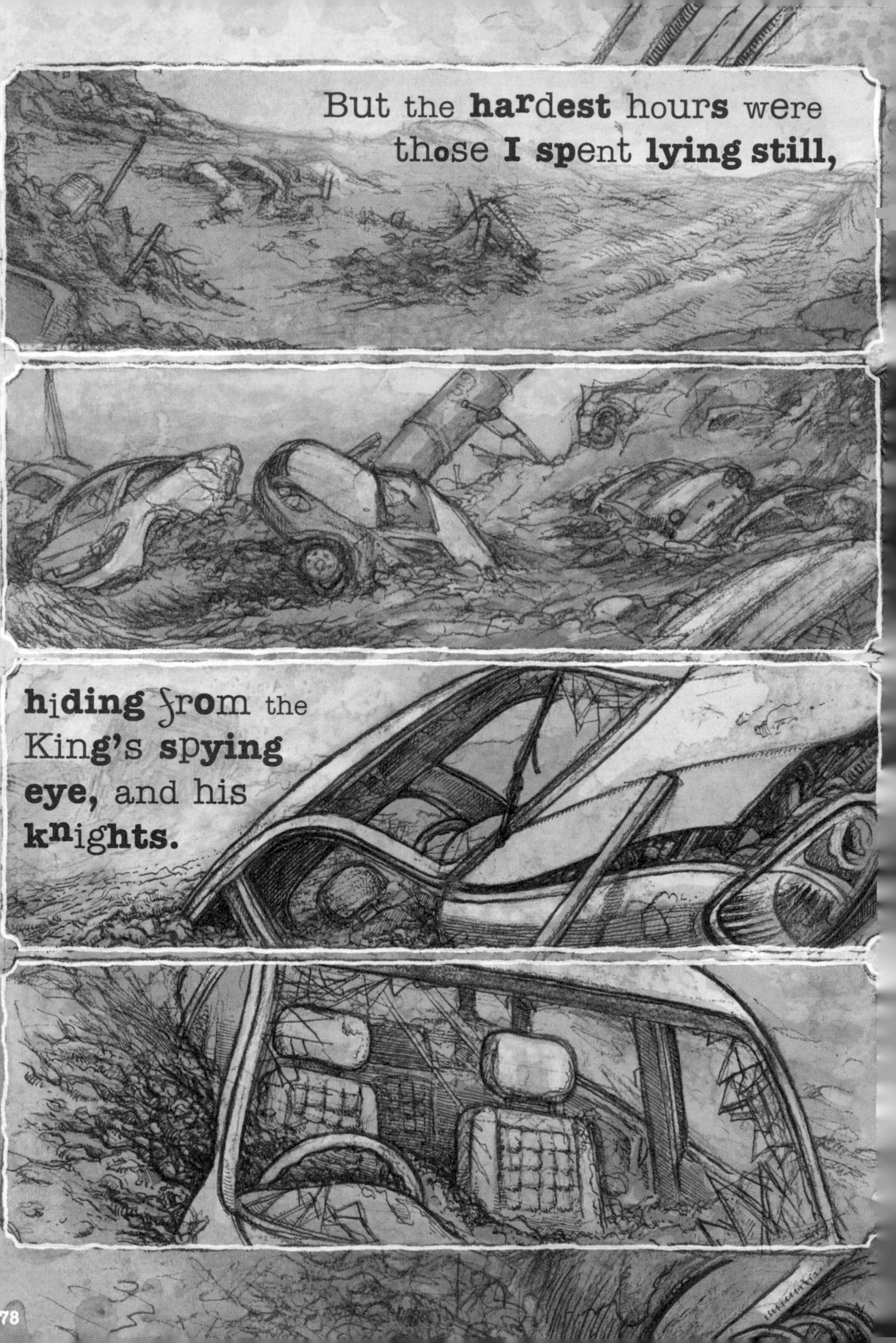
But the hardest hours were those I spent lying still,
hiding from the King's spying eye, and his knights.

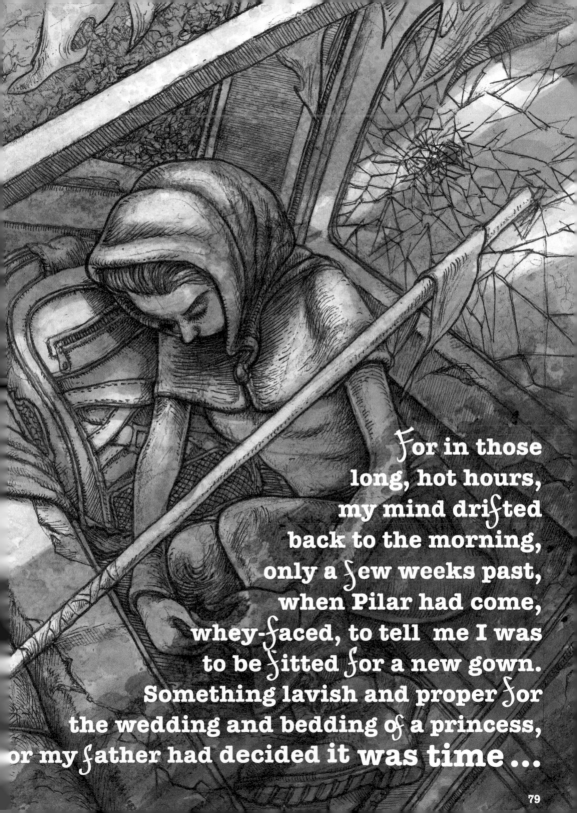

For in those
long, hot hours,
my mind drifted
back to the morning,
only a few weeks past,
when Pilar had come,
whey-faced, to tell me I was
to be fitted for a new gown.
Something lavish and proper for
the wedding and bedding of a princess,
or my father had decided it was time...

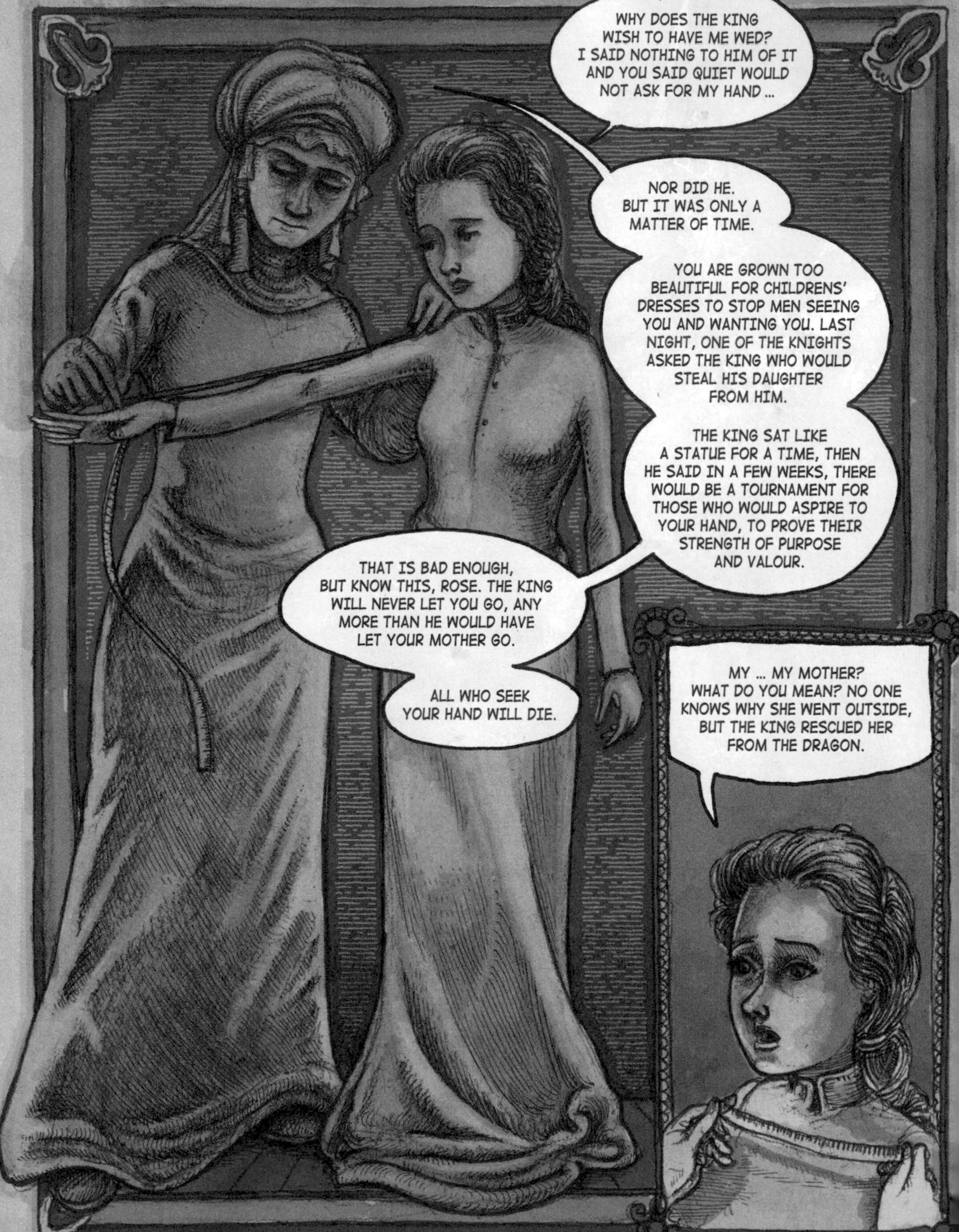
WHY DOES THE KING WISH TO HAVE ME WED? I SAID NOTHING TO HIM OF IT AND YOU SAID QUIET WOULD NOT ASK FOR MY HAND ...
NOR DID HE. BUT IT WAS ONLY A MATTER OF TIME.
YOU ARE GROWN TOO BEAUTIFUL FOR CHILDRENS' DRESSES TO STOP MEN SEEING YOU AND WANTING YOU. LAST NIGHT, ONE OF THE KNIGHTS ASKED THE KING WHO WOULD STEAL HIS DAUGHTER FROM HIM.
THE KING SAT LIKE A STATUE FOR A TIME, THEN HE SAID IN A FEW WEEKS, THERE WOULD BE A TOURNAMENT FOR THOSE WHO WOULD ASPIRE TO YOUR HAND, TO PROVE THEIR STRENGTH OF PURPOSE AND VALOUR.
THAT IS BAD ENOUGH, BUT KNOW THIS, ROSE. THE KING WILL NEVER LET YOU GO, ANY MORE THAN HE WOULD HAVE LET YOUR MOTHER GO.
ALL WHO SEEK YOUR HAND WILL DIE.
MY ... MY MOTHER? WHAT DO YOU MEAN? NO ONE KNOWS WHY SHE WENT OUTSIDE, BUT THE KING RESCUED HER FROM THE DRAGON.

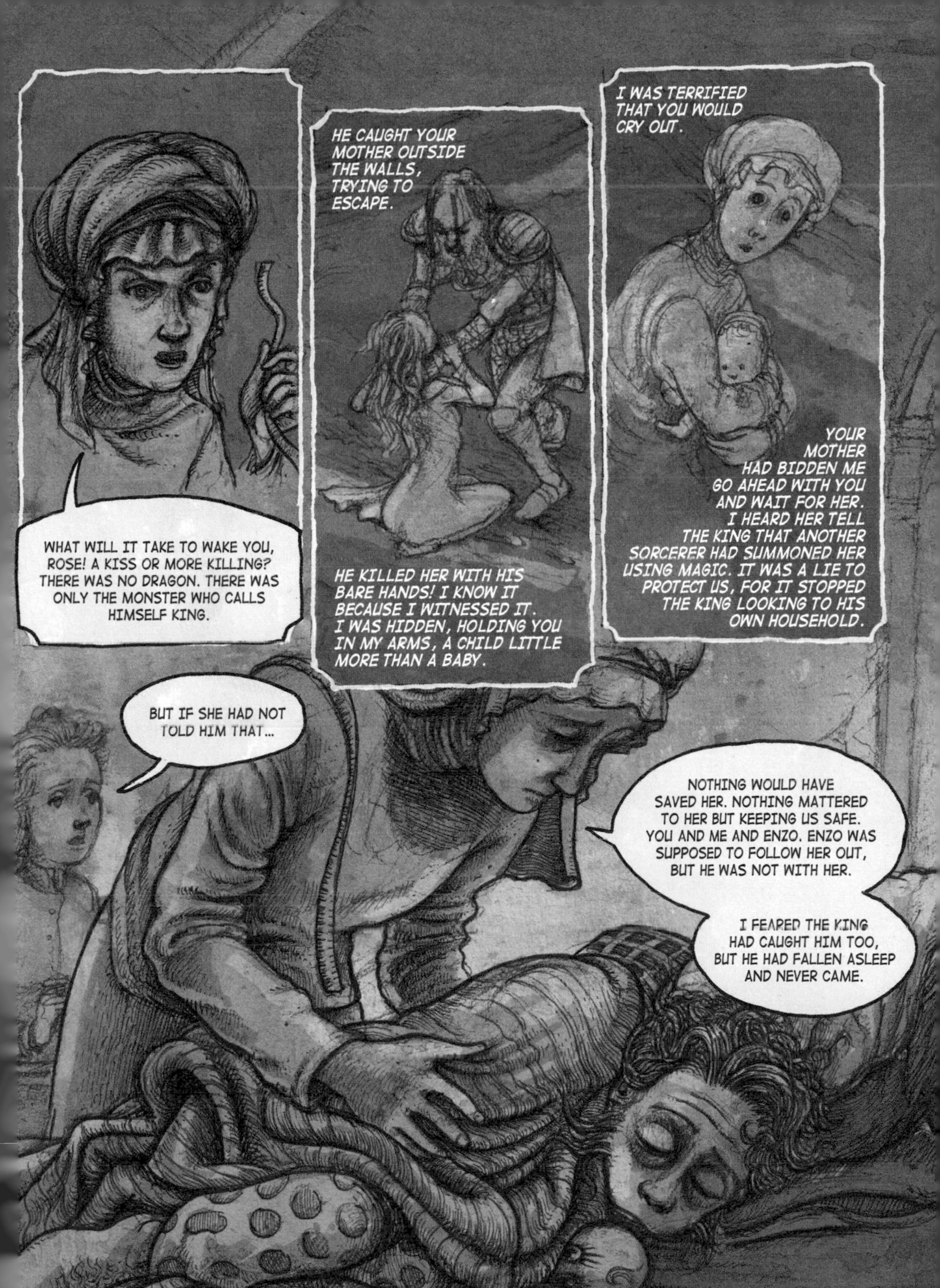

WHAT WILL IT TAKE TO WAKE YOU, ROSE! A KISS OR MORE KILLING? THERE WAS NO DRAGON. THERE WAS ONLY THE MONSTER WHO CALLS HIMSELF KING.
HE CAUGHT YOUR MOTHER OUTSIDE THE WALLS, TRYING TO ESCAPE.
HE KILLED HER WITH HIS BARE HANDS! I KNOW IT BECAUSE I WITNESSED IT. I WAS HIDDEN, HOLDING YOU IN MY ARMS, A CHILD LITTLE MORE THAN A BABY.
I WAS TERRIFIED THAT YOU WOULD CRY OUT.
YOUR MOTHER HAD BIDDEN ME GO AHEAD WITH YOU AND WAIT FOR HER. I HEARD HER TELL THE KING THAT ANOTHER SORCERER HAD SUMMONED HER USING MAGIC. IT WAS A LIE TO PROTECT US, FOR IT STOPPED THE KING LOOKING TO HIS OWN HOUSEHOLD.
BUT IF SHE HAD NOT TOLD HIM THAT...
NOTHING WOULD HAVE SAVED HER. NOTHING MATTERED TO HER BUT KEEPING US SAFE. YOU AND ME AND ENZO. ENZO WAS SUPPOSED TO FOLLOW HER OUT, BUT HE WAS NOT WITH HER.
I FEARED THE KING HAD CAUGHT HIM TOO, BUT HE HAD FALLEN ASLEEP AND NEVER CAME.

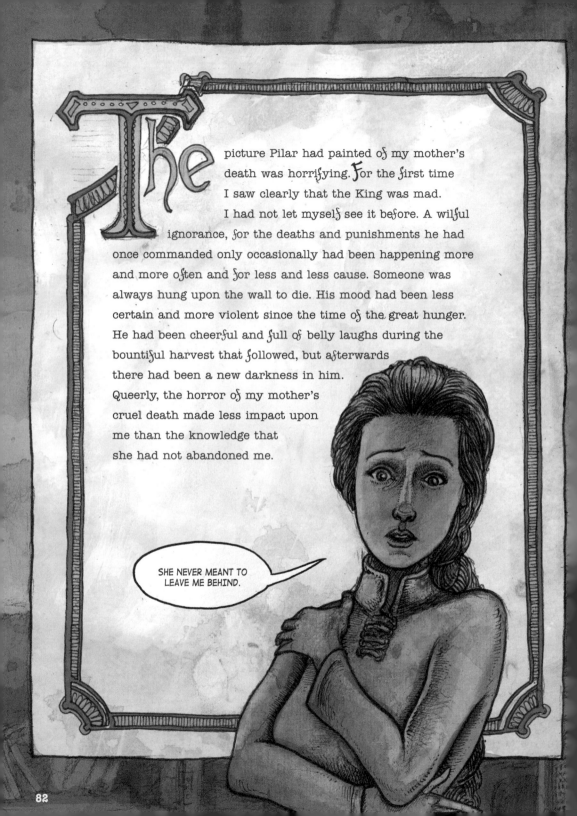

The picture Pilar had painted of my mother's death was horrifying. For the first time I saw clearly that the King was mad.

I had not let myself see it before. A wilful ignorance, for the deaths and punishments he had once commanded only occasionally had been happening more and more often and for less and less cause. Someone was always hung upon the wall to die. His mood had been less certain and more violent since the time of the great hunger. He had been cheerful and full of belly laughs during the bountiful harvest that followed, but afterwards there had been a new darkness in him. Queerly, the horror of my mother's cruel death made less impact upon me than the knowledge that she had not abandoned me.

SHE NEVER MEANT TO LEAVE ME BEHIND.

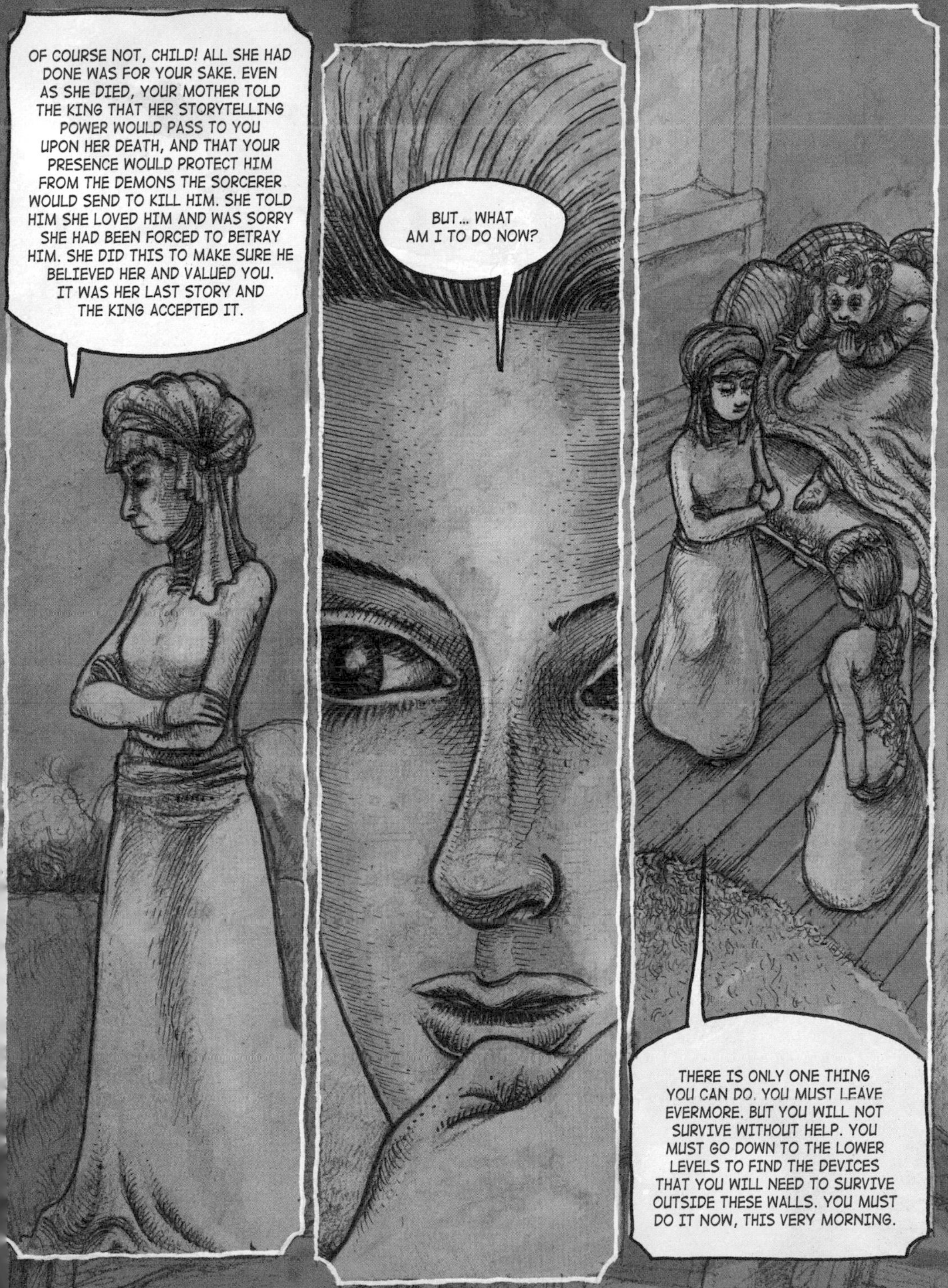
OF COURSE NOT, CHILD! ALL SHE HAD DONE WAS FOR YOUR SAKE. EVEN AS SHE DIED, YOUR MOTHER TOLD THE KING THAT HER STORYTELLING POWER WOULD PASS TO YOU UPON HER DEATH, AND THAT YOUR PRESENCE WOULD PROTECT HIM FROM THE DEMONS THE SORCERER WOULD SEND TO KILL HIM. SHE TOLD HIM SHE LOVED HIM AND WAS SORRY SHE HAD BEEN FORCED TO BETRAY HIM. SHE DID THIS TO MAKE SURE HE BELIEVED HER AND VALUED YOU. IT WAS HER LAST STORY AND THE KING ACCEPTED IT.
BUT... WHAT AM I TO DO NOW?
THERE IS ONLY ONE THING YOU CAN DO. YOU MUST LEAVE EVERMORE. BUT YOU WILL NOT SURVIVE WITHOUT HELP. YOU MUST GO DOWN TO THE LOWER LEVELS TO FIND THE DEVICES THAT YOU WILL NEED TO SURVIVE OUTSIDE THESE WALLS. YOU MUST DO IT NOW, THIS VERY MORNING.

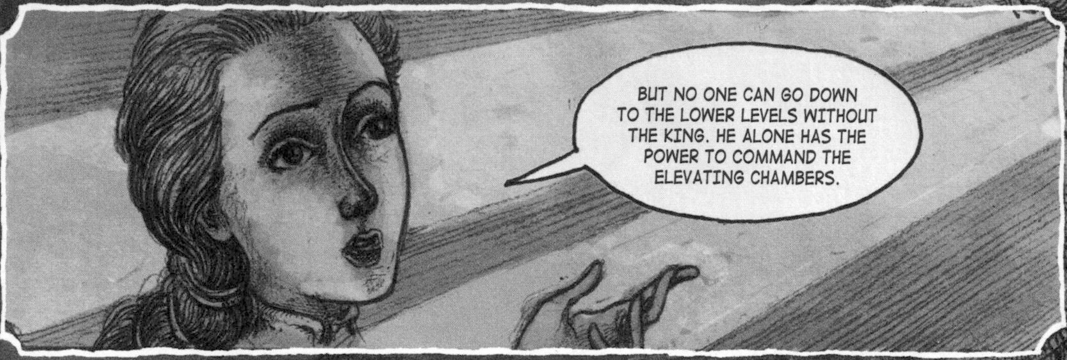
BUT NO ONE CAN GO DOWN TO THE LOWER LEVELS WITHOUT THE KING. HE ALONE HAS THE POWER TO COMMAND THE ELEVATING CHAMBERS.

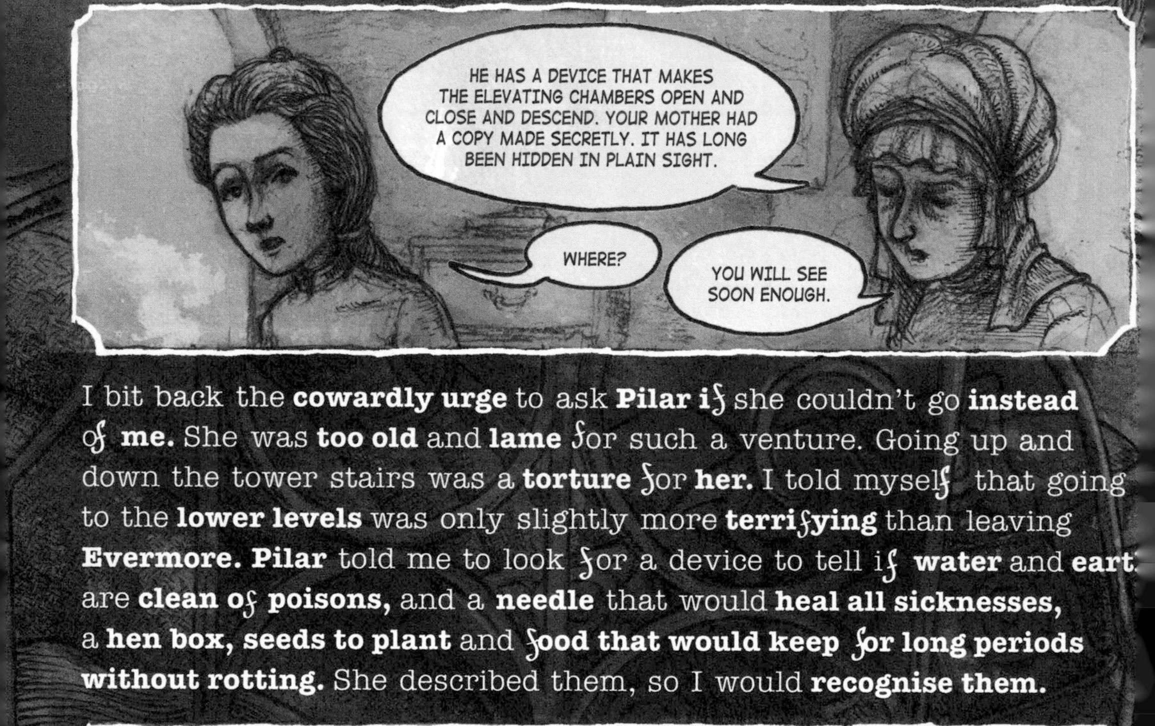
HE HAS A DEVICE THAT MAKES THE ELEVATING CHAMBERS OPEN AND CLOSE AND DESCEND. YOUR MOTHER HAD A COPY MADE SECRETLY. IT HAS LONG BEEN HIDDEN IN PLAIN SIGHT.
WHERE?
YOU WILL SEE SOON ENOUGH.

I bit back the **cowardly urge** to ask **Pilar if** she couldn't go **instead of me.** She was **too old** and **lame** for such a venture. Going up and down the tower stairs was a **torture for her.** I told myself that going to the **lower levels** was only slightly more **terrifying** than leaving **Evermore. Pilar** told me to look for a device to tell if **water** and **eart** are **clean of poisons,** and a **needle** that would **heal all sicknesses,** a **hen box, seeds to plant** and **food that would keep for long periods without rotting.** She described them, so I would **recognise them.**

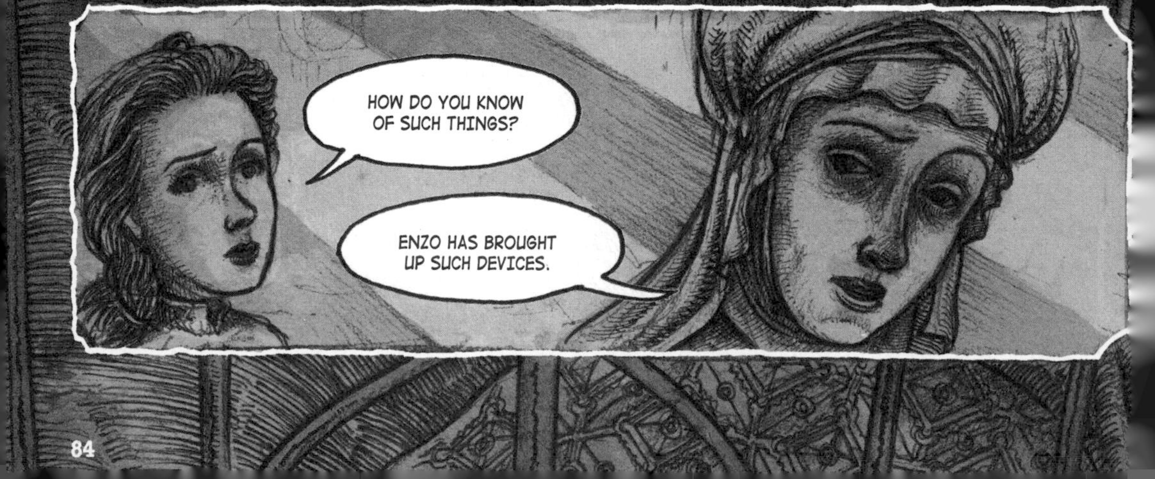
HOW DO YOU KNOW OF SUCH THINGS?
ENZO HAS BROUGHT UP SUCH DEVICES.

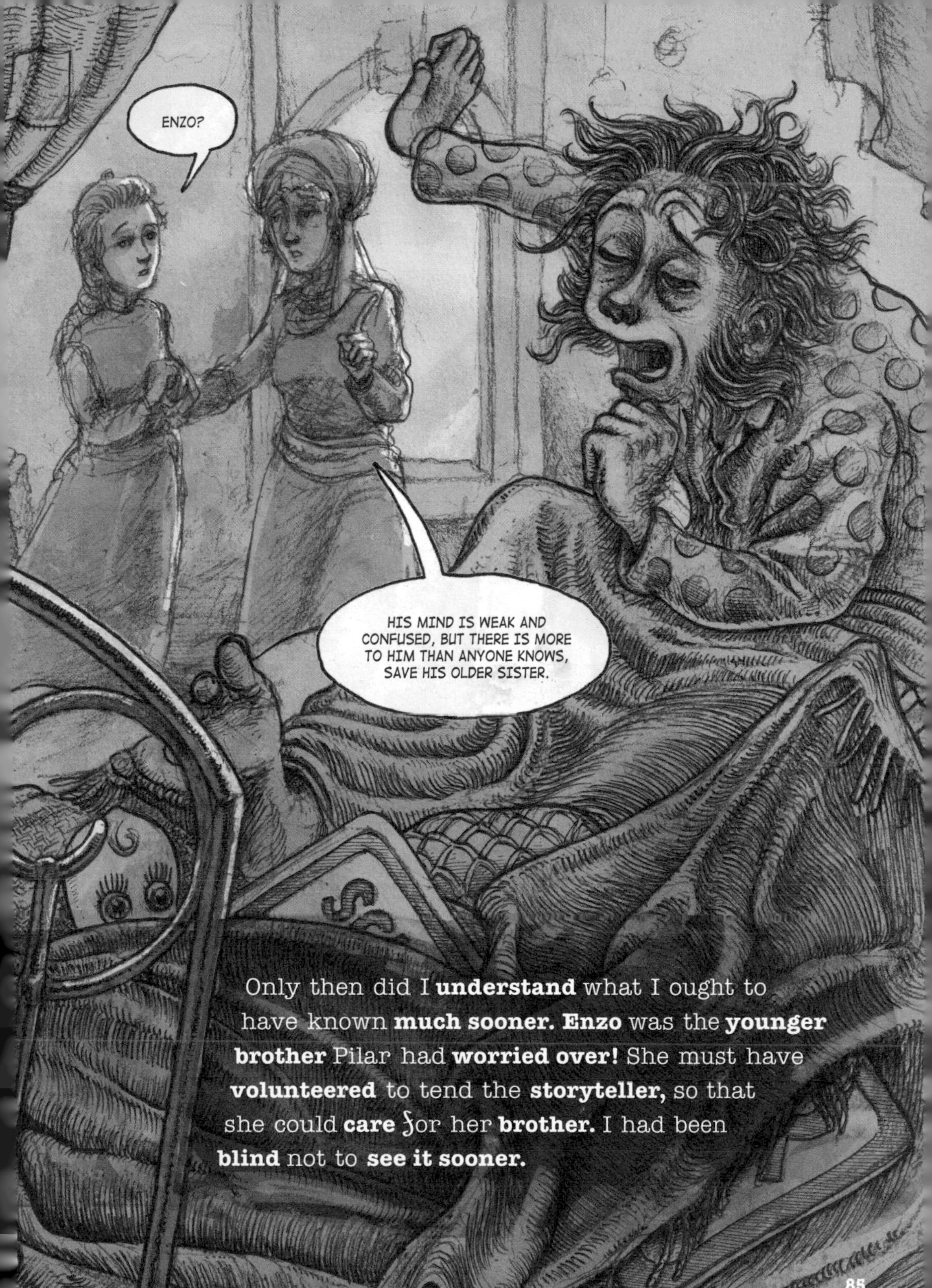
ENZO?
HIS MIND IS WEAK AND CONFUSED, BUT THERE IS MORE TO HIM THAN ANYONE KNOWS, SAVE HIS OLDER SISTER.
Only then did I **understand** what I ought to have known **much sooner. Enzo** was the **younger brother** Pilar had **worried over!** She must have **volunteered** to tend the **storyteller,** so that she could **care** for her **brother.** I had been **blind** not to **see it sooner.**

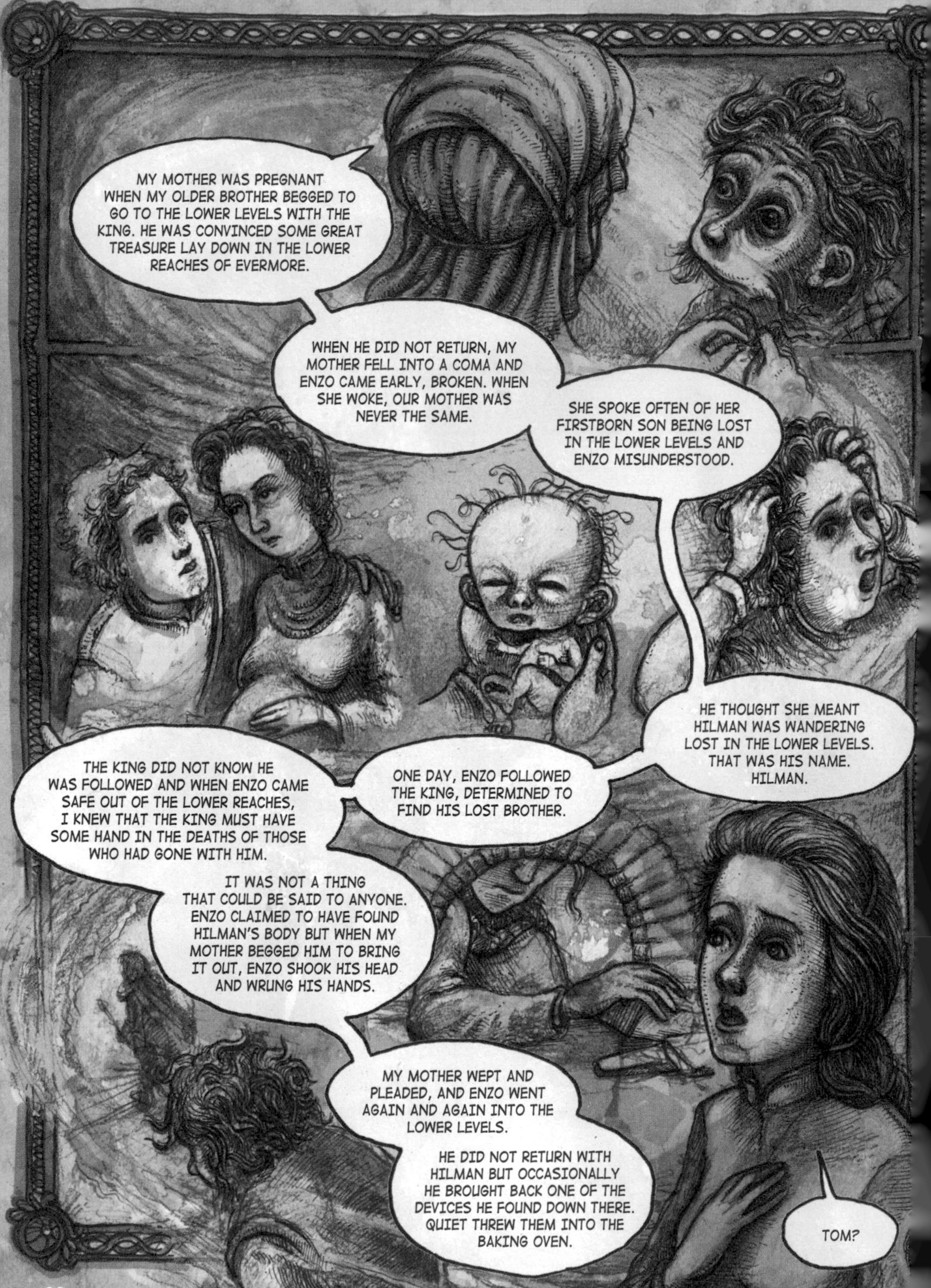

MY MOTHER WAS PREGNANT WHEN MY OLDER BROTHER BEGGED TO GO TO THE LOWER LEVELS WITH THE KING. HE WAS CONVINCED SOME GREAT TREASURE LAY DOWN IN THE LOWER REACHES OF EVERMORE.
WHEN HE DID NOT RETURN, MY MOTHER FELL INTO A COMA AND ENZO CAME EARLY, BROKEN. WHEN SHE WOKE, OUR MOTHER WAS NEVER THE SAME.
SHE SPOKE OFTEN OF HER FIRSTBORN SON BEING LOST IN THE LOWER LEVELS AND ENZO MISUNDERSTOOD.
HE THOUGHT SHE MEANT HILMAN WAS WANDERING LOST IN THE LOWER LEVELS. THAT WAS HIS NAME. HILMAN.
ONE DAY, ENZO FOLLOWED THE KING, DETERMINED TO FIND HIS LOST BROTHER.
THE KING DID NOT KNOW HE WAS FOLLOWED AND WHEN ENZO CAME SAFE OUT OF THE LOWER REACHES, I KNEW THAT THE KING MUST HAVE SOME HAND IN THE DEATHS OF THOSE WHO HAD GONE WITH HIM.
IT WAS NOT A THING THAT COULD BE SAID TO ANYONE. ENZO CLAIMED TO HAVE FOUND HILMAN'S BODY BUT WHEN MY MOTHER BEGGED HIM TO BRING IT OUT, ENZO SHOOK HIS HEAD AND WRUNG HIS HANDS.
MY MOTHER WEPT AND PLEADED, AND ENZO WENT AGAIN AND AGAIN INTO THE LOWER LEVELS.
HE DID NOT RETURN WITH HILMAN BUT OCCASIONALLY HE BROUGHT BACK ONE OF THE DEVICES HE FOUND DOWN THERE. QUIET THREW THEM INTO THE BAKING OVEN.
TOM?

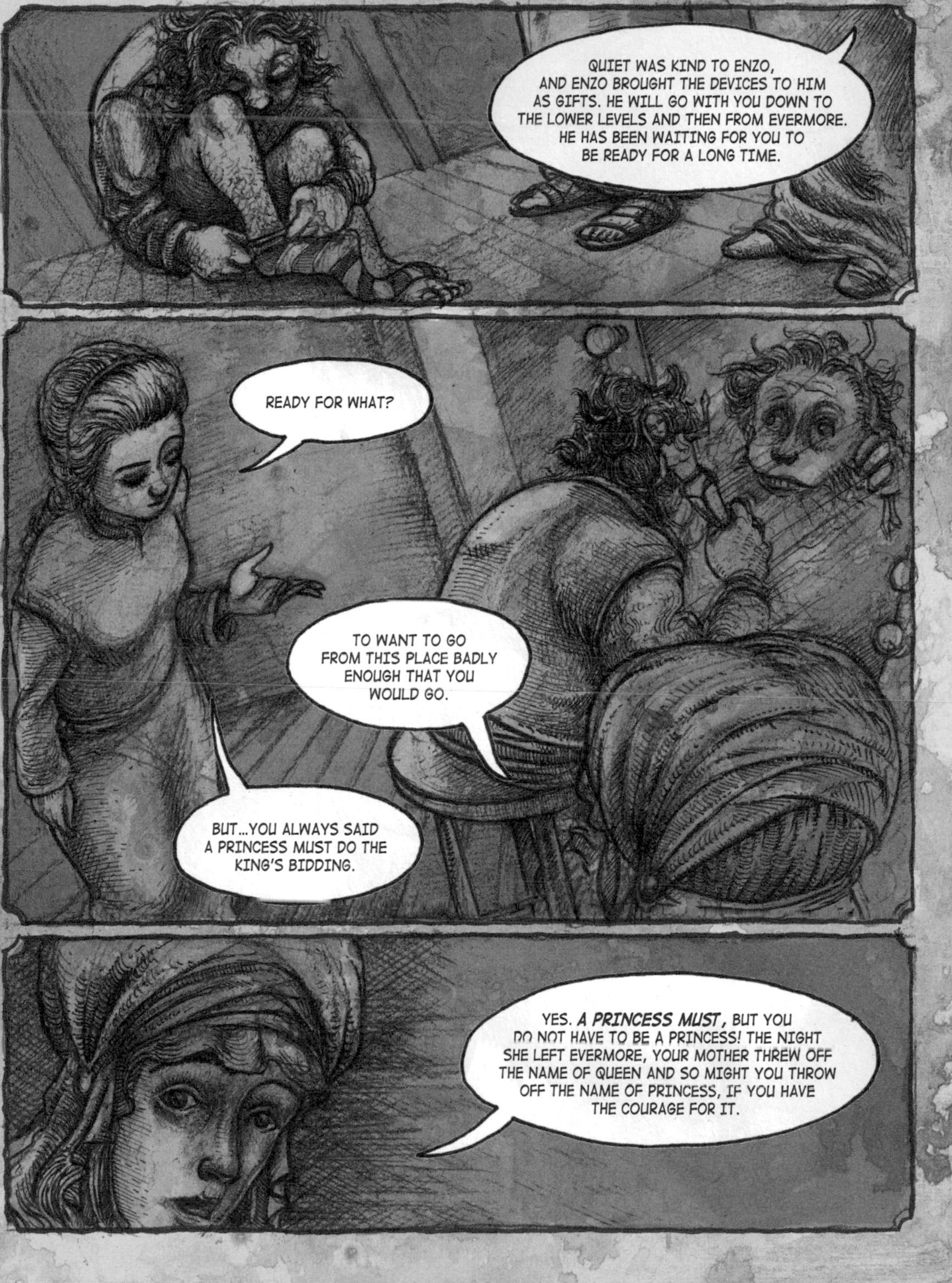
QUIET WAS KIND TO ENZO, AND ENZO BROUGHT THE DEVICES TO HIM AS GIFTS. HE WILL GO WITH YOU DOWN TO THE LOWER LEVELS AND THEN FROM EVERMORE. HE HAS BEEN WAITING FOR YOU TO BE READY FOR A LONG TIME.
READY FOR WHAT?
TO WANT TO GO FROM THIS PLACE BADLY ENOUGH THAT YOU WOULD GO.
BUT...YOU ALWAYS SAID A PRINCESS MUST DO THE KING'S BIDDING.
YES. *A PRINCESS MUST,* BUT YOU DO NOT HAVE TO BE A PRINCESS! THE NIGHT SHE LEFT EVERMORE, YOUR MOTHER THREW OFF THE NAME OF QUEEN AND SO MIGHT YOU THROW OFF THE NAME OF PRINCESS, IF YOU HAVE THE COURAGE FOR IT.

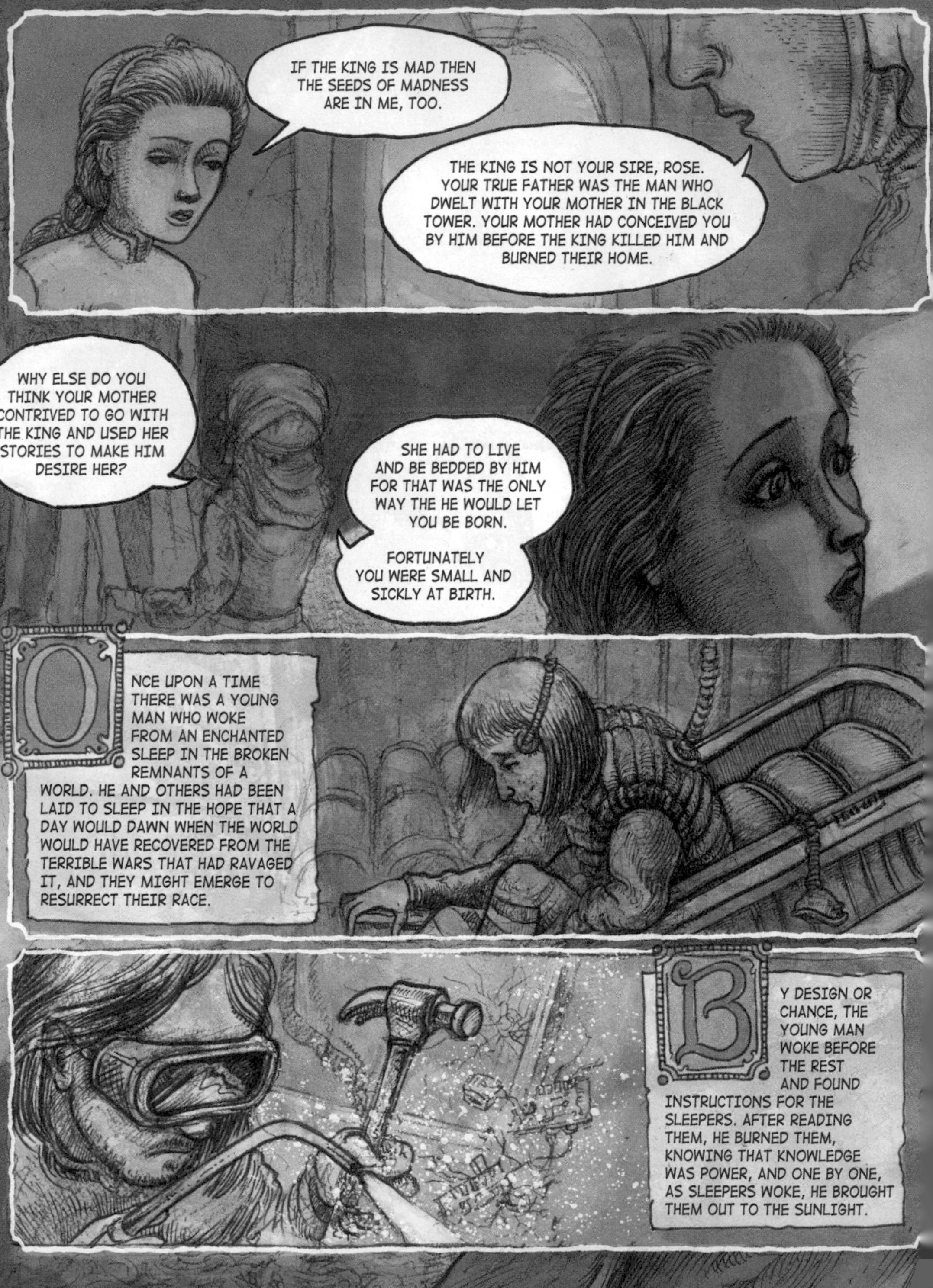
IF THE KING IS MAD THEN THE SEEDS OF MADNESS ARE IN ME, TOO.
THE KING IS NOT YOUR SIRE, ROSE. YOUR TRUE FATHER WAS THE MAN WHO DWELT WITH YOUR MOTHER IN THE BLACK TOWER. YOUR MOTHER HAD CONCEIVED YOU BY HIM BEFORE THE KING KILLED HIM AND BURNED THEIR HOME.
WHY ELSE DO YOU THINK YOUR MOTHER CONTRIVED TO GO WITH THE KING AND USED HER STORIES TO MAKE HIM DESIRE HER?
SHE HAD TO LIVE AND BE BEDDED BY HIM FOR THAT WAS THE ONLY WAY THE HE WOULD LET YOU BE BORN.
FORTUNATELY YOU WERE SMALL AND SICKLY AT BIRTH.
ONCE UPON A TIME THERE WAS A YOUNG MAN WHO WOKE FROM AN ENCHANTED SLEEP IN THE BROKEN REMNANTS OF A WORLD. HE AND OTHERS HAD BEEN LAID TO SLEEP IN THE HOPE THAT A DAY WOULD DAWN WHEN THE WORLD WOULD HAVE RECOVERED FROM THE TERRIBLE WARS THAT HAD RAVAGED IT, AND THEY MIGHT EMERGE TO RESURRECT THEIR RACE.
BY DESIGN OR CHANCE, THE YOUNG MAN WOKE BEFORE THE REST AND FOUND INSTRUCTIONS FOR THE SLEEPERS. AFTER READING THEM, HE BURNED THEM, KNOWING THAT KNOWLEDGE WAS POWER, AND ONE BY ONE, AS SLEEPERS WOKE, HE BROUGHT THEM OUT TO THE SUNLIGHT.

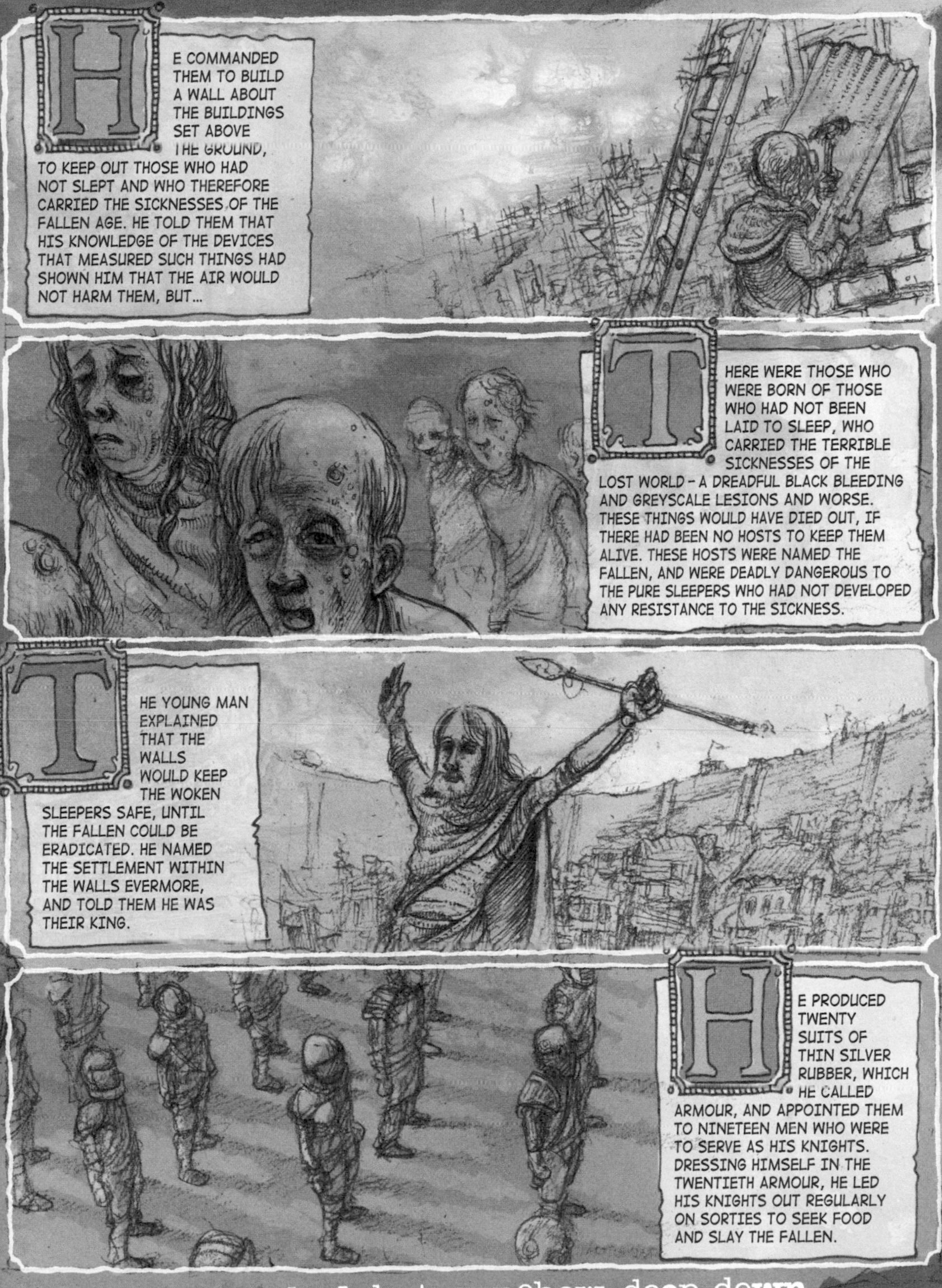
HE COMMANDED THEM TO BUILD A WALL ABOUT THE BUILDINGS SET ABOVE THE GROUND, TO KEEP OUT THOSE WHO HAD NOT SLEPT AND WHO THEREFORE CARRIED THE SICKNESSES OF THE FALLEN AGE. HE TOLD THEM THAT HIS KNOWLEDGE OF THE DEVICES THAT MEASURED SUCH THINGS HAD SHOWN HIM THAT THE AIR WOULD NOT HARM THEM, BUT...
THERE WERE THOSE WHO WERE BORN OF THOSE WHO HAD NOT BEEN LAID TO SLEEP, WHO CARRIED THE TERRIBLE SICKNESSES OF THE LOST WORLD – A DREADFUL BLACK BLEEDING AND GREYSCALE LESIONS AND WORSE. THESE THINGS WOULD HAVE DIED OUT, IF THERE HAD BEEN NO HOSTS TO KEEP THEM ALIVE. THESE HOSTS WERE NAMED THE FALLEN, AND WERE DEADLY DANGEROUS TO THE PURE SLEEPERS WHO HAD NOT DEVELOPED ANY RESISTANCE TO THE SICKNESS.
THE YOUNG MAN EXPLAINED THAT THE WALLS WOULD KEEP THE WOKEN SLEEPERS SAFE, UNTIL THE FALLEN COULD BE ERADICATED. HE NAMED THE SETTLEMENT WITHIN THE WALLS EVERMORE, AND TOLD THEM HE WAS THEIR KING.
HE PRODUCED TWENTY SUITS OF THIN SILVER RUBBER, WHICH HE CALLED ARMOUR, AND APPOINTED THEM TO NINETEEN MEN WHO WERE TO SERVE AS HIS KNIGHTS. DRESSING HIMSELF IN THE TWENTIETH ARMOUR, HE LED HIS KNIGHTS OUT REGULARLY ON SORTIES TO SEEK FOOD AND SLAY THE FALLEN.

I was **shocked**, but somehow, deep down
I had known the **truth** all along ...

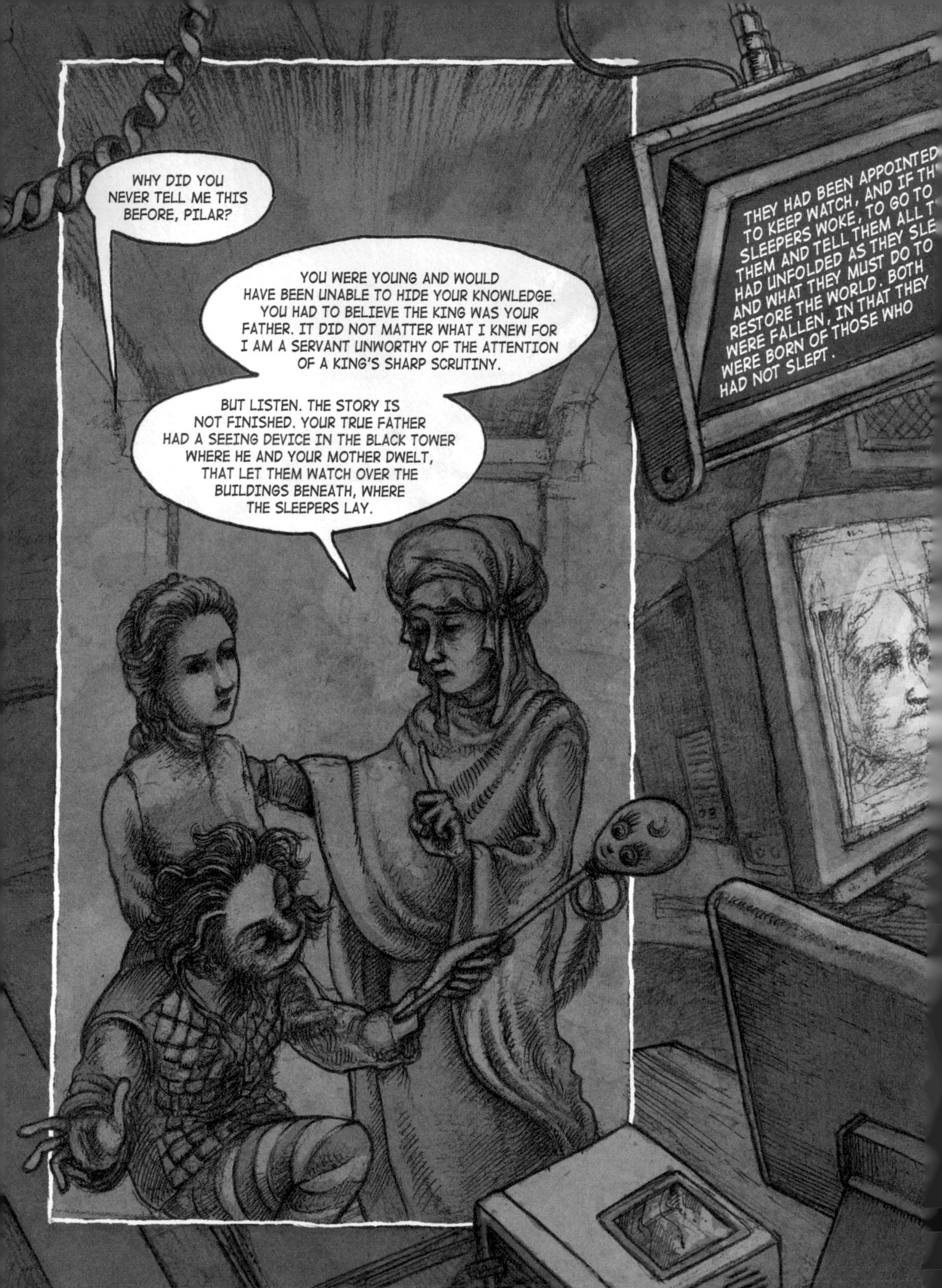
WHY DID YOU NEVER TELL ME THIS BEFORE, PILAR?
YOU WERE YOUNG AND WOULD HAVE BEEN UNABLE TO HIDE YOUR KNOWLEDGE. YOU HAD TO BELIEVE THE KING WAS YOUR FATHER. IT DID NOT MATTER WHAT I KNEW FOR I AM A SERVANT UNWORTHY OF THE ATTENTION OF A KING'S SHARP SCRUTINY.
BUT LISTEN. THE STORY IS NOT FINISHED. YOUR TRUE FATHER HAD A SEEING DEVICE IN THE BLACK TOWER WHERE HE AND YOUR MOTHER DWELT, THAT LET THEM WATCH OVER THE BUILDINGS BENEATH, WHERE THE SLEEPERS LAY.
THEY HAD BEEN APPOINTED TO KEEP WATCH, AND IF TH SLEEPERS WOKE, TO GO TO THEM AND TELL THEM ALL T HAD UNFOLDED AS THEY SLE AND WHAT THEY MUST DO TO RESTORE THE WORLD. BOTH WERE FALLEN, IN THAT THEY WERE BORN OF THOSE WHO HAD NOT SLEPT.

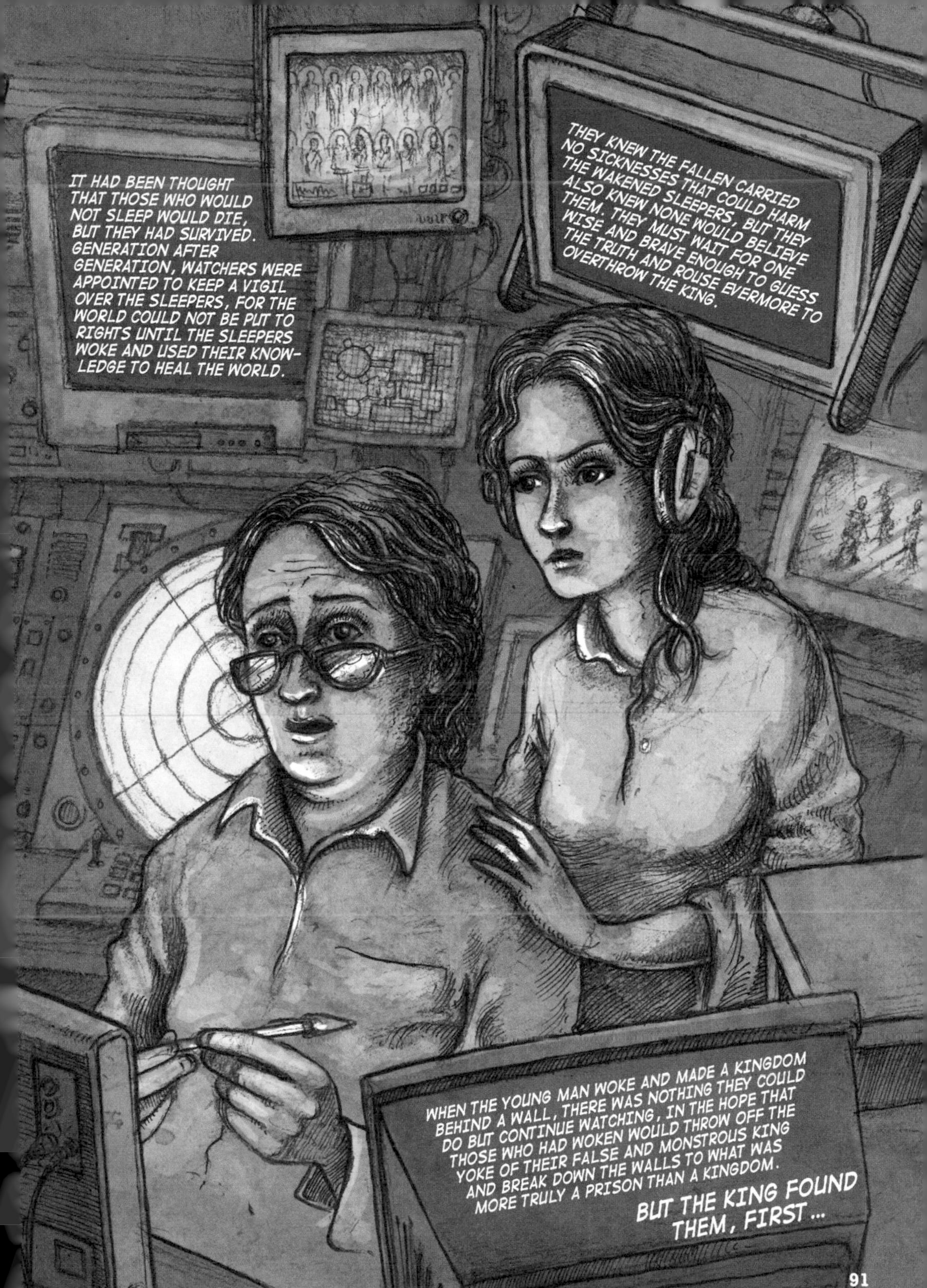
IT HAD BEEN THOUGHT THAT THOSE WHO WOULD NOT SLEEP WOULD DIE, BUT THEY HAD SURVIVED. GENERATION AFTER GENERATION, WATCHERS WERE APPOINTED TO KEEP A VIGIL OVER THE SLEEPERS, FOR THE WORLD COULD NOT BE PUT TO RIGHTS UNTIL THE SLEEPERS WOKE AND USED THEIR KNOWLEDGE TO HEAL THE WORLD.
THEY KNEW THE FALLEN CARRIED NO SICKNESSES THAT COULD HARM THE WAKENED SLEEPERS, BUT THEY ALSO KNEW NONE WOULD BELIEVE THEM. THEY MUST WAIT FOR ONE WISE AND BRAVE ENOUGH TO GUESS THE TRUTH AND ROUSE EVERMORE TO OVERTHROW THE KING.
WHEN THE YOUNG MAN WOKE AND MADE A KINGDOM BEHIND A WALL, THERE WAS NOTHING THEY COULD DO BUT CONTINUE WATCHING, IN THE HOPE THAT THOSE WHO HAD WOKEN WOULD THROW OFF THE YOKE OF THEIR FALSE AND MONSTROUS KING AND BREAK DOWN THE WALLS TO WHAT WAS MORE TRULY A PRISON THAN A KINGDOM.
BUT THE KING FOUND THEM, FIRST...

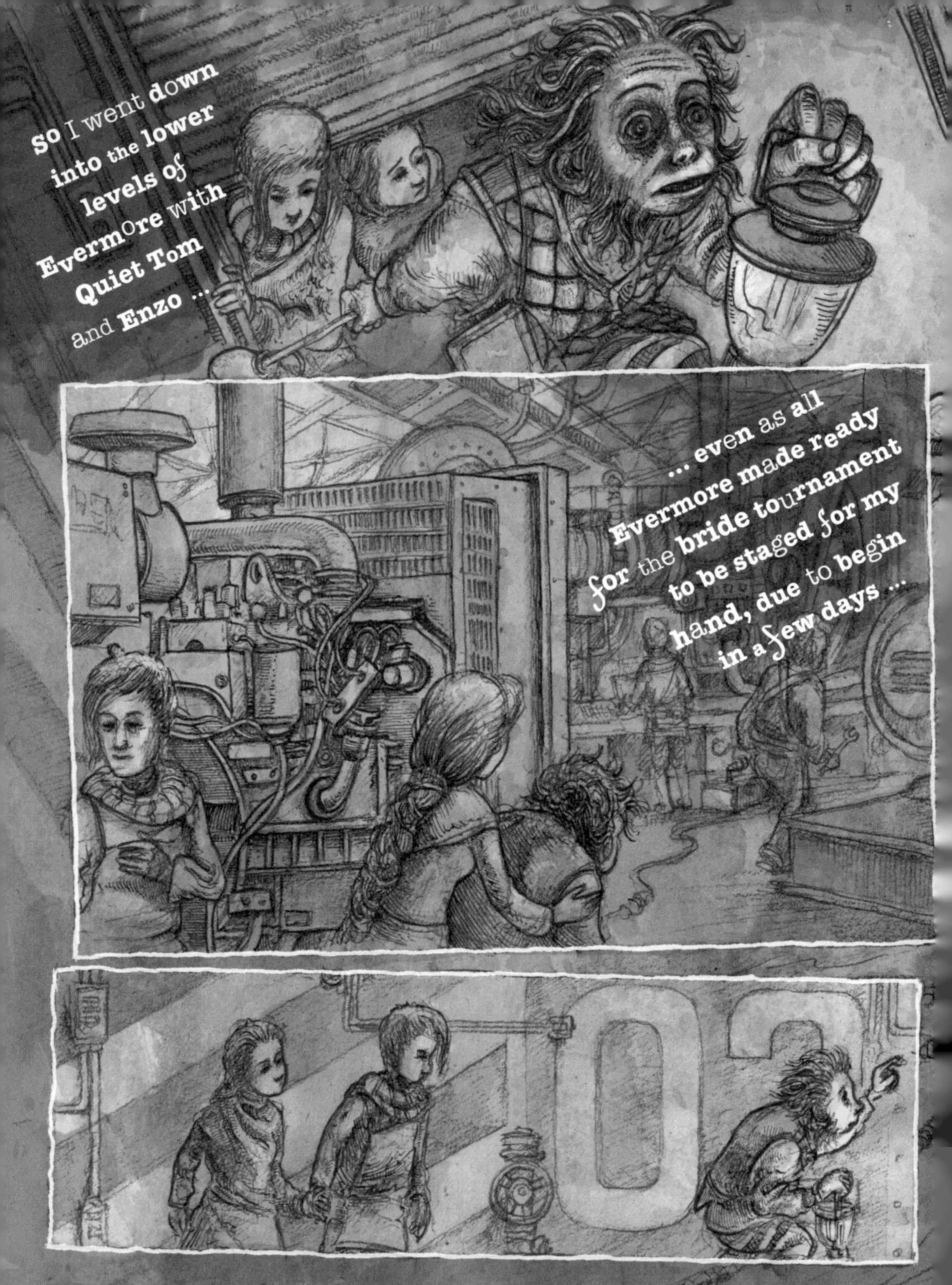
So I went down into the lower levels of Evermore with Quiet Tom and Enzo ...
... even as all Evermore made ready for the bride tournament to be staged for my hand, due to begin in a few days ...

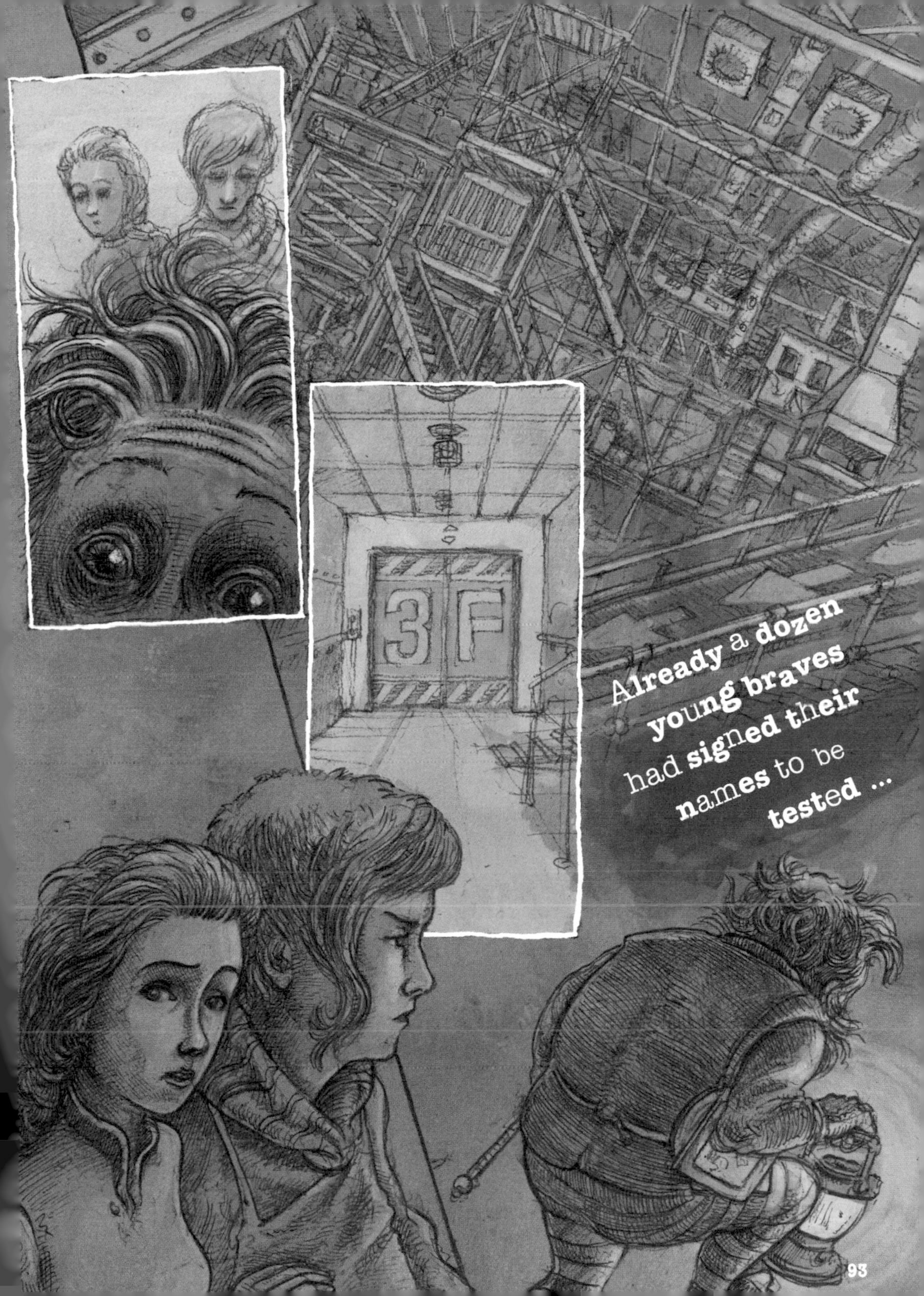
3F
Already a dozen young braves had signed their names to be tested ...

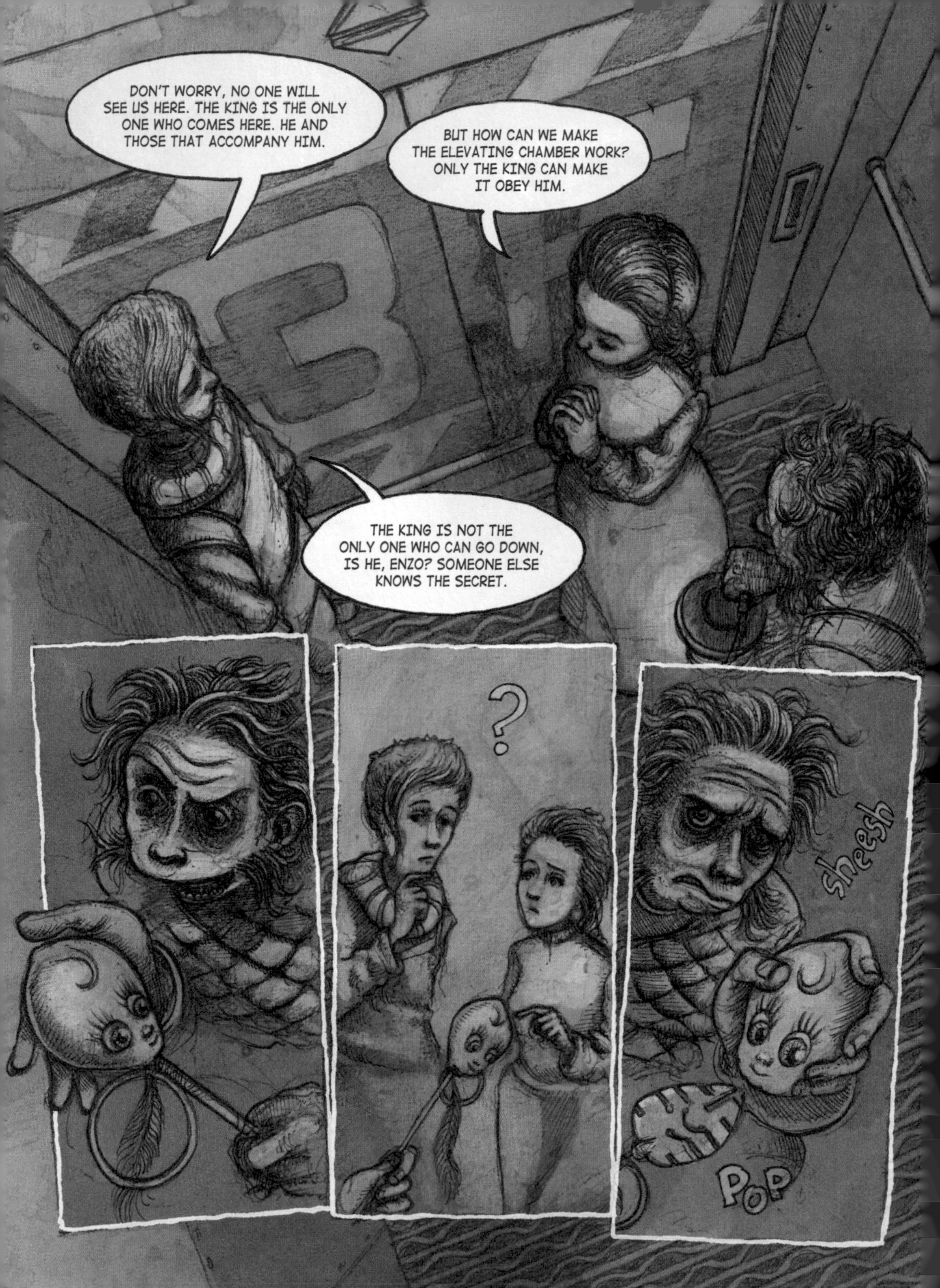
DON'T WORRY, NO ONE WILL SEE US HERE. THE KING IS THE ONLY ONE WHO COMES HERE. HE AND THOSE THAT ACCOMPANY HIM.
BUT HOW CAN WE MAKE THE ELEVATING CHAMBER WORK? ONLY THE KING CAN MAKE IT OBEY HIM.
THE KING IS NOT THE ONLY ONE WHO CAN GO DOWN, IS HE, ENZO? SOMEONE ELSE KNOWS THE SECRET.
?
sheesh
POP

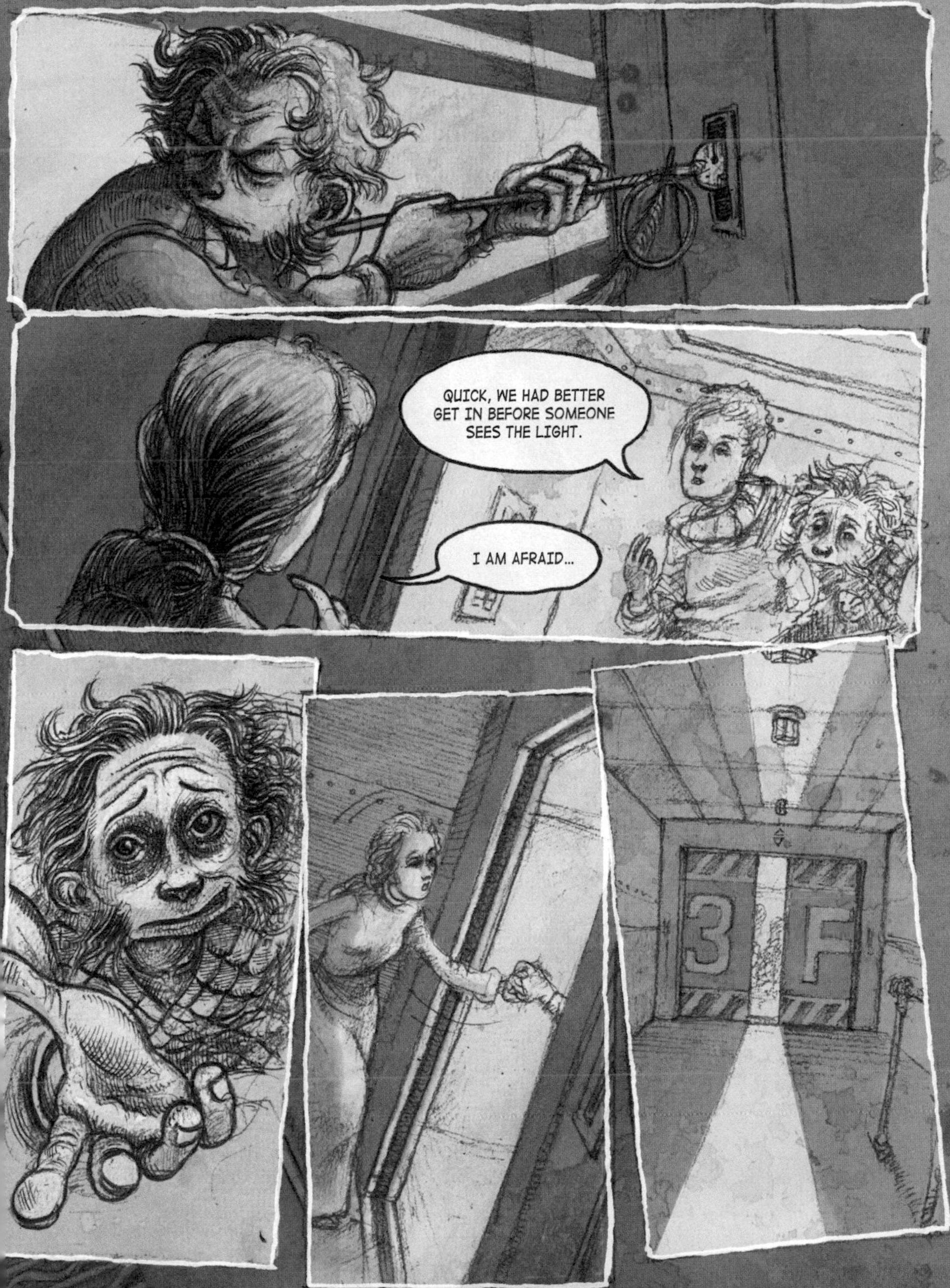
QUICK, WE HAD BETTER GET IN BEFORE SOMEONE SEES THE LIGHT.
I AM AFRAID...
3 F

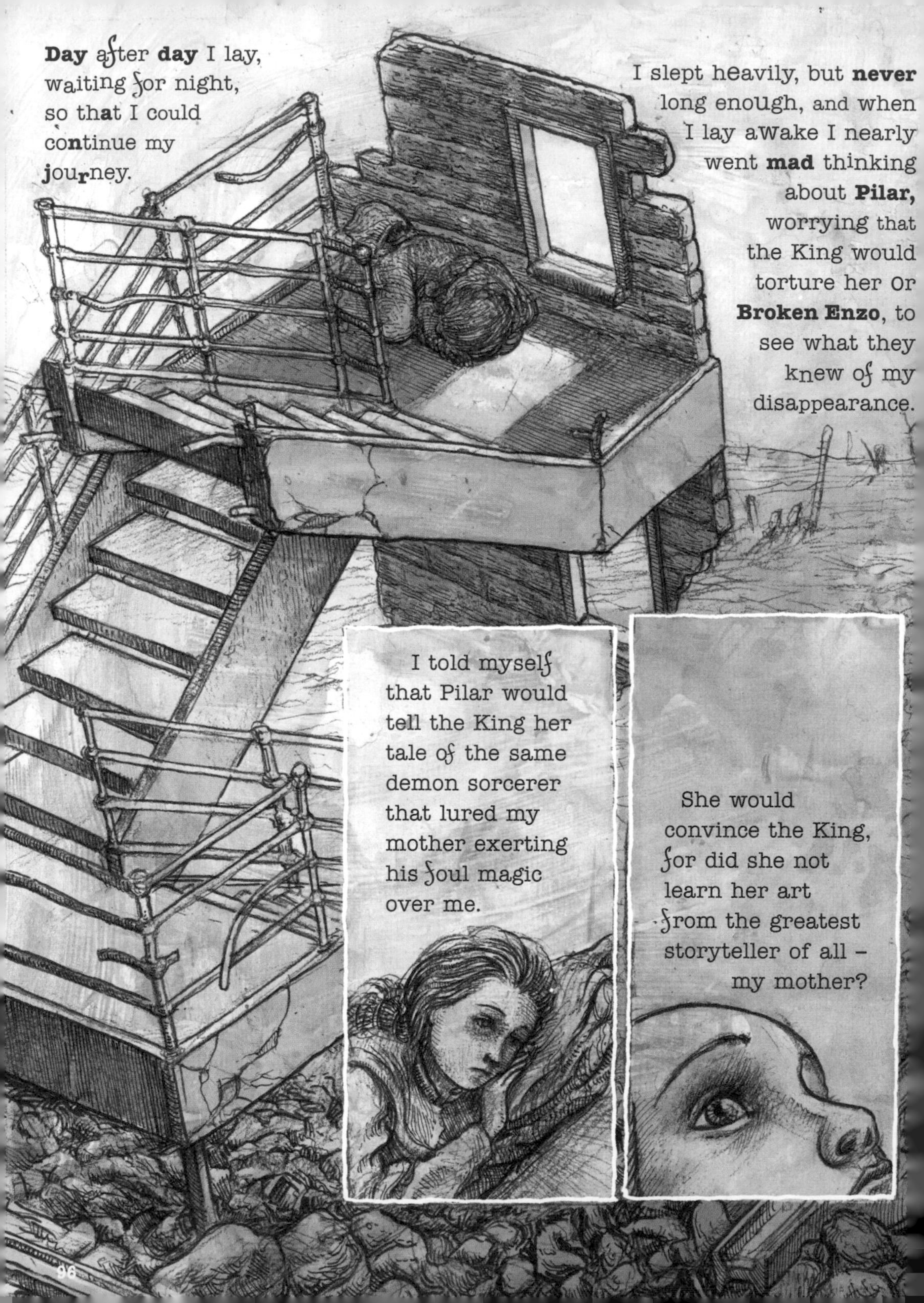
Day after day I lay, waiting for night, so that I could continue my journey.
I slept heavily, but never long enough, and when I lay awake I nearly went mad thinking about Pilar, worrying that the King would torture her or Broken Enzo, to see what they knew of my disappearance.
I told myself that Pilar would tell the King her tale of the same demon sorcerer that lured my mother exerting his foul magic over me.
She would convince the King, for did she not learn her art from the greatest storyteller of all – my mother?

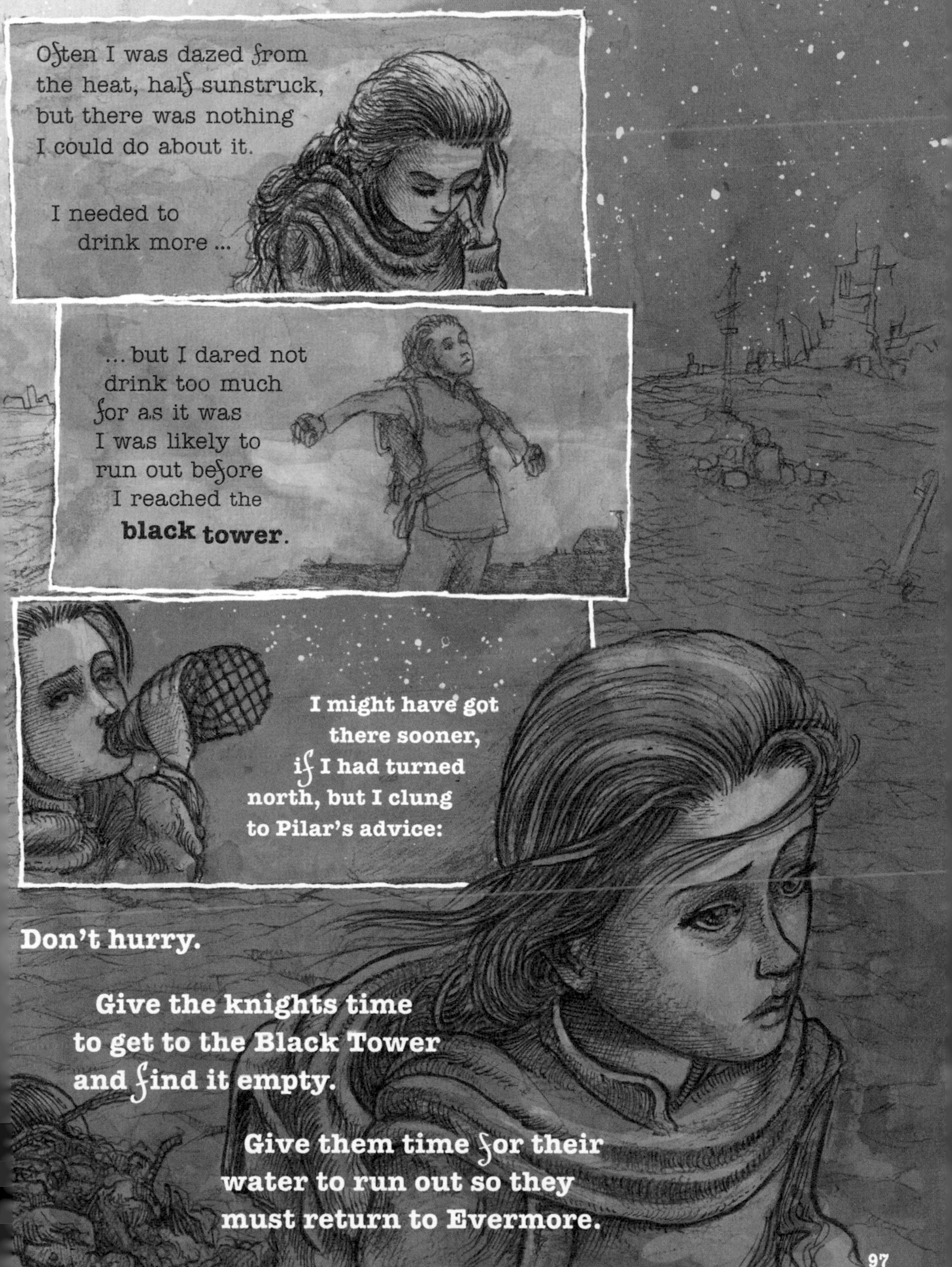
Often I was dazed from the heat, half sunstruck, but there was nothing I could do about it.
I needed to drink more ...
... but I dared not drink too much for as it was I was likely to run out before I reached the black tower.
I might have got there sooner, if I had turned north, but I clung to Pilar's advice:
Don't hurry.
Give the knights time to get to the Black Tower and find it empty.
Give them time for their water to run out so they must return to Evermore.

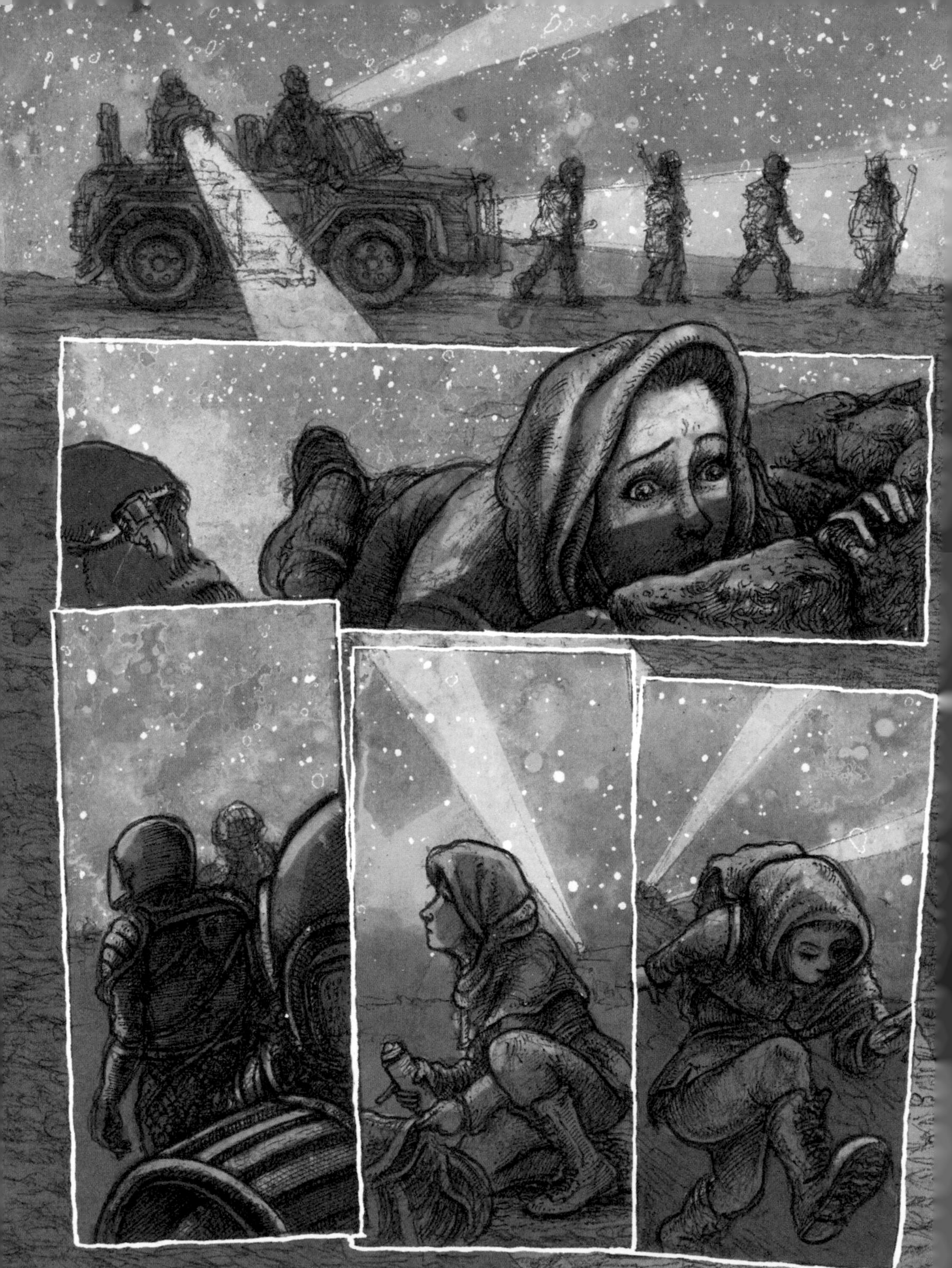

At last I turned north, still moving on only when it was moonless dark. The rest of the time I lay motionless under my blanket. I wove endless nets of fear for myself, some connected to what I would find at the black tower. I knew that if Pilar had been wrong about me being able to cleanse the water in the well, I would die a slow death there. She had warned me the water was poisonous but this had been my parents' doing to keep anyone from lingering. There was a device hidden which, once made to work, would purify the water. But what if the well had dried out? Or if the cleansing device had been taken or broken. Nor did I dare to think of activating any of the devices and boxes I had brought up from the lower levels of Evermore, for they could only be used once and I must be far from Evermore and its tyrant King before using them to make a place for myself to stay.

It was a relief when, the second night travelling north, the light breeze that had been blowing gained force and grew into a windstorm so fierce and blinding that it was impossible to breathe, let alone to see. I lost a day for I could not use the stars to guide me and it was impossible to light a match to see the compass. There was nothing but to lie down, wrapped in the blanket. Even then, the air was so thick with sand dust that I could scarce draw a breath. I prayed I would not suffocate before it was over.

When the gritty tempest passed, it was near dawn and I was trapped for another day. That night when I emerged from my temporary grave, I finished the last drop of water but I was still far from the Black Tower. There was no use in thinking about it, and I set off, refusing to give way to fear. Pilar and Enzo had risked themselves to save me and Tom…well, I could not bear to think of what had happened to Tom in the deadly lower levels of Evermore. No more can I bear to write that story now. But I knew all their suffering had come to pass because they had wanted to help me escape the King and Evermore. It would be a poor way to honour their sacrifices if I simply lay down and died. That would be a bad ending to my story.

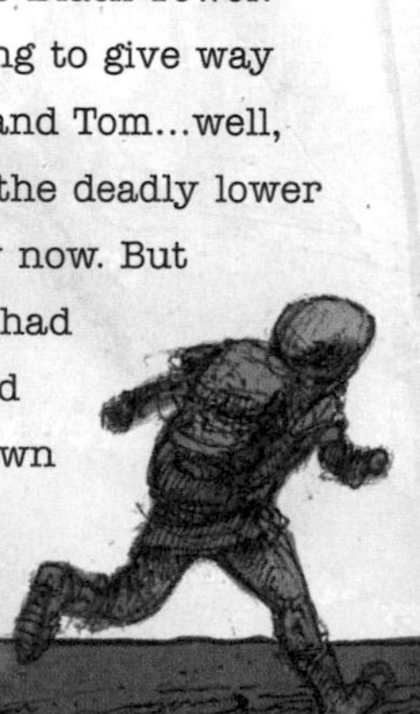

How I survived that last part of the walk I do not know, any more than I know how I managed the dark and terrifying climb down from the White Tower of Evermore. But by the end of it, I was stumbling along in the broad daylight, too stupid with thirst to care if I was seen. My head clamoured with pain and my tongue lay cracked in my dust-dry mouth. If the King's knights had seen me, they could have taken me without a murmur. The thought did not frighten me. The heat had sucked all fear from me, and when night came, I had neither the strength nor the wit to do anything but fall headlong in the sand and sleep.

I did not think I would wake.

I dreamed of Tom.

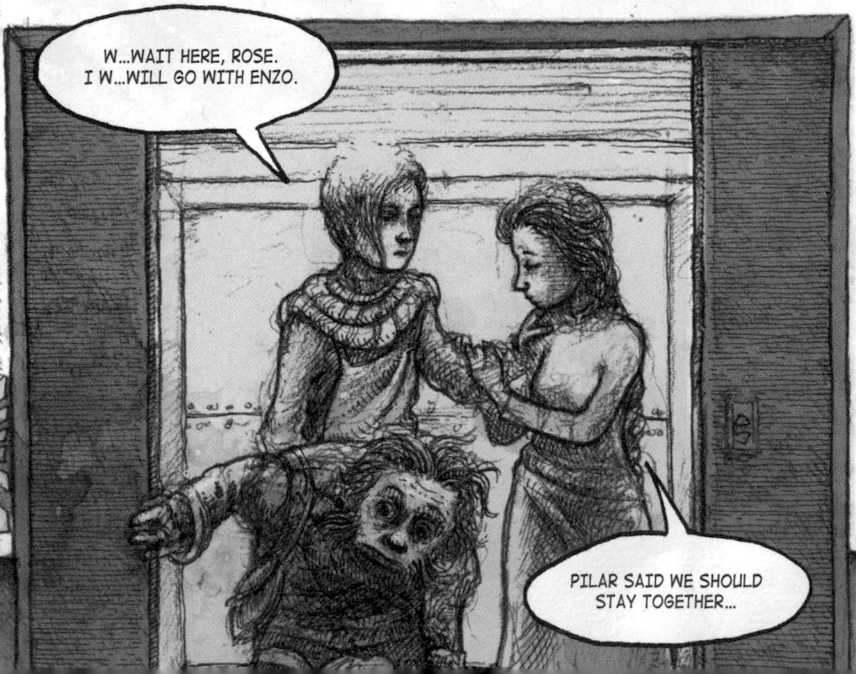
W...WAIT HERE, ROSE. I W...WILL GO WITH ENZO.
PILAR SAID WE SHOULD STAY TOGETHER...

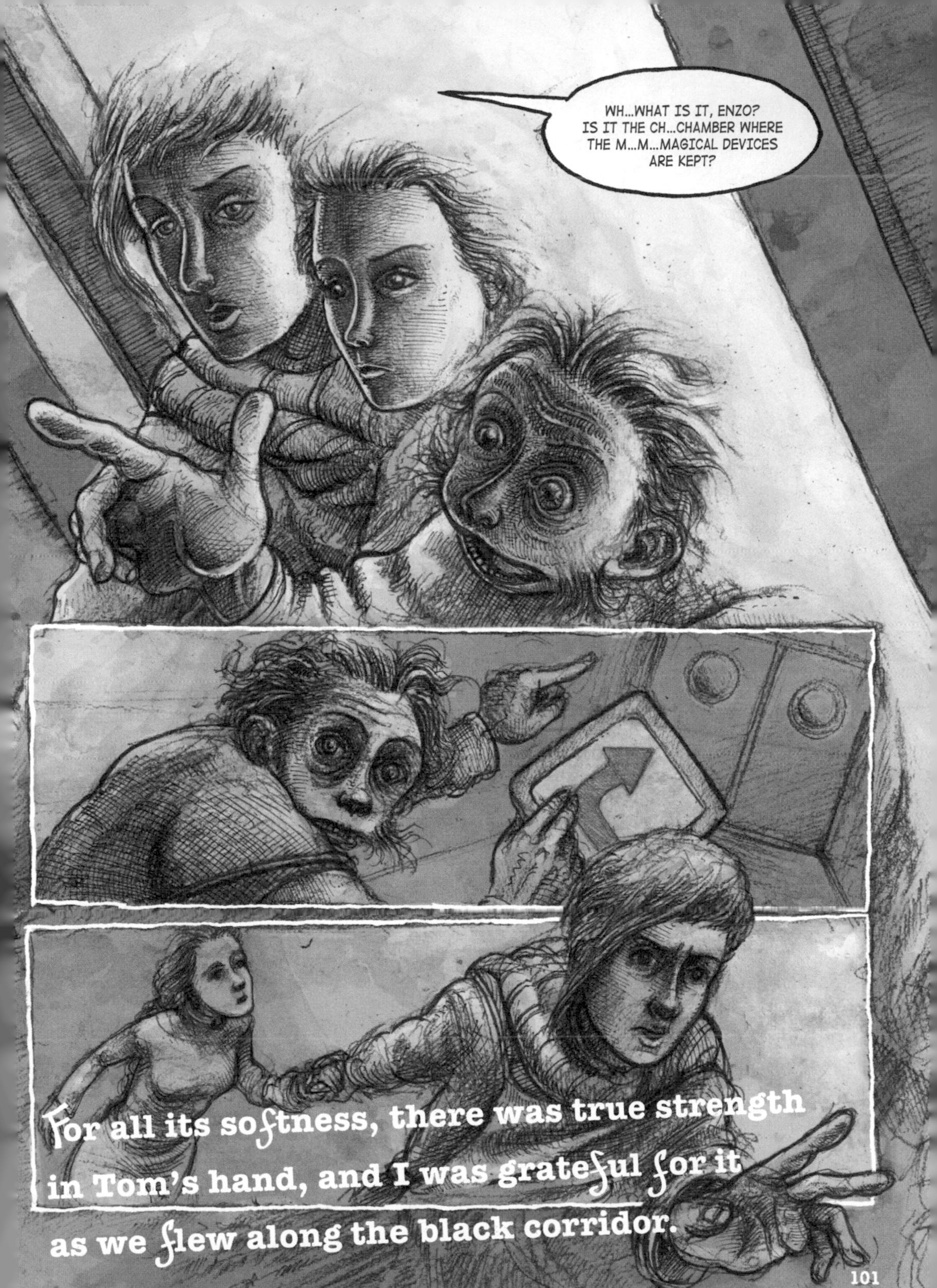
WH...WHAT IS IT, ENZO? IS IT THE CH...CHAMBER WHERE THE M...M...MAGICAL DEVICES ARE KEPT?
For all its softness, there was true strength in Tom's hand, and I was grateful for it as we flew along the black corridor.

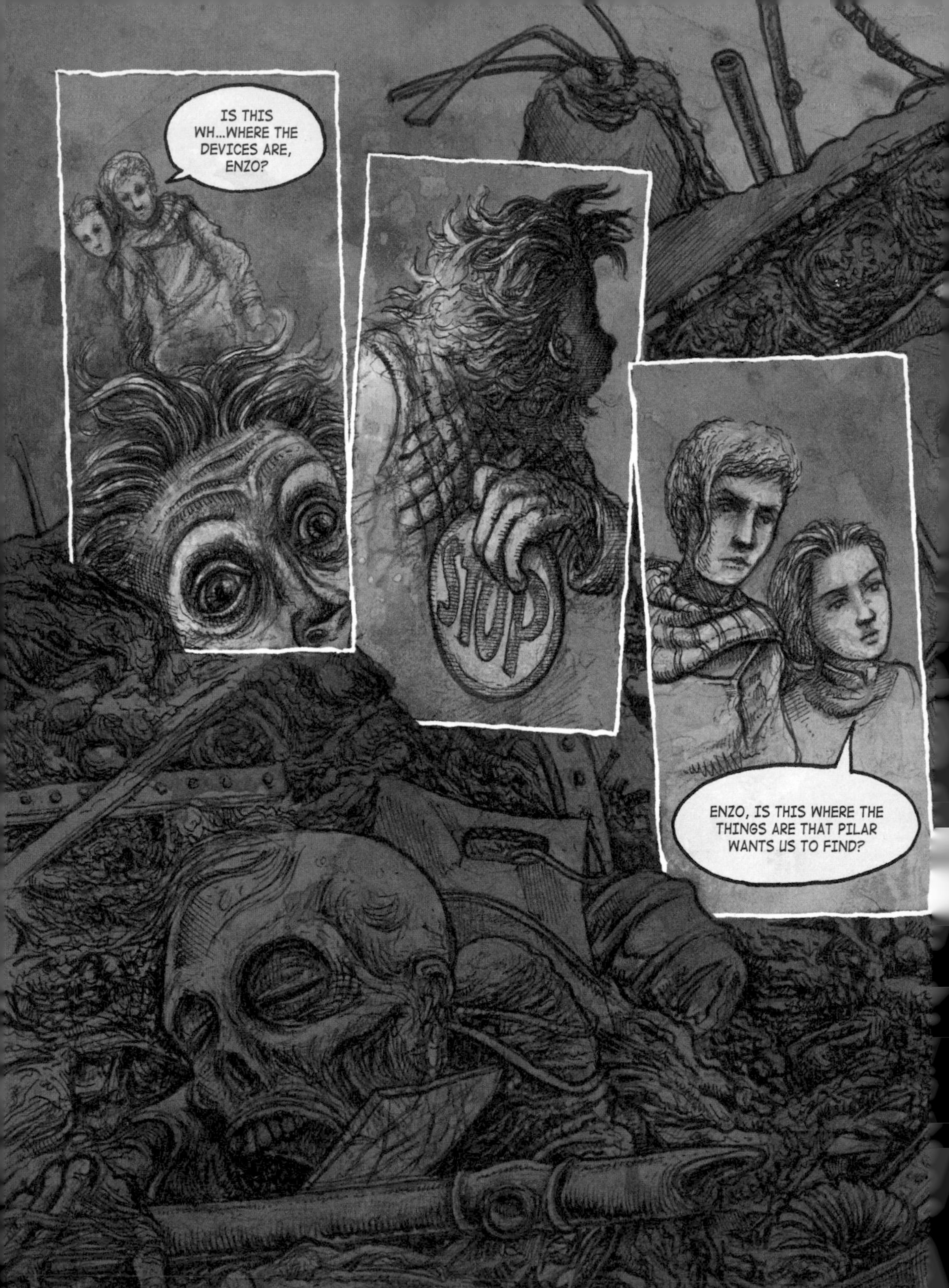
IS THIS WH...WHERE THE DEVICES ARE, ENZO?
STOP
ENZO, IS THIS WHERE THE THINGS ARE THAT PILAR WANTS US TO FIND?

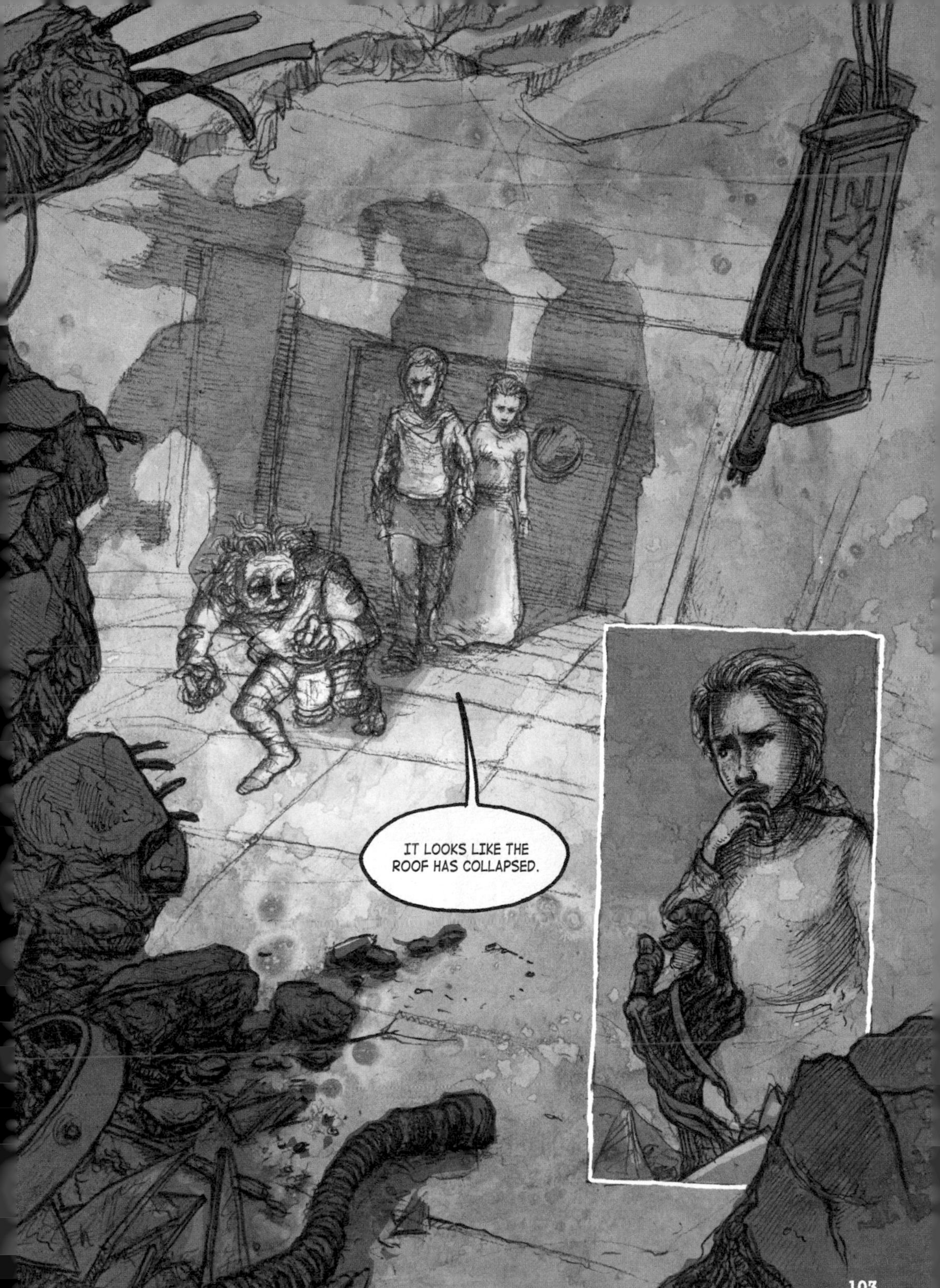
EXIT
IT LOOKS LIKE THE ROOF HAS COLLAPSED.

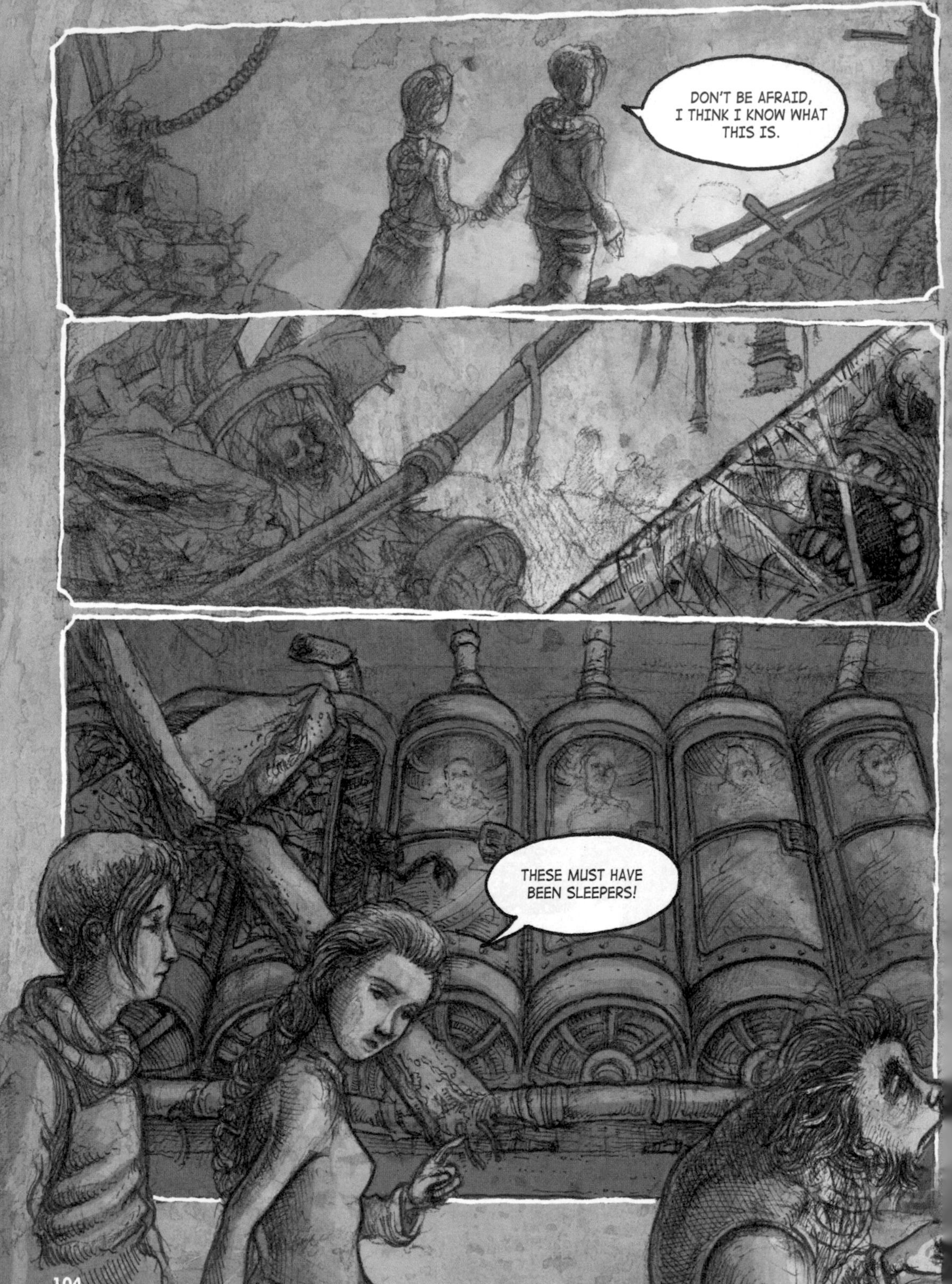
DON'T BE AFRAID, I THINK I KNOW WHAT THIS IS.
THESE MUST HAVE BEEN SLEEPERS!

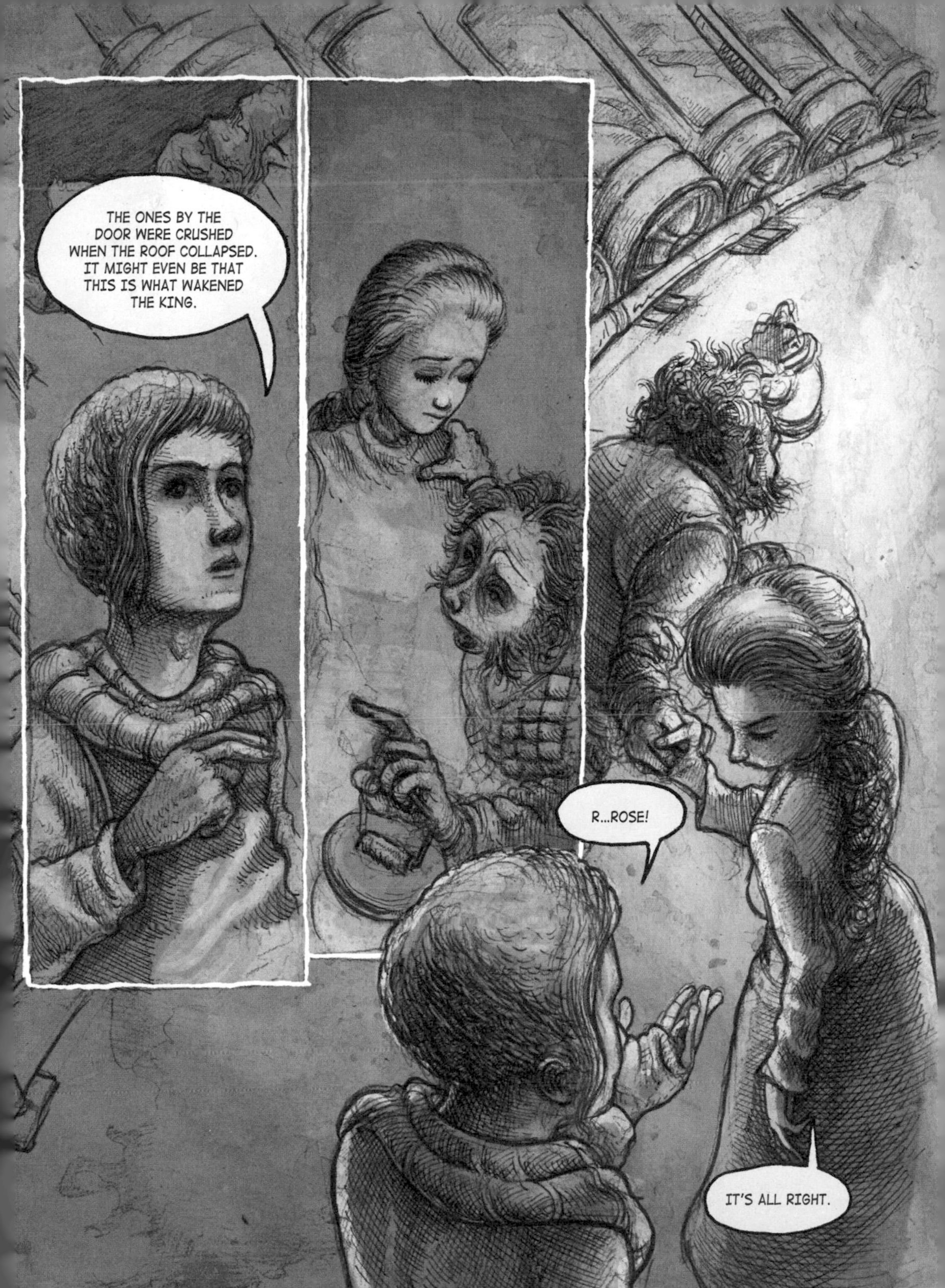
THE ONES BY THE DOOR WERE CRUSHED WHEN THE ROOF COLLAPSED. IT MIGHT EVEN BE THAT THIS IS WHAT WAKENED THE KING.
R...ROSE!
IT'S ALL RIGHT.

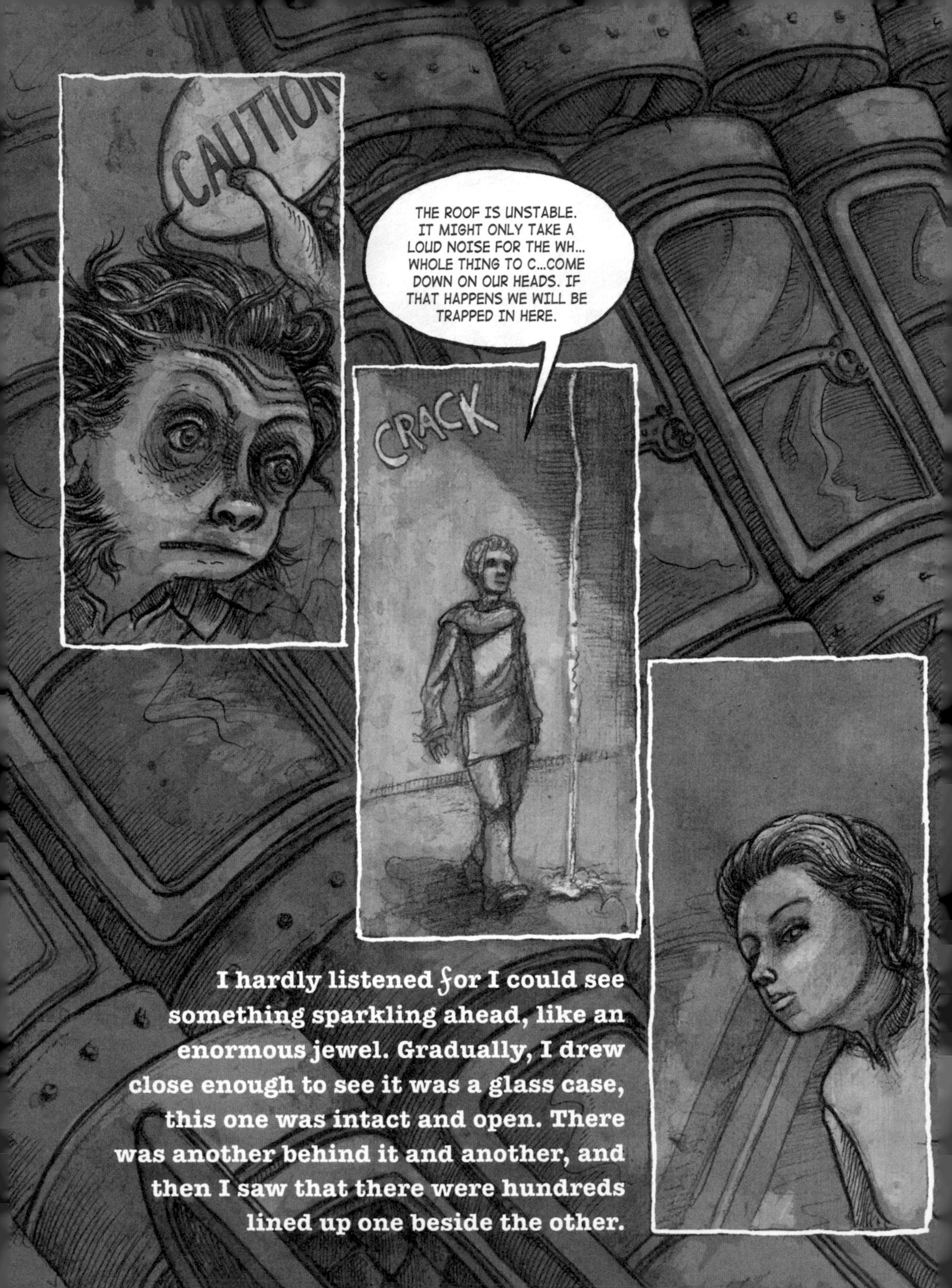
CAUTION
THE ROOF IS UNSTABLE. IT MIGHT ONLY TAKE A LOUD NOISE FOR THE WH... WHOLE THING TO C...COME DOWN ON OUR HEADS. IF THAT HAPPENS WE WILL BE TRAPPED IN HERE.
CRACK
I hardly listened for I could see something sparkling ahead, like an enormous jewel. Gradually, I drew close enough to see it was a glass case, this one was intact and open. There was another behind it and another, and then I saw that there were hundreds lined up one beside the other.

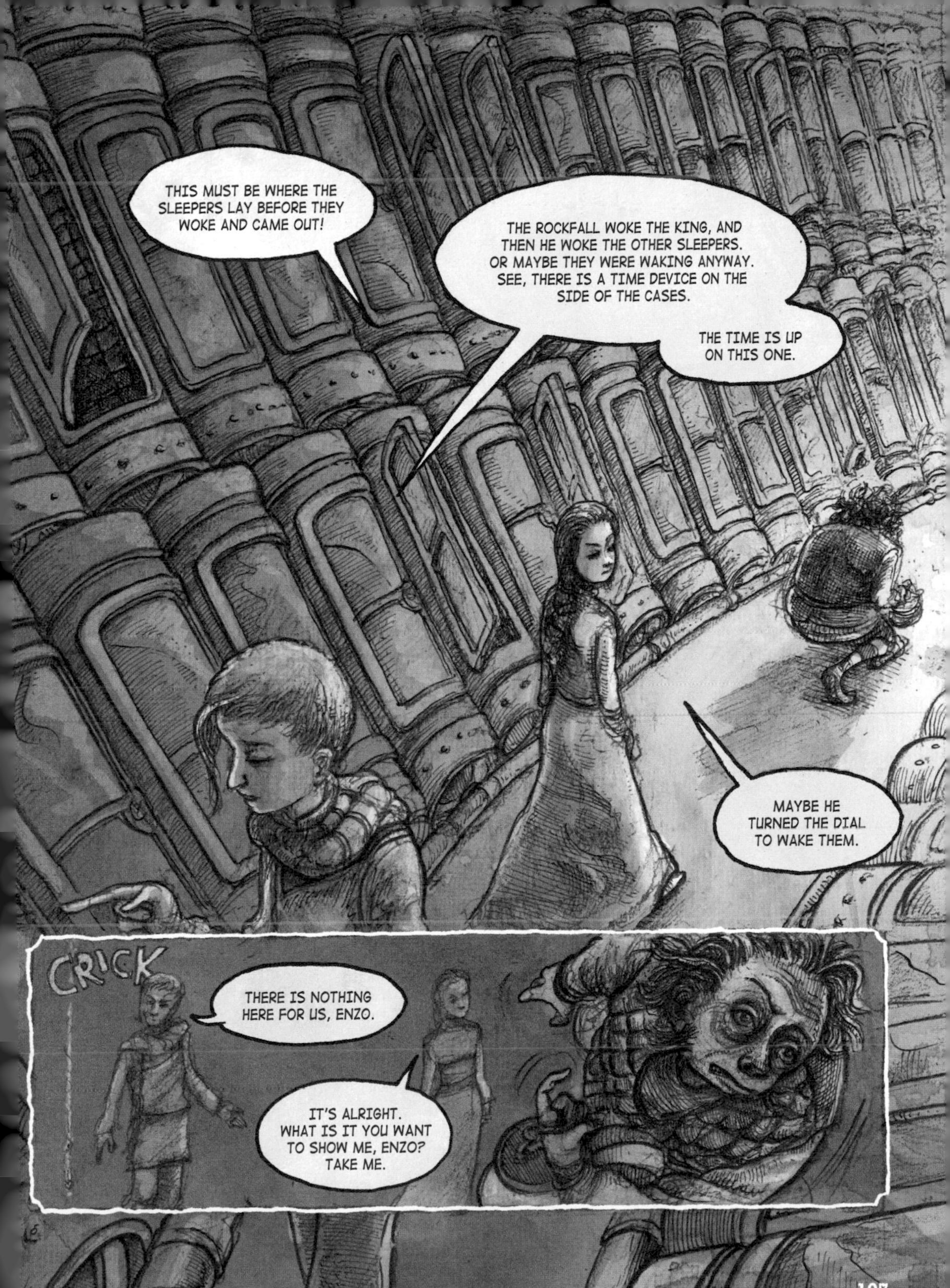
THIS MUST BE WHERE THE SLEEPERS LAY BEFORE THEY WOKE AND CAME OUT!
THE ROCKFALL WOKE THE KING, AND THEN HE WOKE THE OTHER SLEEPERS. OR MAYBE THEY WERE WAKING ANYWAY. SEE, THERE IS A TIME DEVICE ON THE SIDE OF THE CASES.
THE TIME IS UP ON THIS ONE.
MAYBE HE TURNED THE DIAL TO WAKE THEM.
CRICK
THERE IS NOTHING HERE FOR US, ENZO.
IT'S ALRIGHT. WHAT IS IT YOU WANT TO SHOW ME, ENZO? TAKE ME.

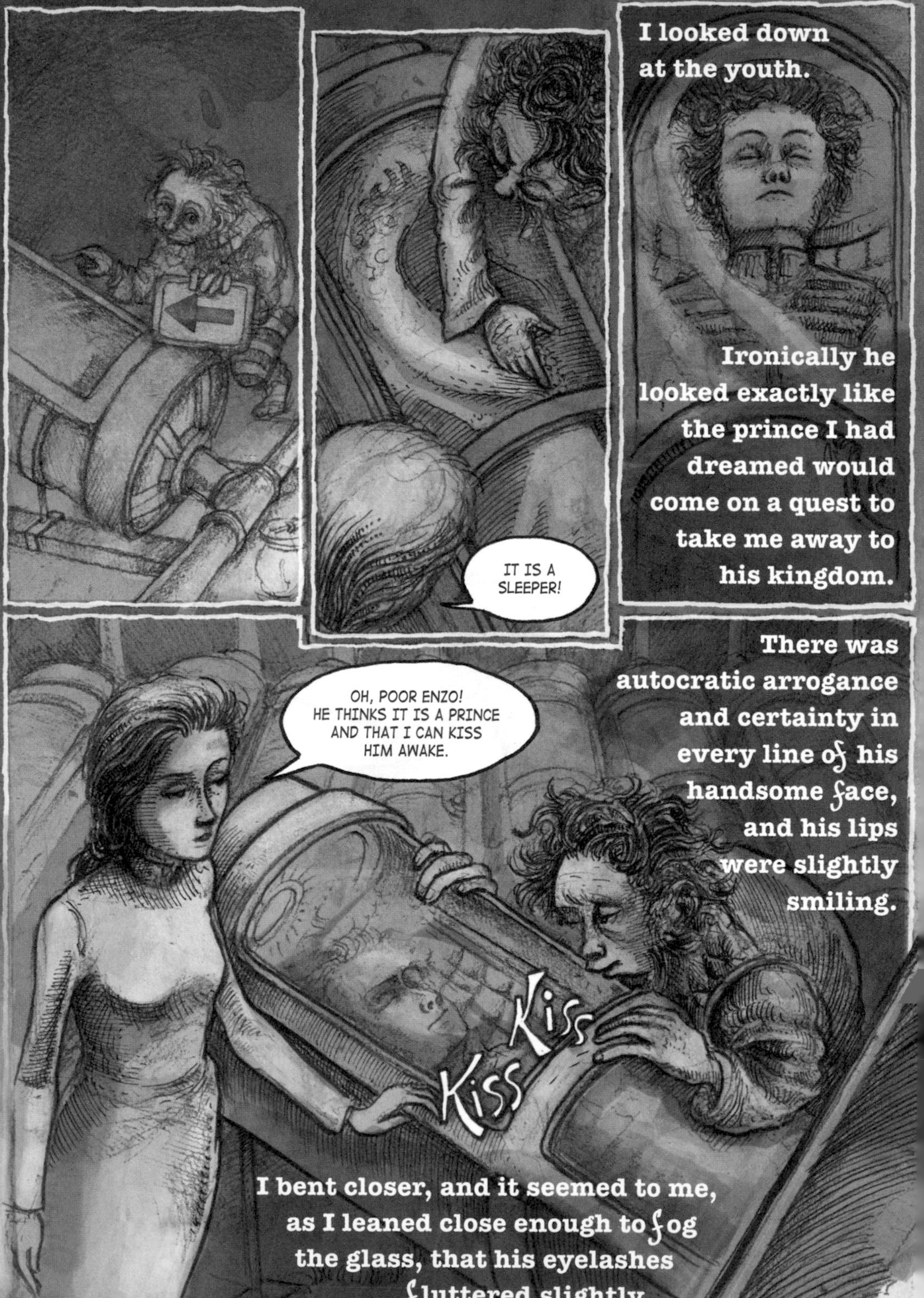
IT IS A SLEEPER!
I looked down at the youth.
Ironically he looked exactly like the prince I had dreamed would come on a quest to take me away to his kingdom.
There was autocratic arrogance and certainty in every line of his handsome face, and his lips were slightly smiling.
OH, POOR ENZO! HE THINKS IT IS A PRINCE AND THAT I CAN KISS HIM AWAKE.
Kiss
Kiss
I bent closer, and it seemed to me, as I leaned close enough to fog the glass, that his eyelashes fluttered slightly.

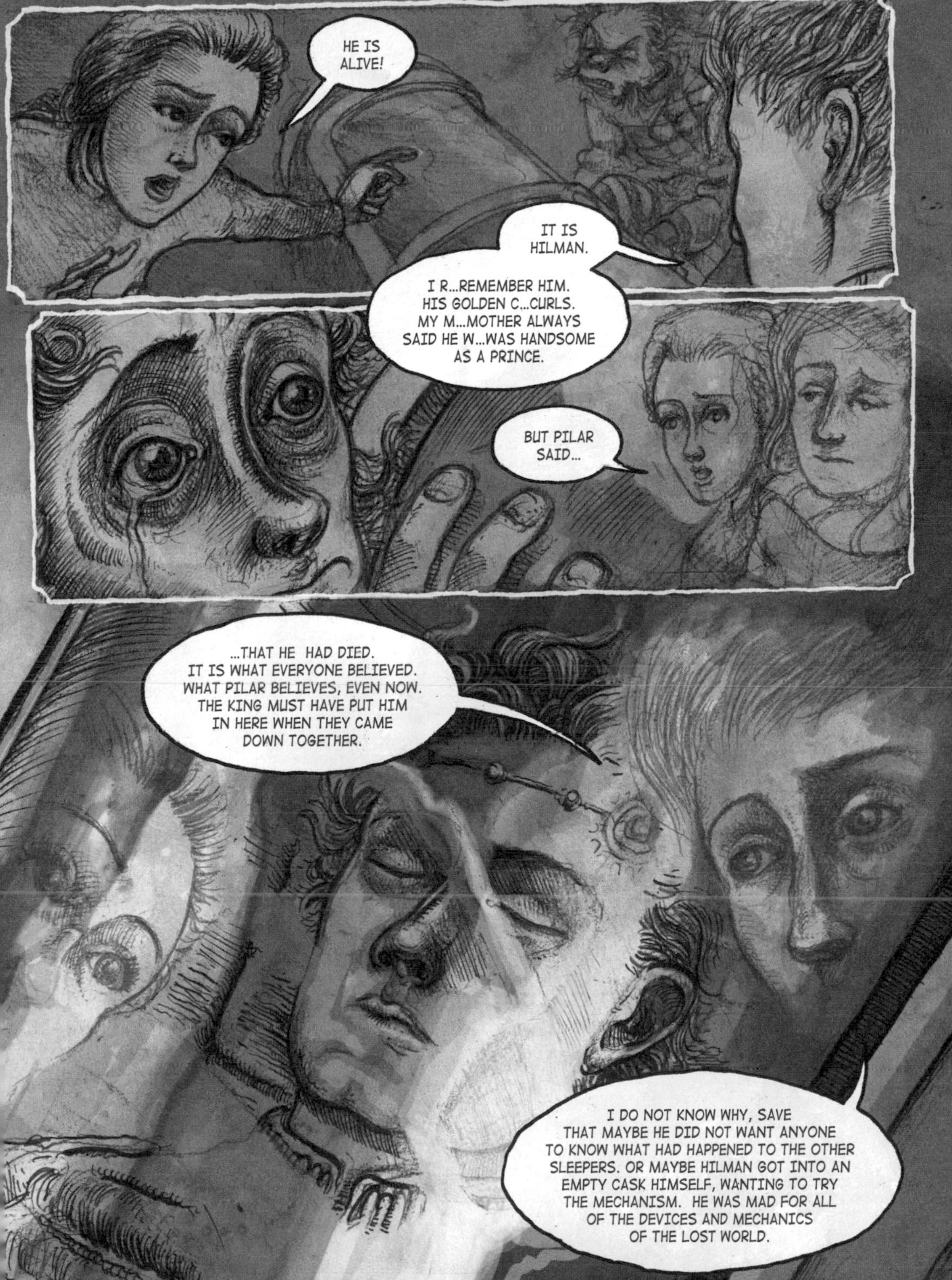
HE IS ALIVE!
IT IS HILMAN.
I R...REMEMBER HIM. HIS GOLDEN C...CURLS. MY M...MOTHER ALWAYS SAID HE W...WAS HANDSOME AS A PRINCE.
BUT PILAR SAID...
...THAT HE HAD DIED. IT IS WHAT EVERYONE BELIEVED. WHAT PILAR BELIEVES, EVEN NOW. THE KING MUST HAVE PUT HIM IN HERE WHEN THEY CAME DOWN TOGETHER.
I DO NOT KNOW WHY, SAVE THAT MAYBE HE DID NOT WANT ANYONE TO KNOW WHAT HAD HAPPENED TO THE OTHER SLEEPERS. OR MAYBE HILMAN GOT INTO AN EMPTY CASK HIMSELF, WANTING TO TRY THE MECHANISM. HE WAS MAD FOR ALL OF THE DEVICES AND MECHANICS OF THE LOST WORLD.

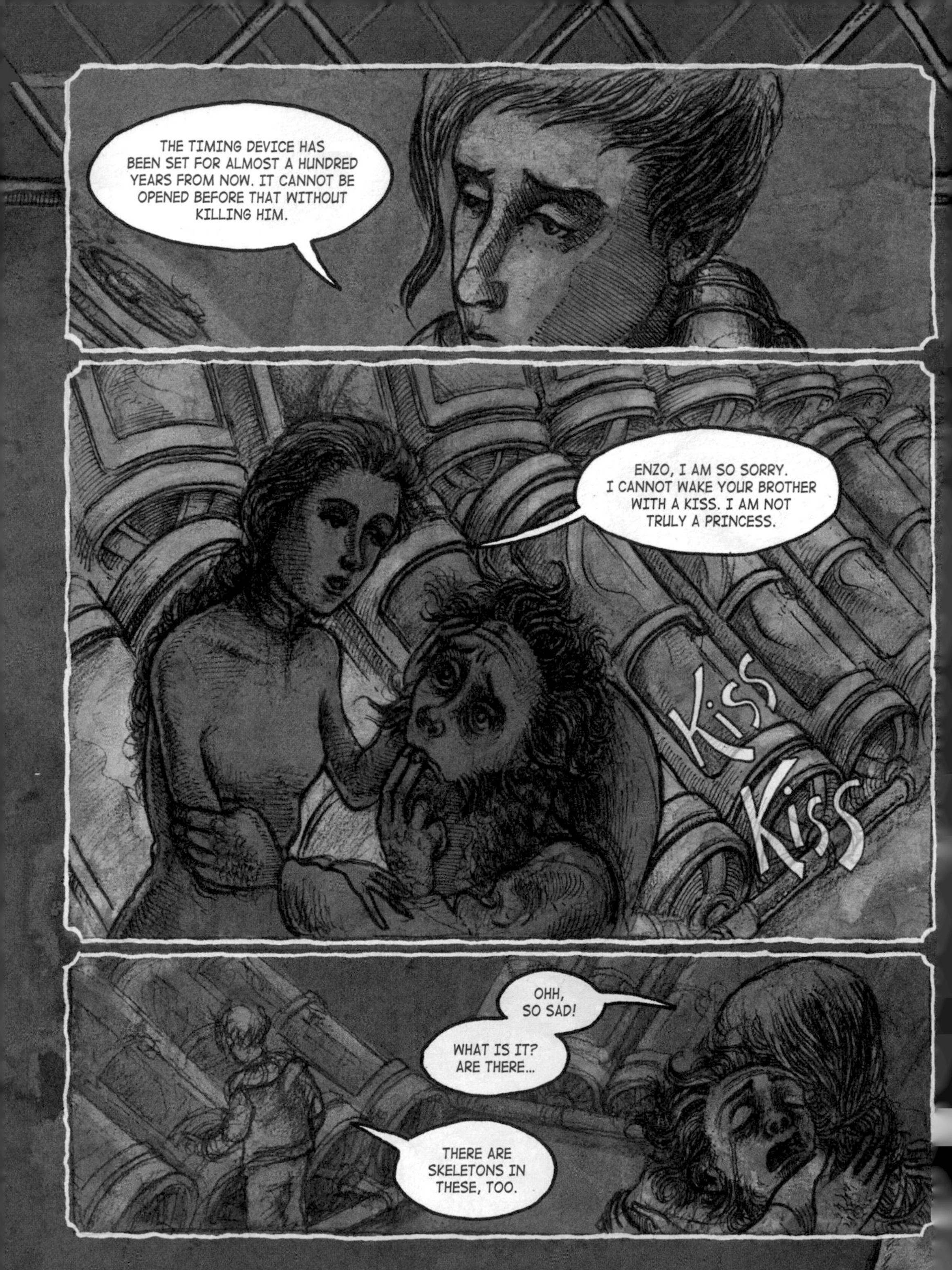
THE TIMING DEVICE HAS BEEN SET FOR ALMOST A HUNDRED YEARS FROM NOW. IT CANNOT BE OPENED BEFORE THAT WITHOUT KILLING HIM.
ENZO, I AM SO SORRY. I CANNOT WAKE YOUR BROTHER WITH A KISS. I AM NOT TRULY A PRINCESS.
KISS
KISS
OHH, SO SAD!
WHAT IS IT? ARE THERE...
THERE ARE SKELETONS IN THESE, TOO.

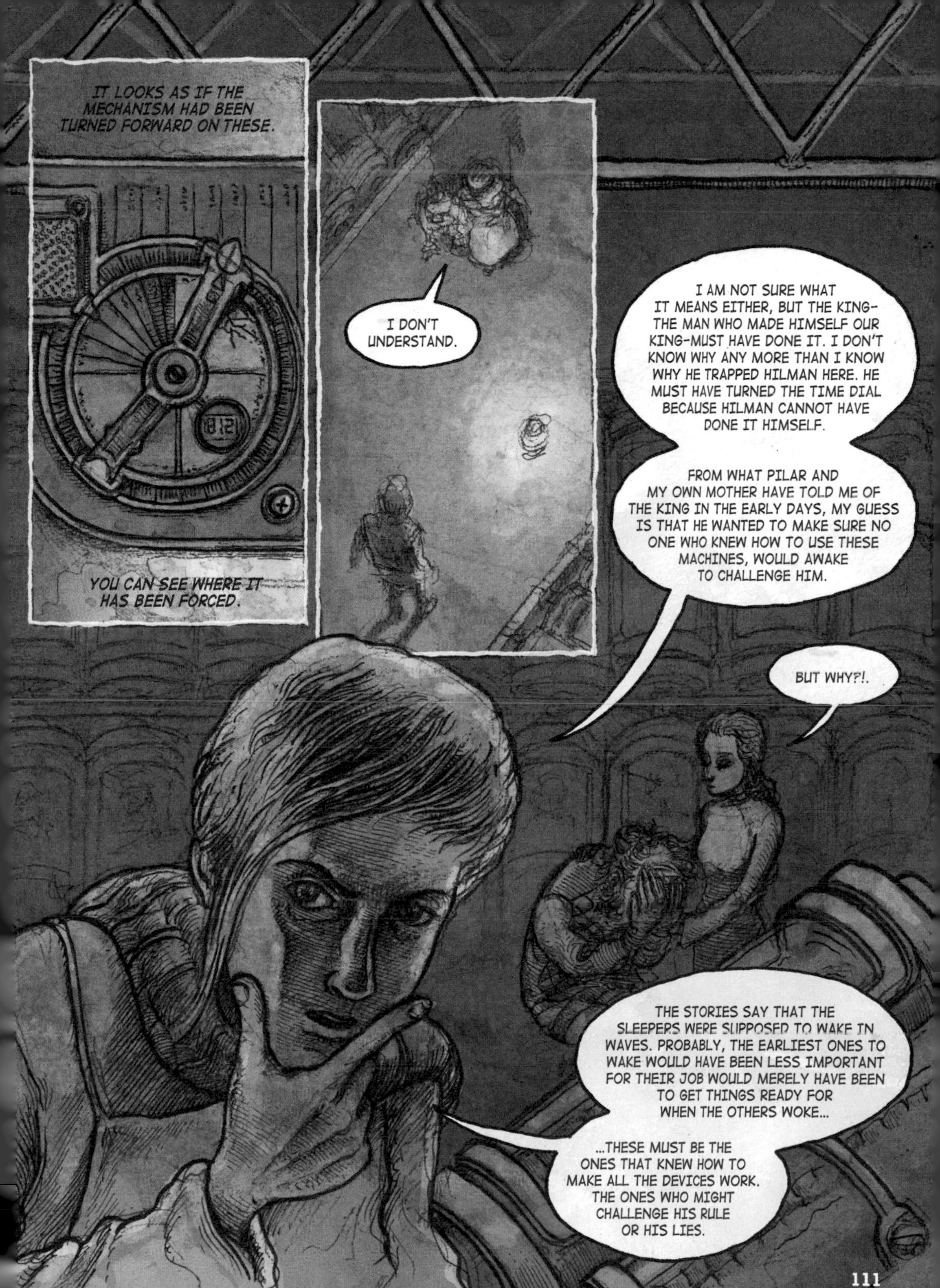
IT LOOKS AS IF THE MECHANISM HAD BEEN TURNED FORWARD ON THESE.
YOU CAN SEE WHERE IT HAS BEEN FORCED.
I DON'T UNDERSTAND.
I AM NOT SURE WHAT IT MEANS EITHER, BUT THE KING- THE MAN WHO MADE HIMSELF OUR KING-MUST HAVE DONE IT. I DON'T KNOW WHY ANY MORE THAN I KNOW WHY HE TRAPPED HILMAN HERE. HE MUST HAVE TURNED THE TIME DIAL BECAUSE HILMAN CANNOT HAVE DONE IT HIMSELF.
FROM WHAT PILAR AND MY OWN MOTHER HAVE TOLD ME OF THE KING IN THE EARLY DAYS, MY GUESS IS THAT HE WANTED TO MAKE SURE NO ONE WHO KNEW HOW TO USE THESE MACHINES, WOULD AWAKE TO CHALLENGE HIM.
BUT WHY?!.
THE STORIES SAY THAT THE SLEEPERS WERE SUPPOSED TO WAKE IN WAVES. PROBABLY, THE EARLIEST ONES TO WAKE WOULD HAVE BEEN LESS IMPORTANT FOR THEIR JOB WOULD MERELY HAVE BEEN TO GET THINGS READY FOR WHEN THE OTHERS WOKE...
...THESE MUST BE THE ONES THAT KNEW HOW TO MAKE ALL THE DEVICES WORK. THE ONES WHO MIGHT CHALLENGE HIS RULE OR HIS LIES.

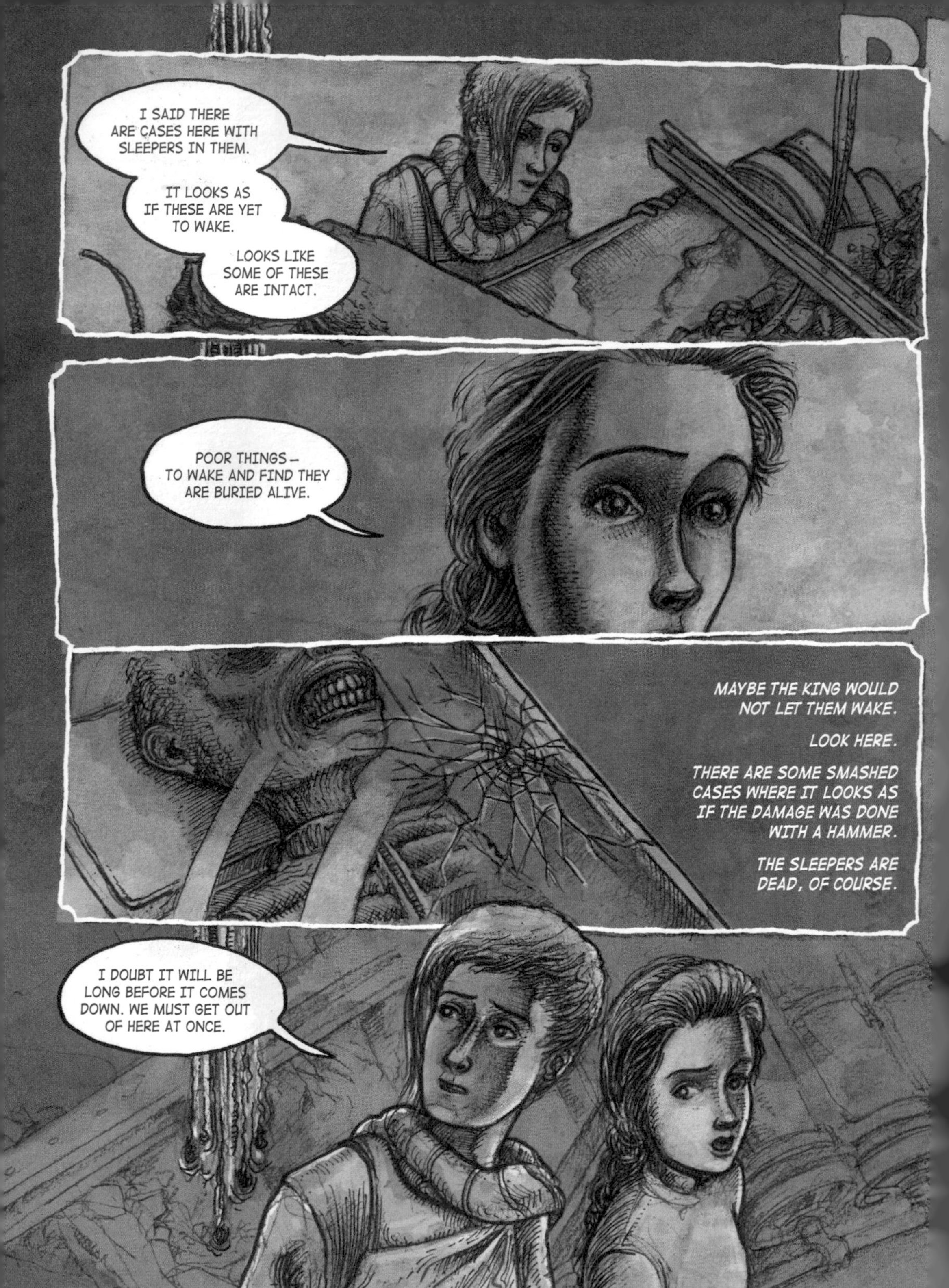
I SAID THERE ARE CASES HERE WITH SLEEPERS IN THEM.
IT LOOKS AS IF THESE ARE YET TO WAKE.
LOOKS LIKE SOME OF THESE ARE INTACT.
POOR THINGS— TO WAKE AND FIND THEY ARE BURIED ALIVE.
MAYBE THE KING WOULD NOT LET THEM WAKE.
LOOK HERE.
THERE ARE SOME SMASHED CASES WHERE IT LOOKS AS IF THE DAMAGE WAS DONE WITH A HAMMER.
THE SLEEPERS ARE DEAD, OF COURSE.
I DOUBT IT WILL BE LONG BEFORE IT COMES DOWN. WE MUST GET OUT OF HERE AT ONCE.

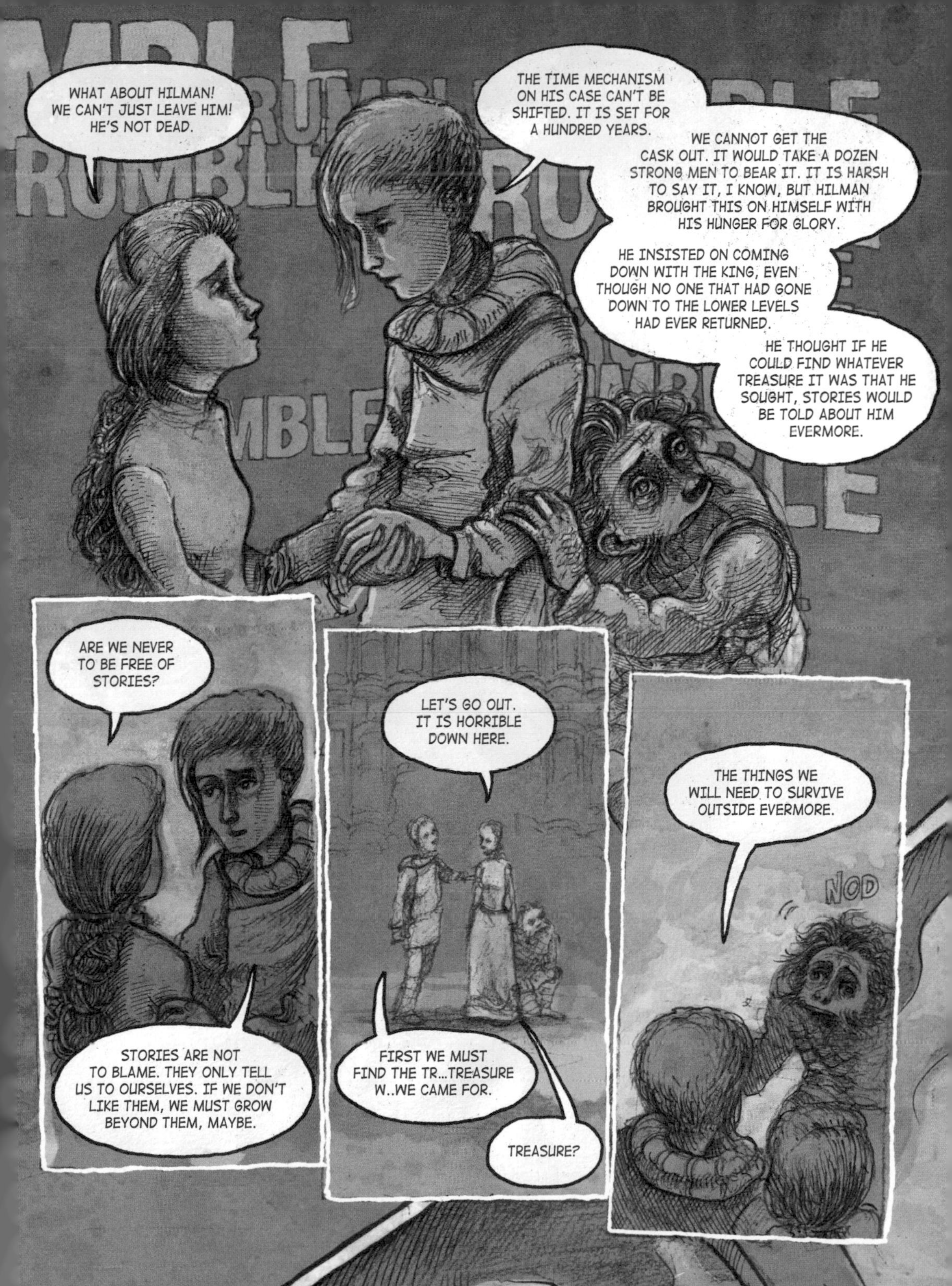
RUMBLE RUMBLE RUMBLE
WHAT ABOUT HILMAN! WE CAN'T JUST LEAVE HIM! HE'S NOT DEAD.
THE TIME MECHANISM ON HIS CASE CAN'T BE SHIFTED. IT IS SET FOR A HUNDRED YEARS.
WE CANNOT GET THE CASK OUT. IT WOULD TAKE A DOZEN STRONG MEN TO BEAR IT. IT IS HARSH TO SAY IT, I KNOW, BUT HILMAN BROUGHT THIS ON HIMSELF WITH HIS HUNGER FOR GLORY.
HE INSISTED ON COMING DOWN WITH THE KING, EVEN THOUGH NO ONE THAT HAD GONE DOWN TO THE LOWER LEVELS HAD EVER RETURNED.
HE THOUGHT IF HE COULD FIND WHATEVER TREASURE IT WAS THAT HE SOUGHT, STORIES WOULD BE TOLD ABOUT HIM EVERMORE.
ARE WE NEVER TO BE FREE OF STORIES?
STORIES ARE NOT TO BLAME. THEY ONLY TELL US TO OURSELVES. IF WE DON'T LIKE THEM, WE MUST GROW BEYOND THEM, MAYBE.
LET'S GO OUT. IT IS HORRIBLE DOWN HERE.
FIRST WE MUST FIND THE TR...TREASURE W..WE CAME FOR.
TREASURE?
THE THINGS WE WILL NEED TO SURVIVE OUTSIDE EVERMORE.
NOD

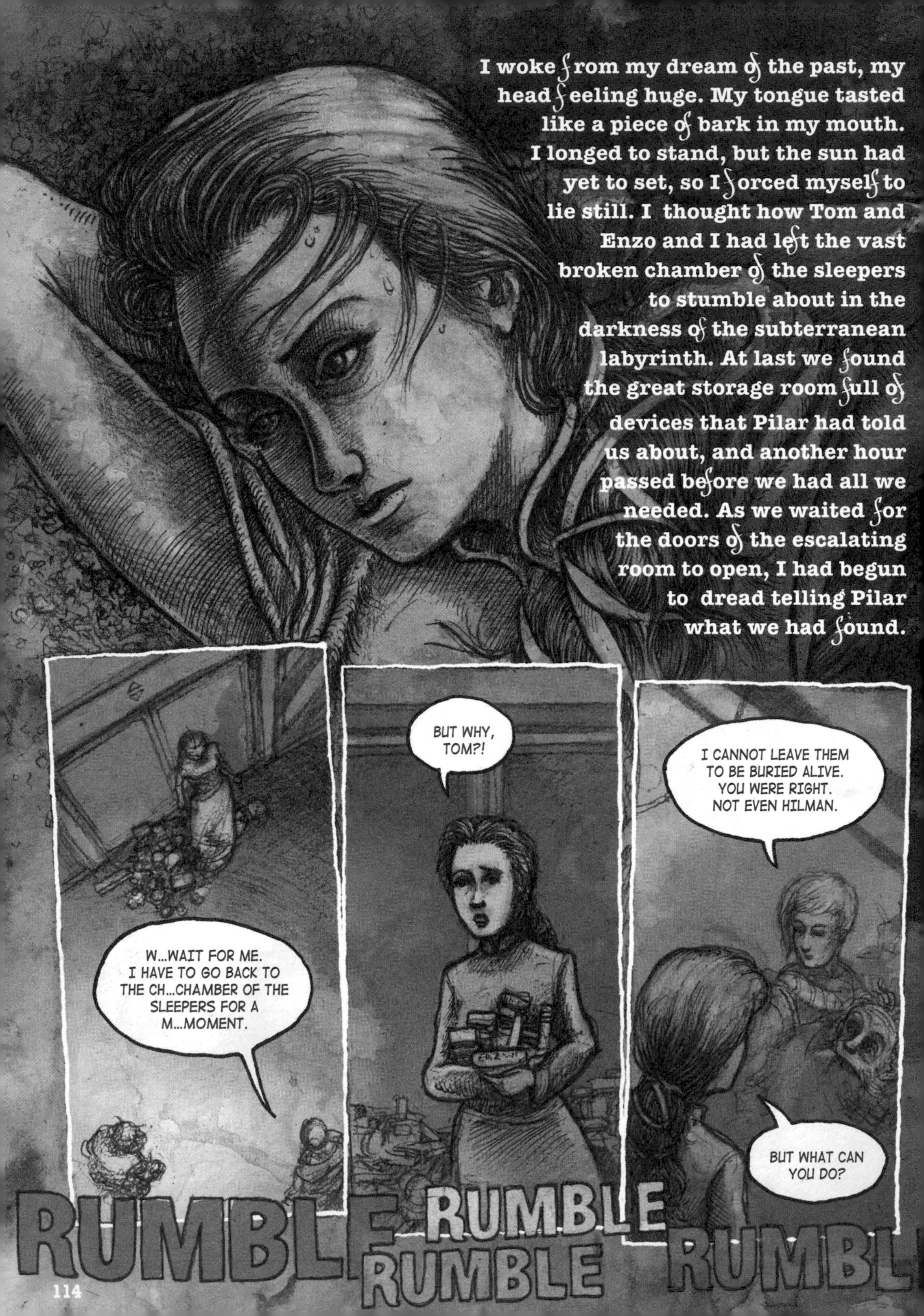
I woke from my dream of the past, my head feeling huge. My tongue tasted like a piece of bark in my mouth. I longed to stand, but the sun had yet to set, so I forced myself to lie still. I thought how Tom and Enzo and I had left the vast broken chamber of the sleepers to stumble about in the darkness of the subterranean labyrinth. At last we found the great storage room full of devices that Pilar had told us about, and another hour passed before we had all we needed. As we waited for the doors of the escalating room to open, I had begun to dread telling Pilar what we had found.
W...WAIT FOR ME. I HAVE TO GO BACK TO THE CH...CHAMBER OF THE SLEEPERS FOR A M...MOMENT.
BUT WHY, TOM?!
I CANNOT LEAVE THEM TO BE BURIED ALIVE. YOU WERE RIGHT. NOT EVEN HILMAN.
BUT WHAT CAN YOU DO?
RUMBLE
RUMBLE
RUMBLE
RUMBL

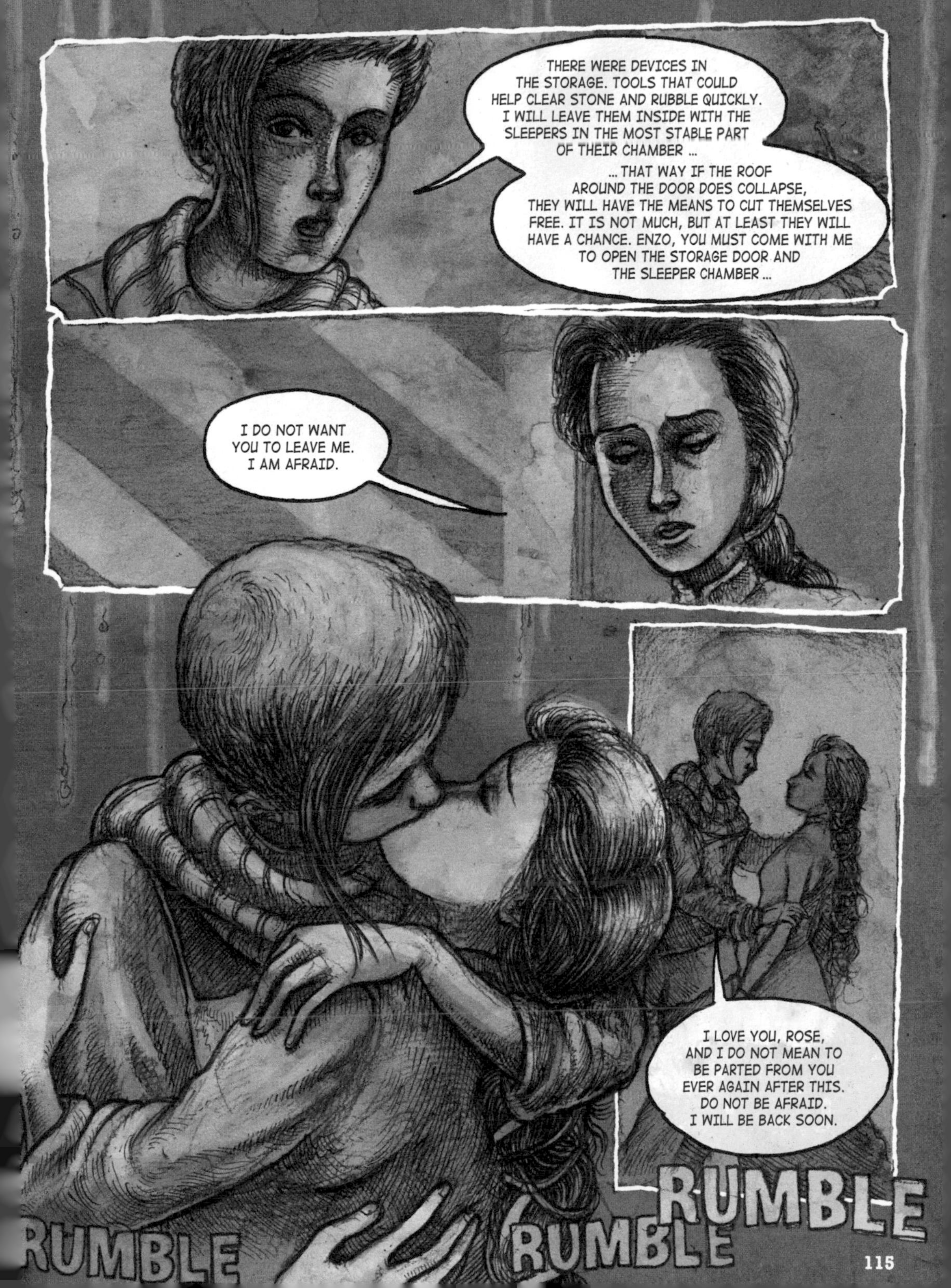
THERE WERE DEVICES IN THE STORAGE. TOOLS THAT COULD HELP CLEAR STONE AND RUBBLE QUICKLY. I WILL LEAVE THEM INSIDE WITH THE SLEEPERS IN THE MOST STABLE PART OF THEIR CHAMBER ...
... THAT WAY IF THE ROOF AROUND THE DOOR DOES COLLAPSE, THEY WILL HAVE THE MEANS TO CUT THEMSELVES FREE. IT IS NOT MUCH, BUT AT LEAST THEY WILL HAVE A CHANCE. ENZO, YOU MUST COME WITH ME TO OPEN THE STORAGE DOOR AND THE SLEEPER CHAMBER ...
I DO NOT WANT YOU TO LEAVE ME. I AM AFRAID.
I LOVE YOU, ROSE, AND I DO NOT MEAN TO BE PARTED FROM YOU EVER AGAIN AFTER THIS. DO NOT BE AFRAID. I WILL BE BACK SOON.
RUMBLE
RUMBLE
RUMBLE

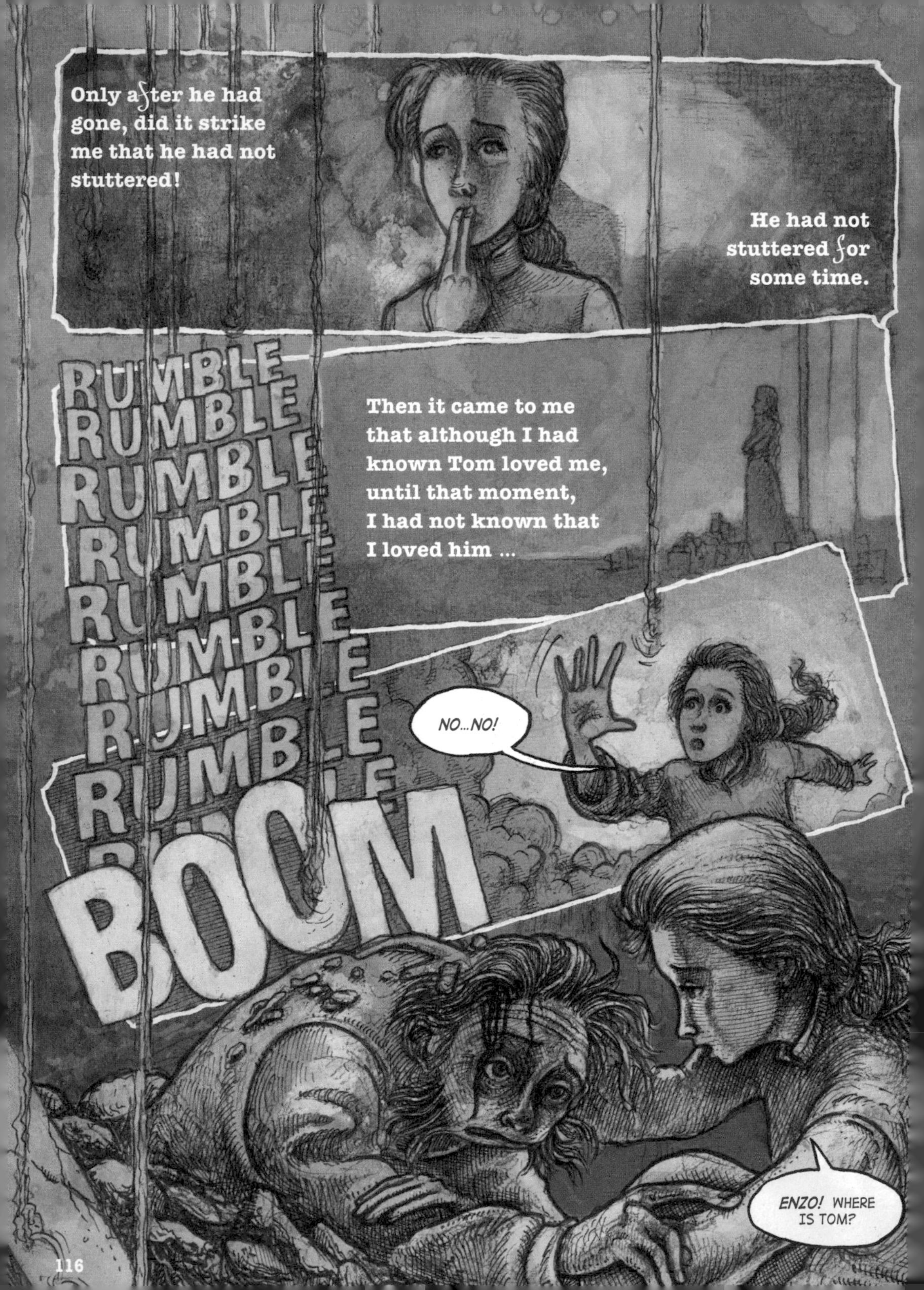

Only after he had gone, did it strike me that he had not stuttered!
He had not stuttered for some time.
RUMBLE RUMBLE RUMBLE RUMBLE RUMBLE RUMBLE RUMBLE RUMBLE RUMBLE RUMBLE
Then it came to me that although I had known Tom loved me, until that moment, I had not known that I loved him ...
NO...NO!
BOOM
ENZO! WHERE IS TOM?

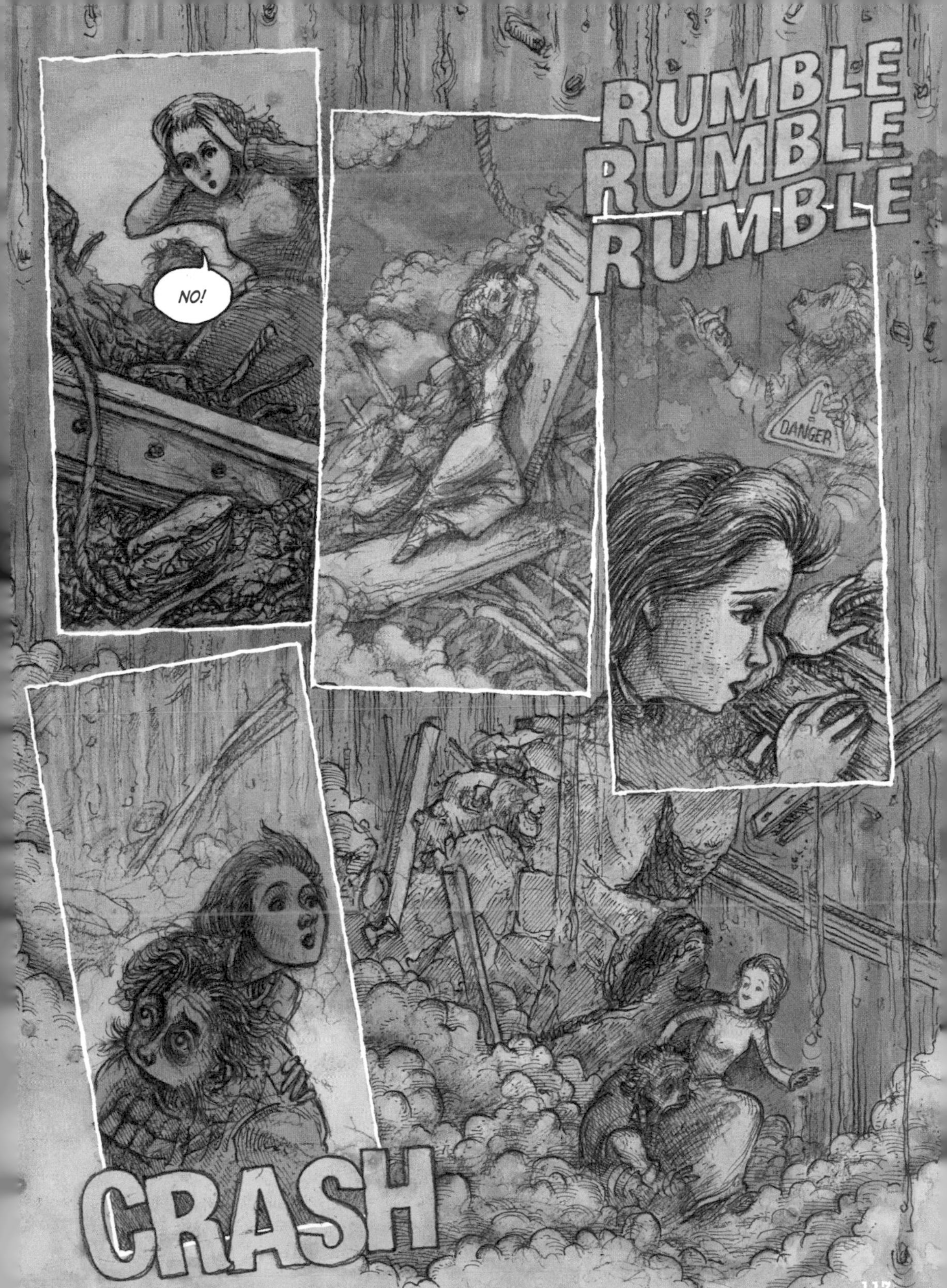
NO!
RUMBLE
RUMBLE
RUMBLE
DANGER
CRASH

It seemed to me as I hobbled through the clouds of dust, half carrying Enzo, that the whole of Evermore was falling about my ears, and so deep was my sorrow for Tom that it seemed right that it should be so. But in fact only a portion of the subterranean labyrinth had collapsed. The rest was intact, along with the walls and towers and buildings of Evermore. The latter has suffered only slight damage and in a few days, other than a single deep crack across the yard, there there was little sign of what had happened. And what had happened was the subject on all lips, until the King came out to address his people, explaining that the damage had come about because of a minor quaking in the earth. Was that true? I did not know. There were slight quakes from time to time, but it mattered not one whit to me. What mattered was that Tom was dead.

There was chaos enough in the days to follow that no one immediately noticed Tom's absence. Then one night his mother sent one of his brothers to ask if I had seen him. I said I had not, feeling as if the tears I dared not shed were a slow and terrible bleeding inside me.

I had told Pilar about Hilman, and it seems to me she took the news with sorrow, but with resignation too. Her grief, like mine, was all for Tom. I no longer had any desire to escape, but after a few days, Pilar insisted that I must go as we had planned. I argued and begged and pleaded, telling her I could not go alone ...

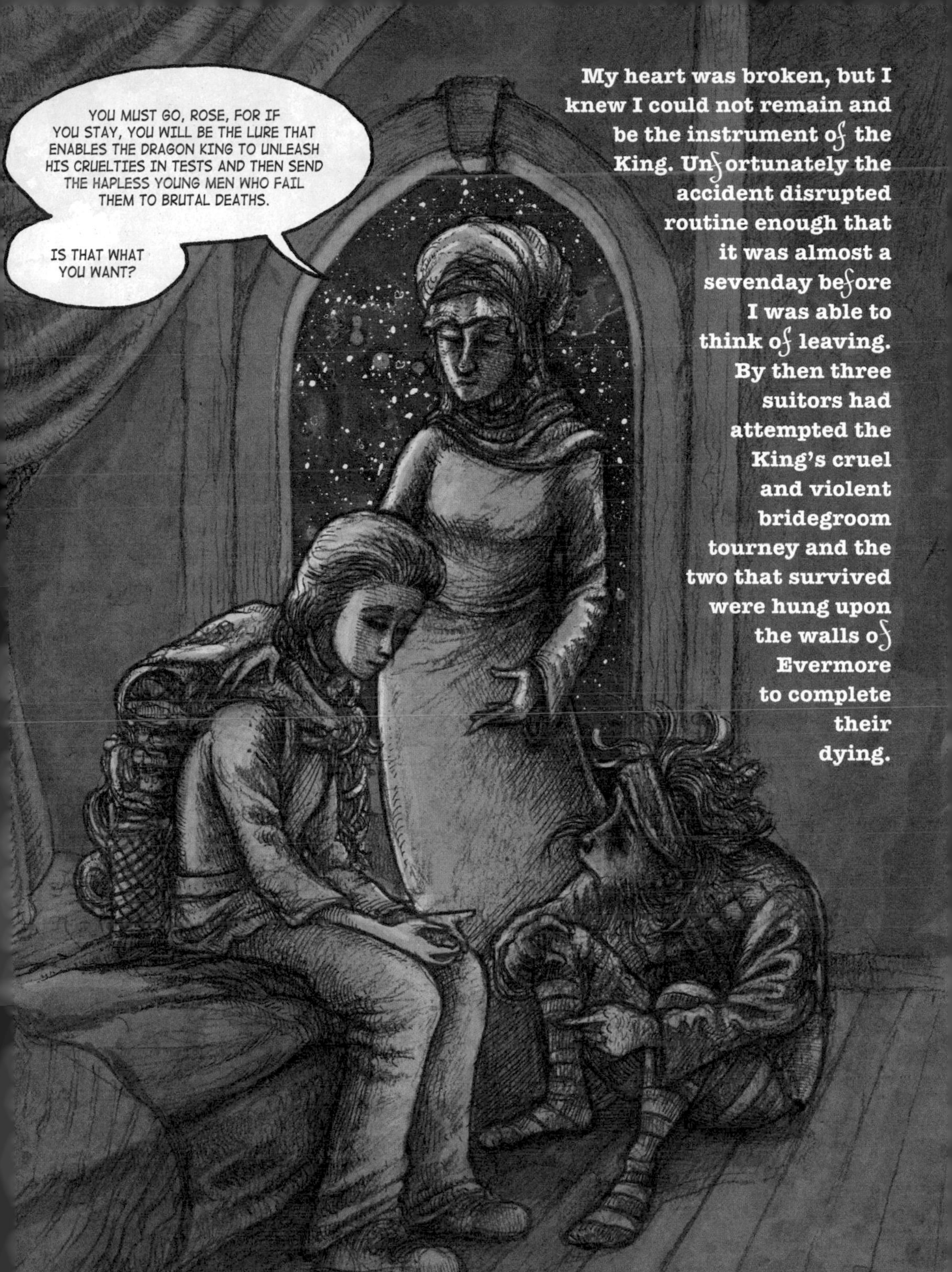
YOU MUST GO, ROSE, FOR IF YOU STAY, YOU WILL BE THE LURE THAT ENABLES THE DRAGON KING TO UNLEASH HIS CRUELTIES IN TESTS AND THEN SEND THE HAPLESS YOUNG MEN WHO FAIL THEM TO BRUTAL DEATHS.
IS THAT WHAT YOU WANT?
My heart was broken, but I knew I could not remain and be the instrument of the King. Unfortunately the accident disrupted routine enough that it was almost a sevenday before I was able to think of leaving. By then three suitors had attempted the King's cruel and violent bridegroom tourney and the two that survived were hung upon the walls of Evermore to complete their dying.

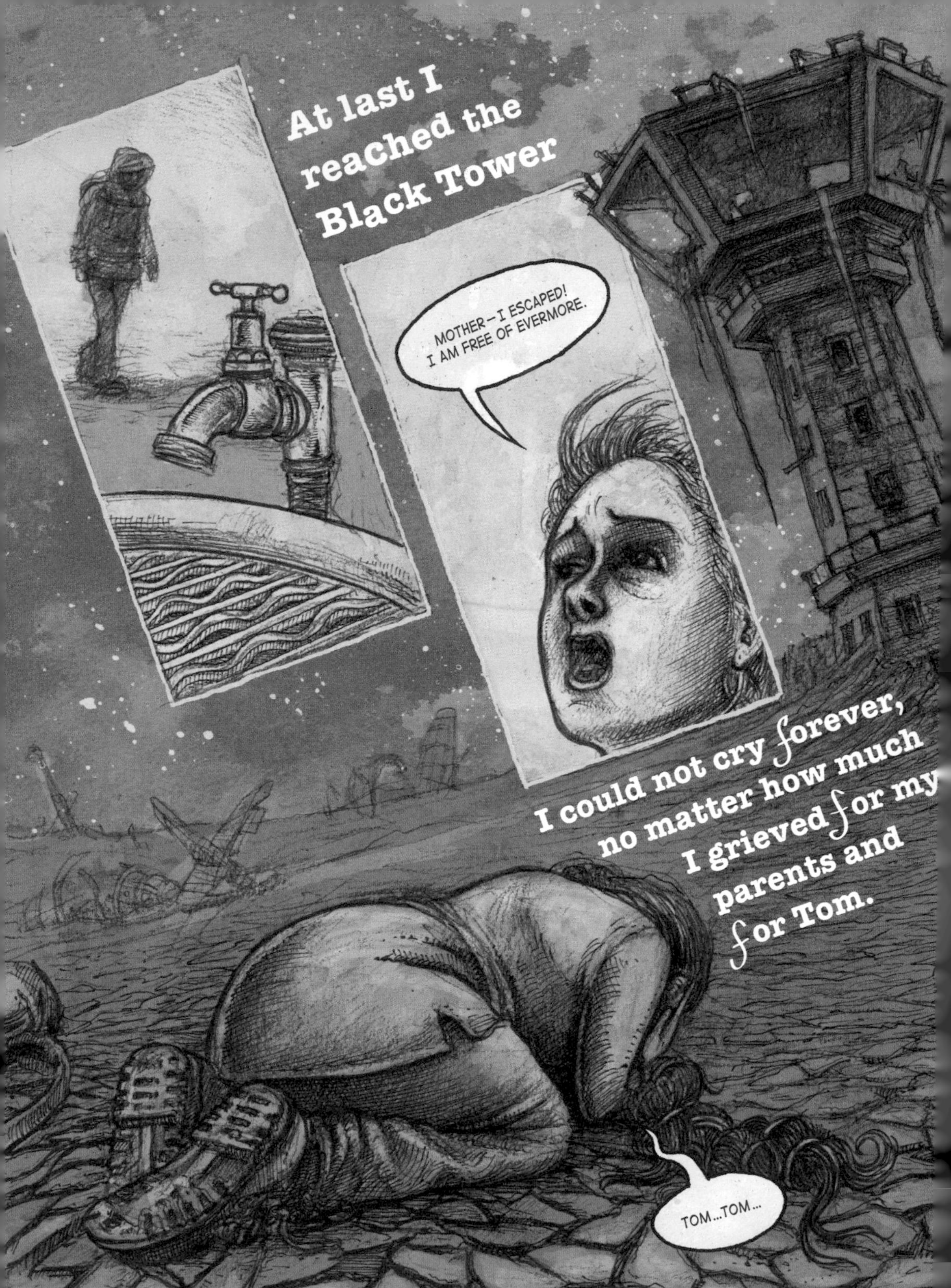
At last I reached the Black Tower
MOTHER—I ESCAPED! I AM FREE OF EVERMORE.
I could not cry forever, no matter how much I grieved for my parents and for Tom.
TOM...TOM...

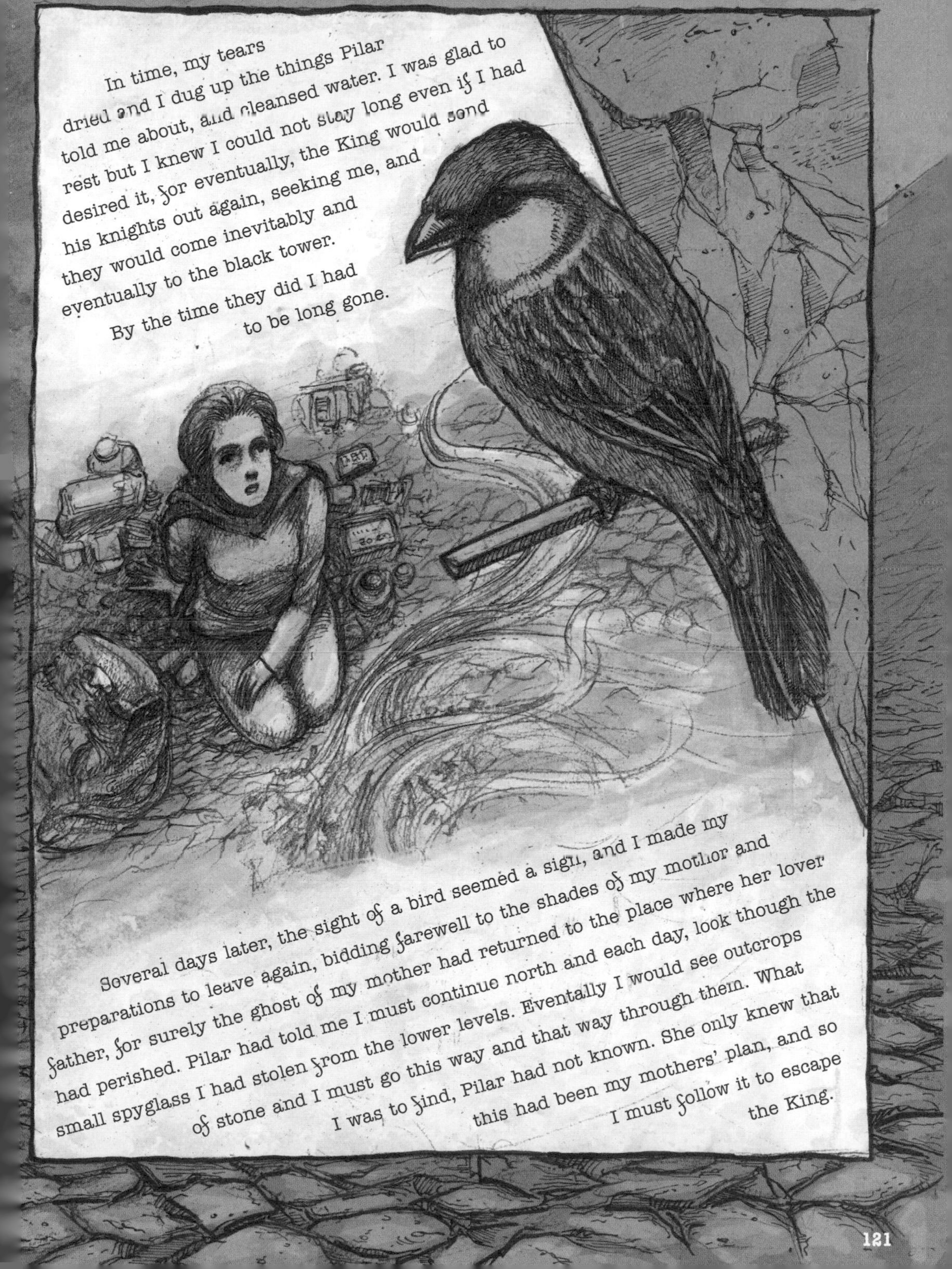

In time, my tears dried and I dug up the things Pilar told me about, and cleansed water. I was glad to rest but I knew I could not stay long even if I had desired it, for eventually, the King would send his knights out again, seeking me, and they would come inevitably and eventually to the black tower.

By the time they did I had to be long gone.

Several days later, the sight of a bird seemed a sign, and I made my preparations to leave again, bidding farewell to the shades of my mother and father, for surely the ghost of my mother had returned to the place where her lover had perished. Pilar had told me I must continue north and each day, look though the small spyglass I had stolen from the lower levels. Eventally I would see outcrops of stone and I must go this way and that way through them. What I was to find, Pilar had not known. She only knew that this had been my mothers' plan, and so I must follow it to escape the King.

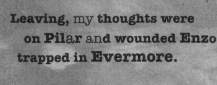

Leaving, my thoughts were
on **Pilar** and wounded **Enzo**
trapped in **Evermore**.

I prayed they had not been
punished because of me.

The moon waxed and waned three times before I came
at last to this little broken tower at the edge of the world.
It was a hard journey, but not near as hard as the terrible
desperate flight from Evermore to the burned tower, and
I could not help but laugh at the irony of it. I had striven
so long and earnestly to put all towers behind me, only to
find one waiting for me at the end of my journey. Gradually I
repaired the tower and made it habitable, and even
comfortable in a spare sort of way, cannibalising bits of other
ruins about. I had some notion of building a better place
eventually, but when I used the water-finding device Tom had
insisted I take, and discovered a pure stream running close by
the tower, I dug a well and then hoed some ground for a garden
bed. Blisters turned into callouses and soft flesh into honed
muscle as I used the various devices to make the earth
fertile enough to accept the precious seeds I had brought.
There was much trial and more error, for I had no
knowledge of my own to rely on, but in time, I had
a few fruiting trees and a little scratchy bed of
vegetables. The fruit was small and often died
before it was ripe enough to eat, but I learned
to replant the seeds of fruitful crops, and
to graft good upon strong so that each
season gave a better return.

Some of the plants produced matter that could be spun and woven, and I did those things when the weather grew cold, for the temperature dropped far lower in this new place than in Evermore. I marvelled the first time I found a thin crust of ice on the surface of the well water, and occasionally a dust of fine white snow would fall. I knew what it was only because of Pilar's stories.

There was endless work to be done and I fell into bed each night, too exhausted to think or dream. I was glad, as for a long time there was only sorrow in quiet hours. On the rare occasions I did dream, and grief and loss assailed me, I fought despair by telling myself that I was preparing a home for when Pilar and Enzo would come.

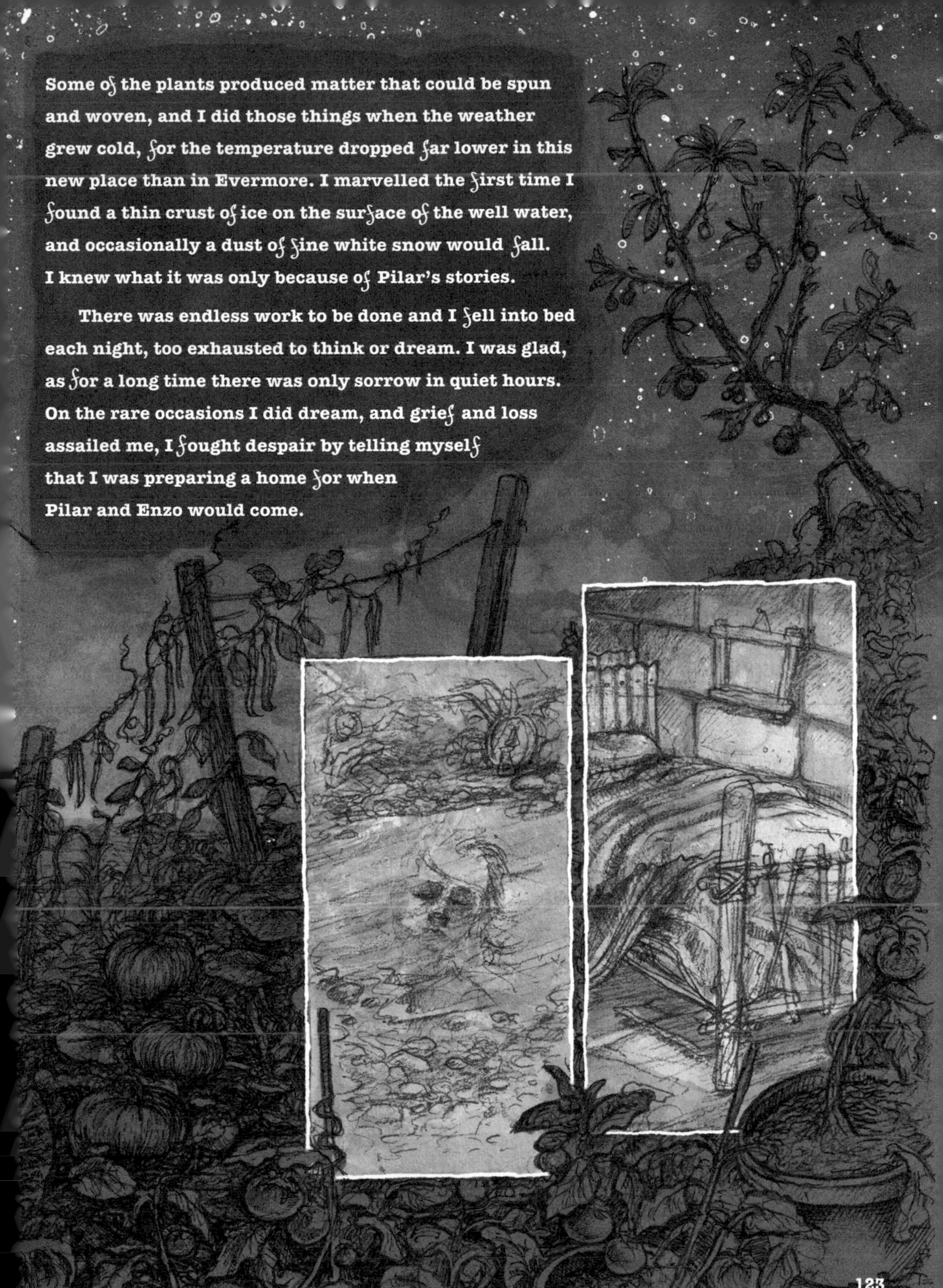

But in time

the stories I told myself grew gentler and deeper, for I poured into them my love and admiration of Pilar, my pity for Enzo and for my mother and father, and most of all, the love I had discovered I felt for Quiet Tom, too late. The stories showed me how shallow and silly and young I had been and how gentle and clever and noble-hearted Tom had been; how he had striven, even at the cost of his own life, to save the sleepers from the mad king, and how well and selflessly he had loved me.

One night, weaving as I sat gazing out my window at the lovely shining sea, I began to tell a tale to myself of a Tom who had not been crushed under a rockfall in the lower levels of Evermore, but who had been trapped within the chamber with the sleepers. The story I wove had him wounded but not killed, and eventually, recovering enough to use the devices he had meant to leave for the sleepers to free themselves to cut his way free. In my story, this took time, and when the sleepers woke, he told them everything.

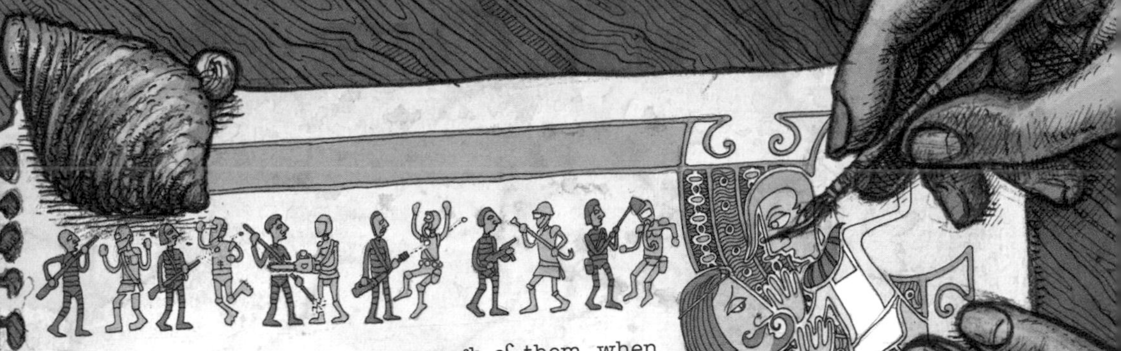

Eventually there were enough of them, when they got free of the lower levels, to burst out to confront and overthrow the dragon king of Evermore.

When all was safe and he could do no more for the sleepers, my story told how Tom would leave to find me. He would bring Enzo and Pilar with him and we would all live happily ever after in a broken tower at the edge of the world.

So did I comfort and woo my heart over the years, until it seemed to me that it must have happened in that way, and that one day, Tom would find me.

When I had basic necessities enough, I began to experiment with the more complex devices Tom had taken from the lower levels. There was a box that made music, and once it worked, I listened, near entranced, for days on end, before it fell abruptly silent. I did not know how to resurrect it, but I missed the music so much that I carved myself a pipe out of a thin hollow bit of branch and learned to play the haunting music the box had taught me.

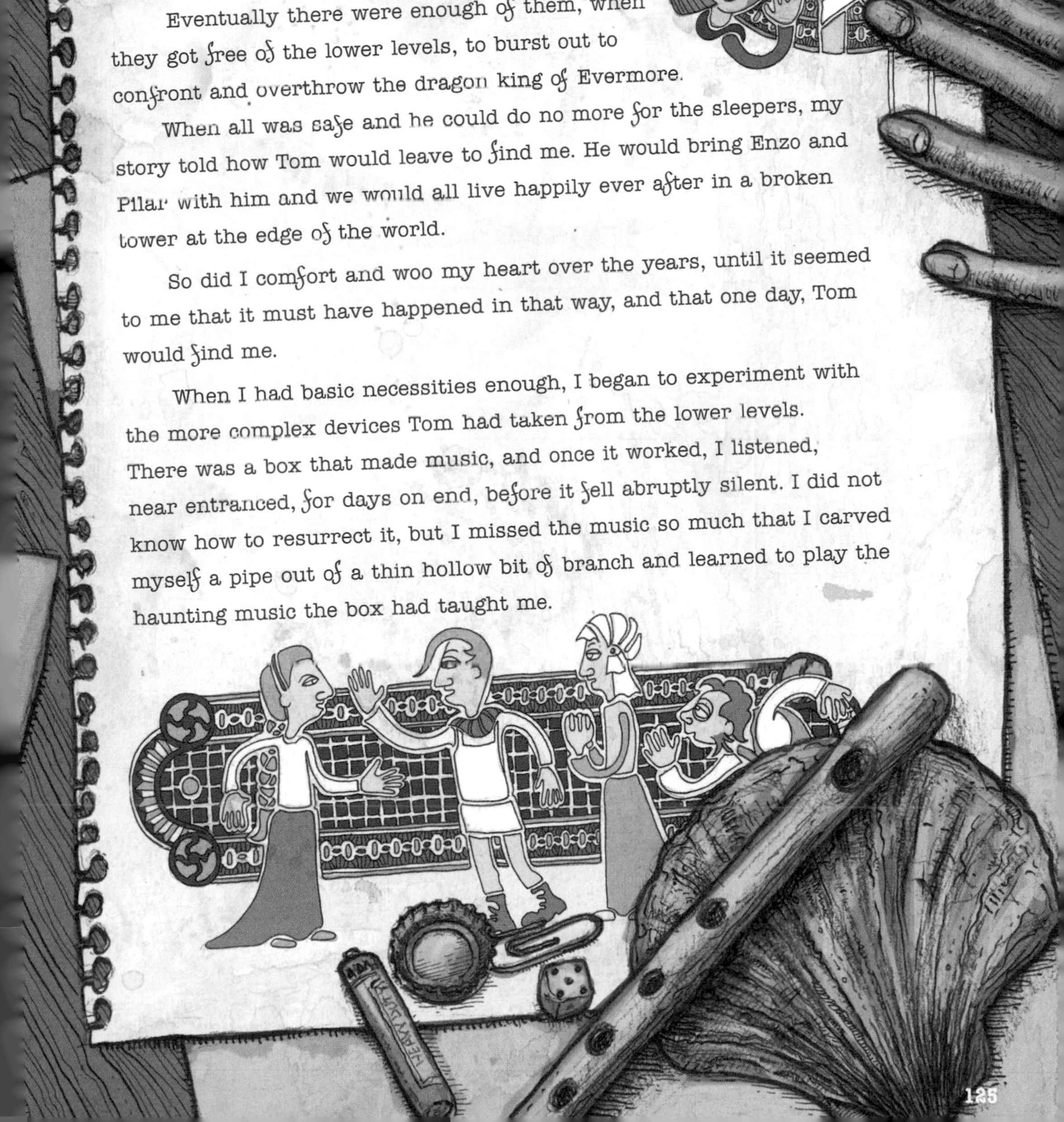

One day

a bird came to peck at a berry in a little tree as I played. I gaped incredulously as it looked down at me with its bright, beady little eye, for there were very few creatures in the world. I hardly dared breathe for fear of frightening it away, but the bird stayed and sang and pecked and in time another bird came and the pair made an odd little nest like a pottery cup, stuck against the side of the tower under its drooping eaves. They laid some eggs, to my wonderment and I watched eagerly as the eggs hatched and the nestlings learned to fly. To my grief, the birds eventually flew away, along with their nestlings.

Inspired by the birds, I finally set up the incubating chamber contained in one of the devices and managed to bring to life an egg in a box, which hatched into Mercy. The rest died but Mercy lived and even gave the occasional egg. There had been many such boxes in the lower levels of Evermore, and I came to lament that I had taken only some hens and a goat. It took me a time to gather the courage to try the goat box, but when I did, Goat was born and lived, though not for long, and she was three-legged and blind. After she died, I came to regret that Tom had made me put the cat box back, saying a cat would be of no practical use.

But then a few months ago, there was a storm and a cat washed up on a spar of wood, half drowned.

Hope, I called her.

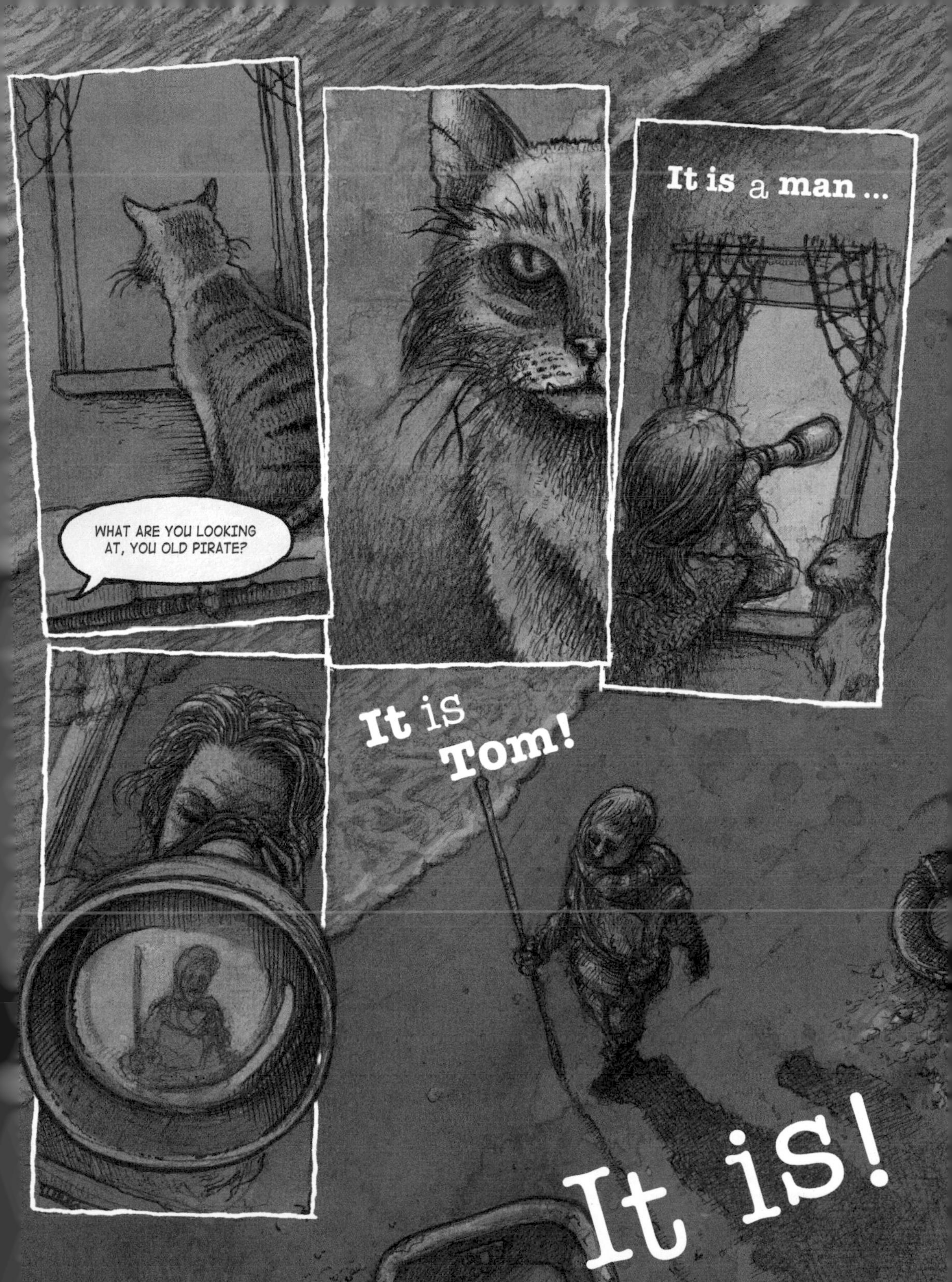
WHAT ARE YOU LOOKING AT, YOU OLD PIRATE?
It is a man ...
It is Tom!
It is!

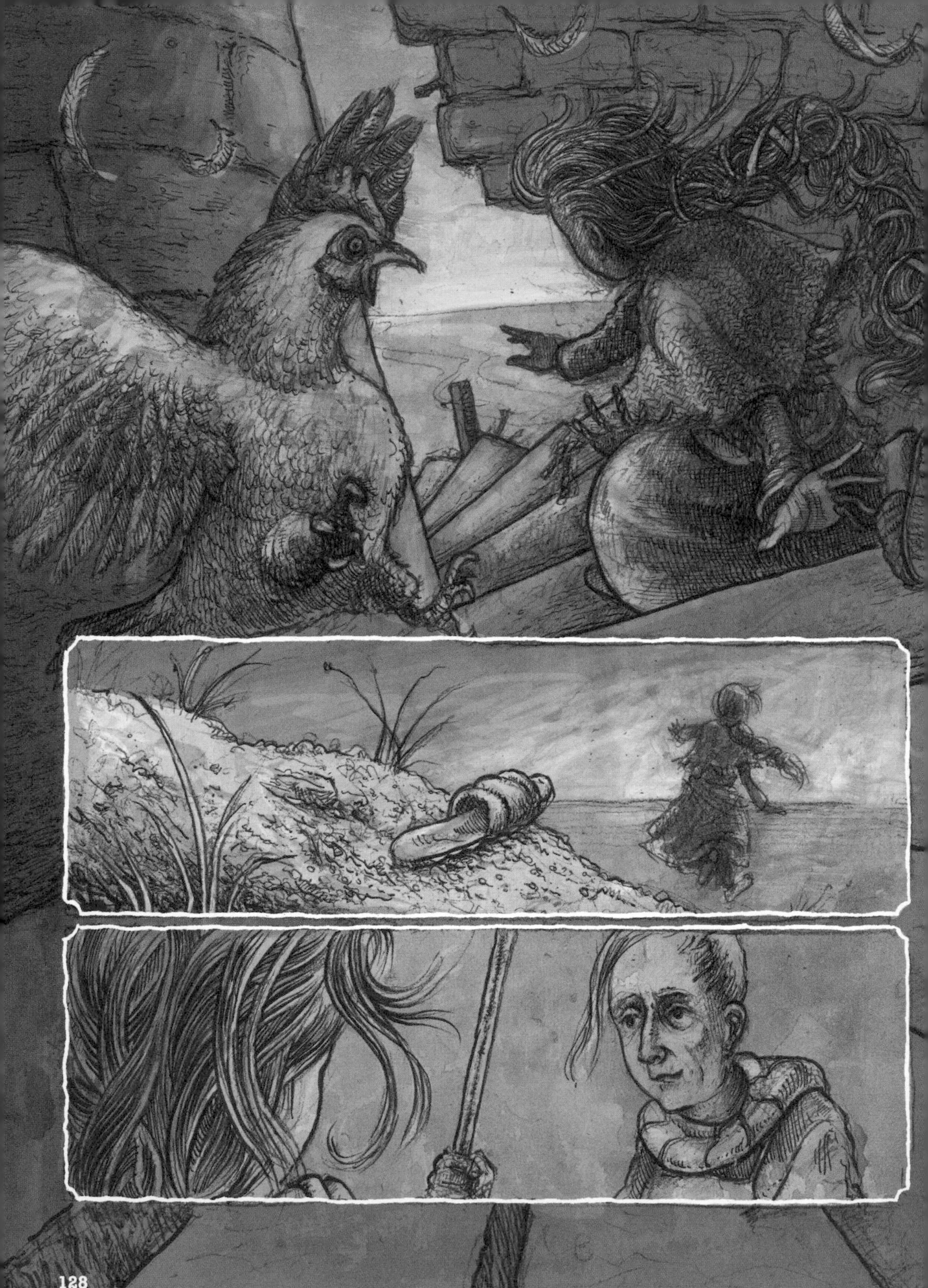

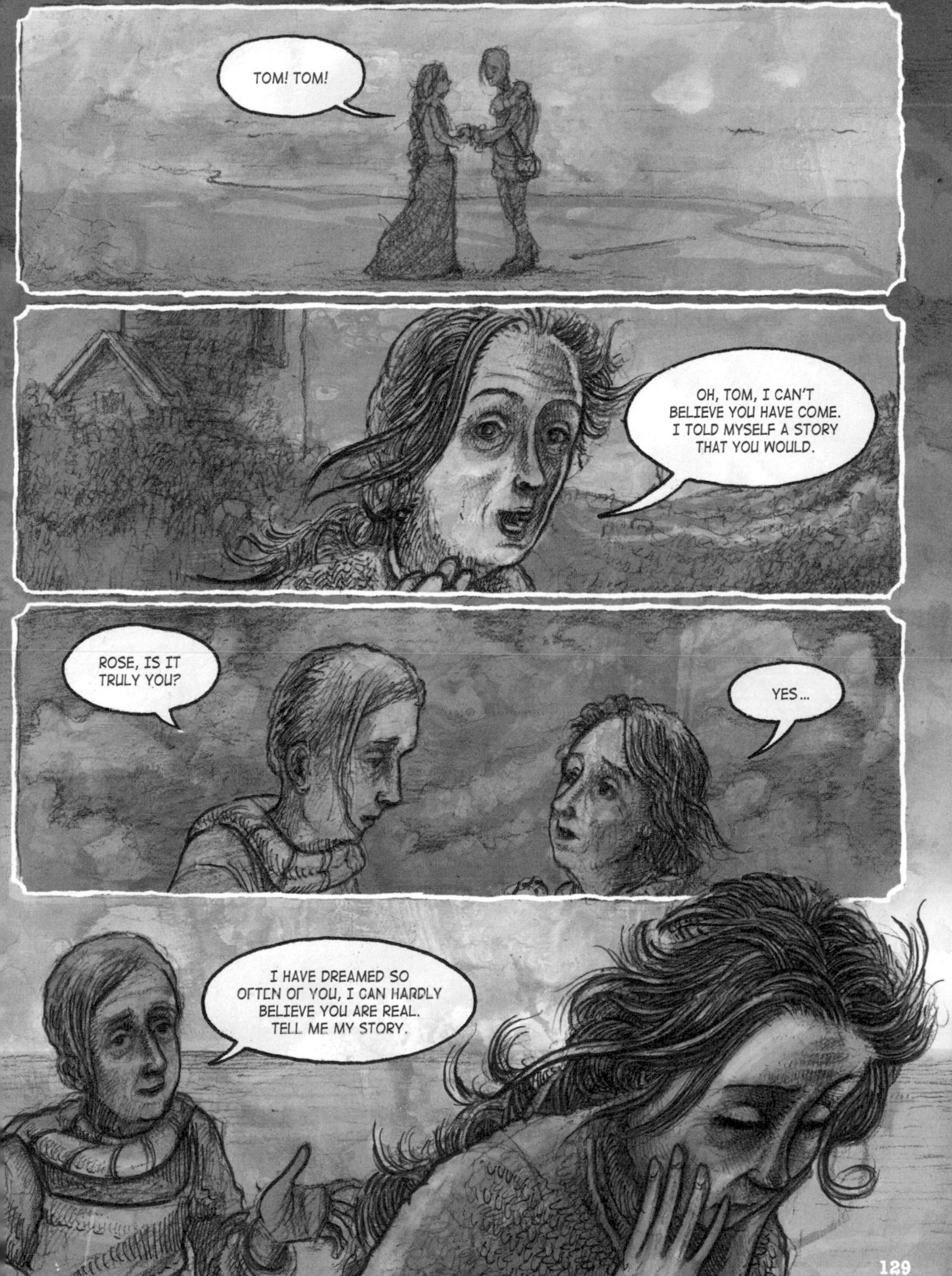
TOM! TOM!
OH, TOM, I CAN'T BELIEVE YOU HAVE COME. I TOLD MYSELF A STORY THAT YOU WOULD.
ROSE, IS IT TRULY YOU?
YES...
I HAVE DREAMED SO OFTEN OF YOU, I CAN HARDLY BELIEVE YOU ARE REAL. TELL ME MY STORY.

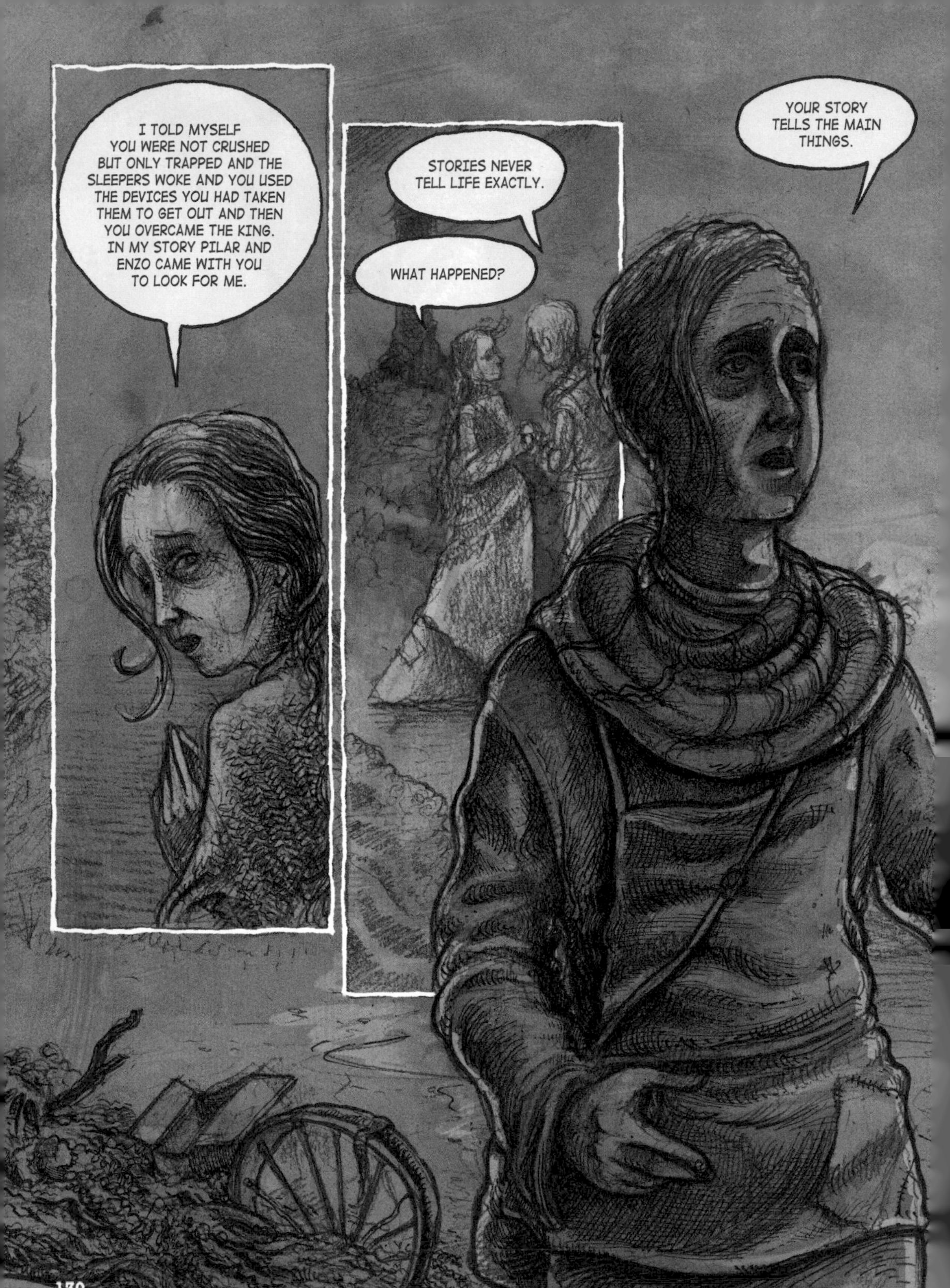
I TOLD MYSELF YOU WERE NOT CRUSHED BUT ONLY TRAPPED AND THE SLEEPERS WOKE AND YOU USED THE DEVICES YOU HAD TAKEN THEM TO GET OUT AND THEN YOU OVERCAME THE KING. IN MY STORY PILAR AND ENZO CAME WITH YOU TO LOOK FOR ME.
STORIES NEVER TELL LIFE EXACTLY.
WHAT HAPPENED?
YOUR STORY TELLS THE MAIN THINGS.

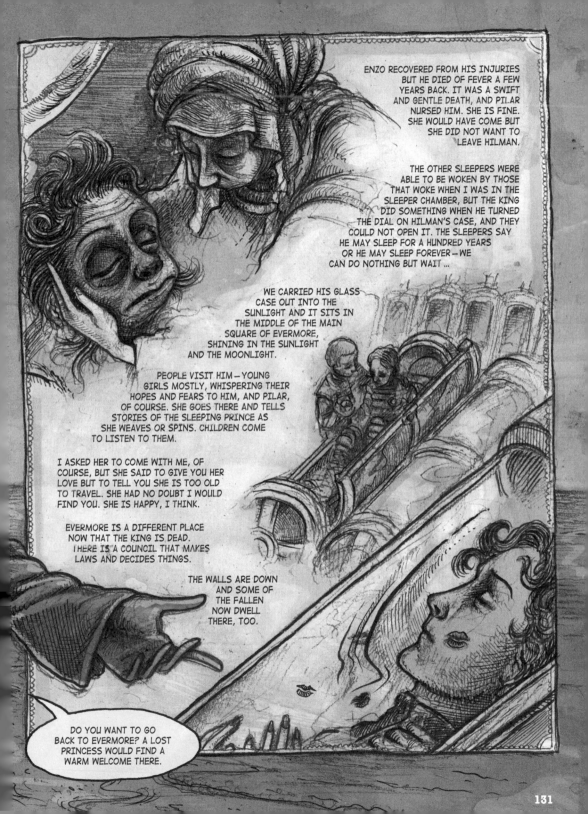

ENZO RECOVERED FROM HIS INJURIES BUT HE DIED OF FEVER A FEW YEARS BACK. IT WAS A SWIFT AND GENTLE DEATH, AND PILAR NURSED HIM. SHE IS FINE. SHE WOULD HAVE COME BUT SHE DID NOT WANT TO LEAVE HILMAN.

THE OTHER SLEEPERS WERE ABLE TO BE WOKEN BY THOSE THAT WOKE WHEN I WAS IN THE SLEEPER CHAMBER, BUT THE KING DID SOMETHING WHEN HE TURNED THE DIAL ON HILMAN'S CASE, AND THEY COULD NOT OPEN IT. THE SLEEPERS SAY HE MAY SLEEP FOR A HUNDRED YEARS OR HE MAY SLEEP FOREVER — WE CAN DO NOTHING BUT WAIT ...

WE CARRIED HIS GLASS CASE OUT INTO THE SUNLIGHT AND IT SITS IN THE MIDDLE OF THE MAIN SQUARE OF EVERMORE, SHINING IN THE SUNLIGHT AND THE MOONLIGHT.

PEOPLE VISIT HIM — YOUNG GIRLS MOSTLY, WHISPERING THEIR HOPES AND FEARS TO HIM, AND PILAR, OF COURSE. SHE GOES THERE AND TELLS STORIES OF THE SLEEPING PRINCE AS SHE WEAVES OR SPINS. CHILDREN COME TO LISTEN TO THEM.

I ASKED HER TO COME WITH ME, OF COURSE, BUT SHE SAID TO GIVE YOU HER LOVE BUT TO TELL YOU SHE IS TOO OLD TO TRAVEL. SHE HAD NO DOUBT I WOULD FIND YOU. SHE IS HAPPY, I THINK.

EVERMORE IS A DIFFERENT PLACE NOW THAT THE KING IS DEAD. THERE IS A COUNCIL THAT MAKES LAWS AND DECIDES THINGS.

THE WALLS ARE DOWN AND SOME OF THE FALLEN NOW DWELL THERE, TOO.

DO YOU WANT TO GO BACK TO EVERMORE? A LOST PRINCESS WOULD FIND A WARM WELCOME THERE.

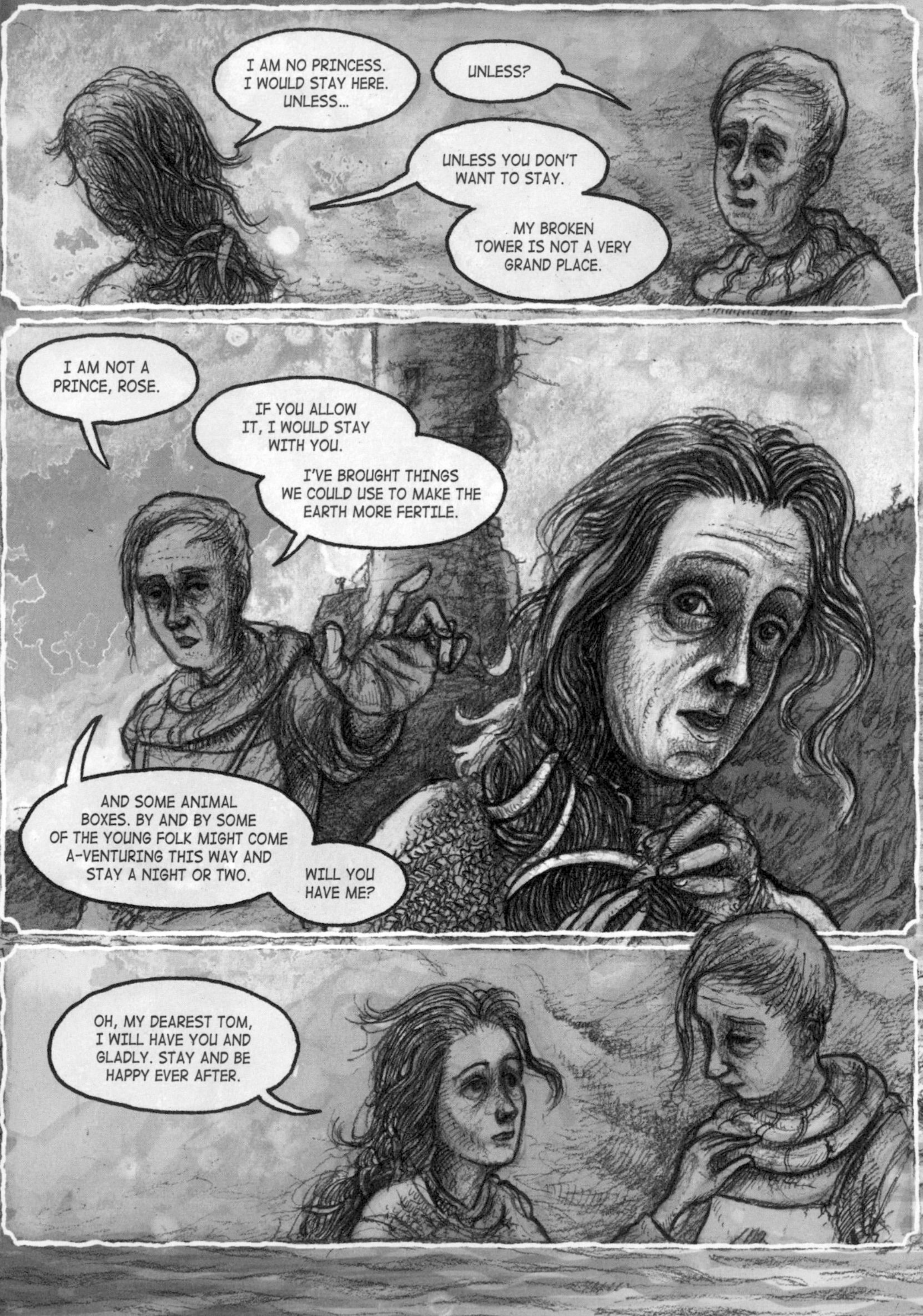
I AM NO PRINCESS. I WOULD STAY HERE. UNLESS...
UNLESS?
UNLESS YOU DON'T WANT TO STAY.
MY BROKEN TOWER IS NOT A VERY GRAND PLACE.
I AM NOT A PRINCE, ROSE.
IF YOU ALLOW IT, I WOULD STAY WITH YOU.
I'VE BROUGHT THINGS WE COULD USE TO MAKE THE EARTH MORE FERTILE.
AND SOME ANIMAL BOXES. BY AND BY SOME OF THE YOUNG FOLK MIGHT COME A-VENTURING THIS WAY AND STAY A NIGHT OR TWO.
WILL YOU HAVE ME?
OH, MY DEAREST TOM, I WILL HAVE YOU AND GLADLY. STAY AND BE HAPPY EVER AFTER.

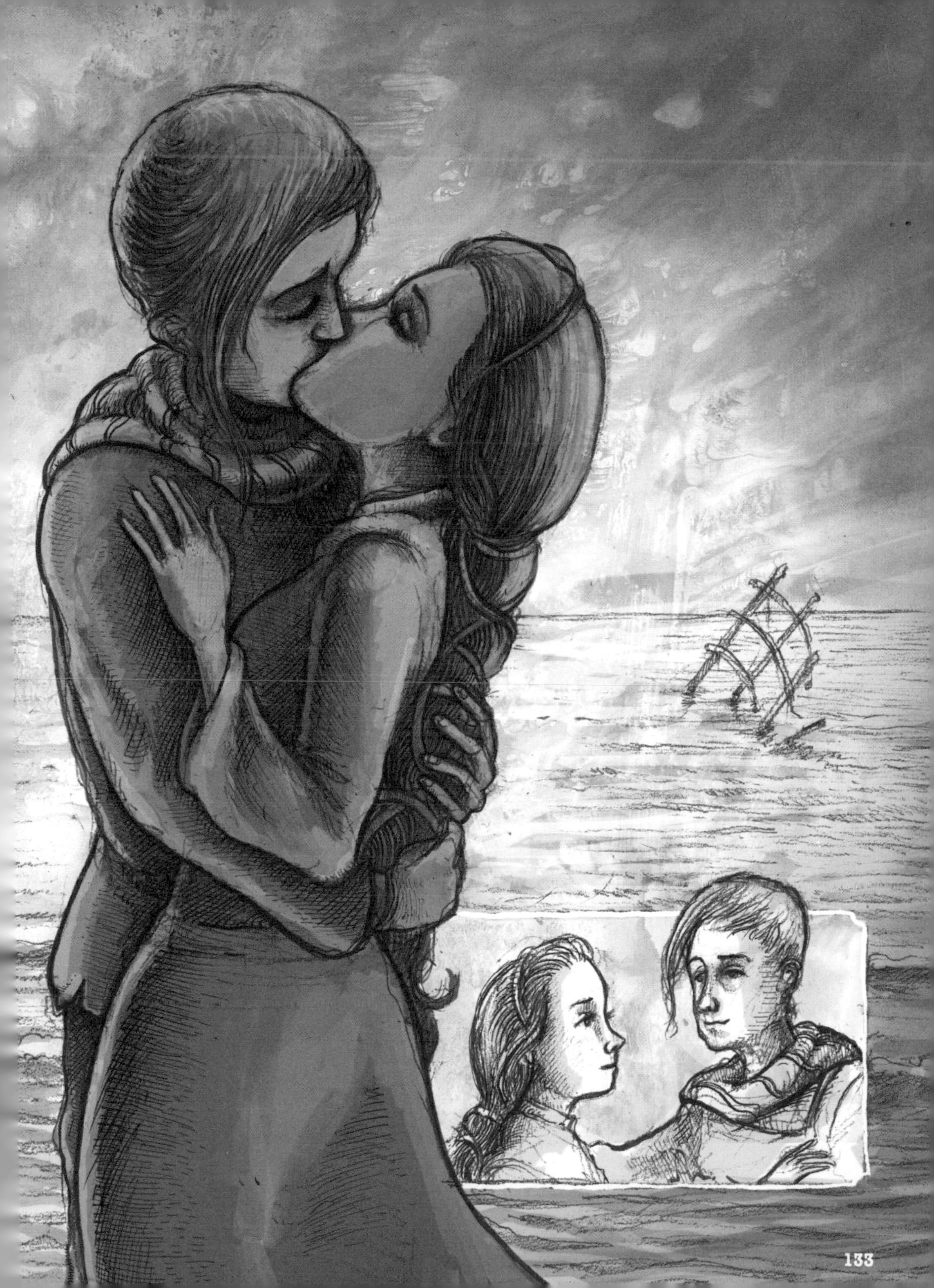

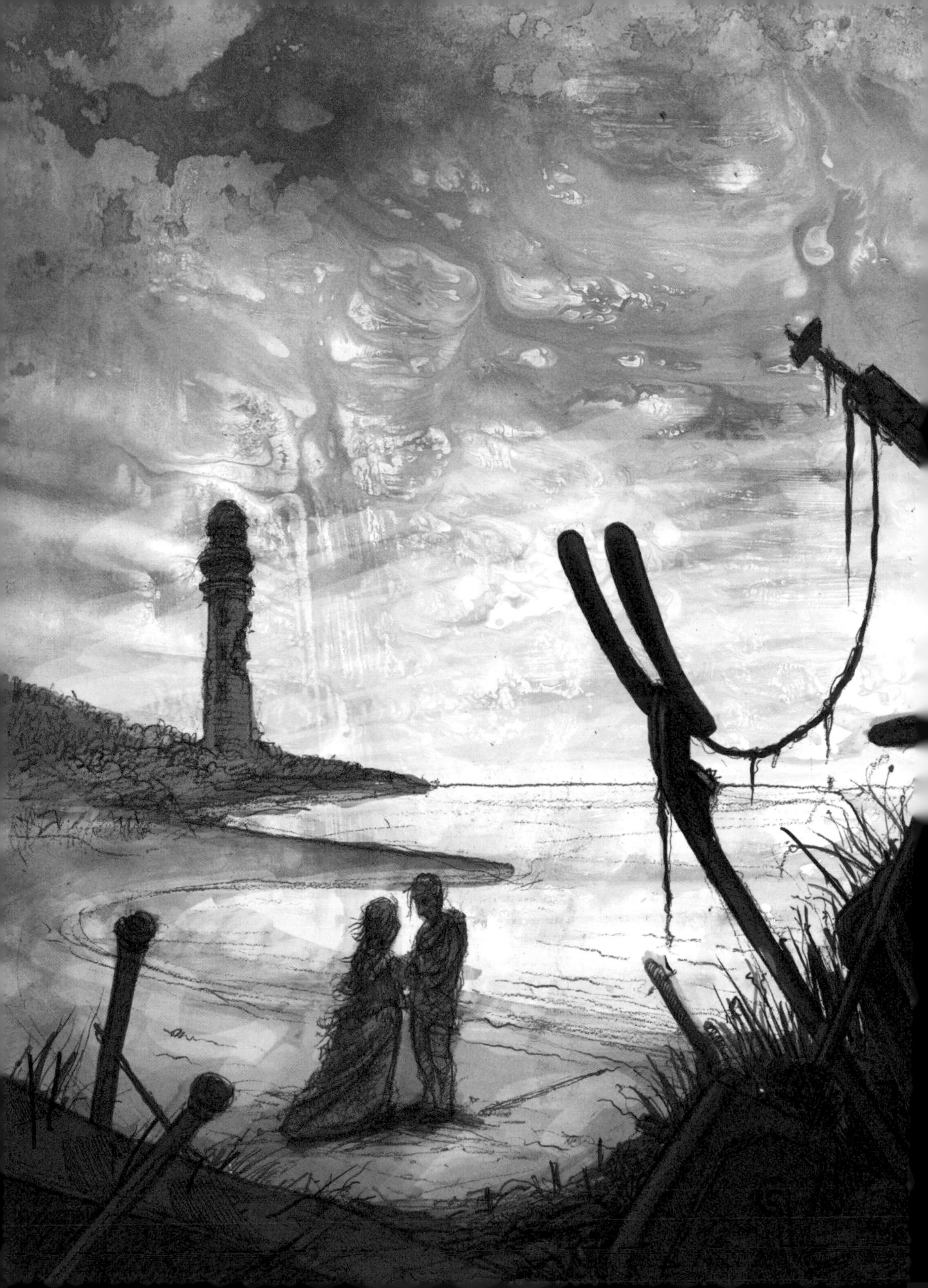

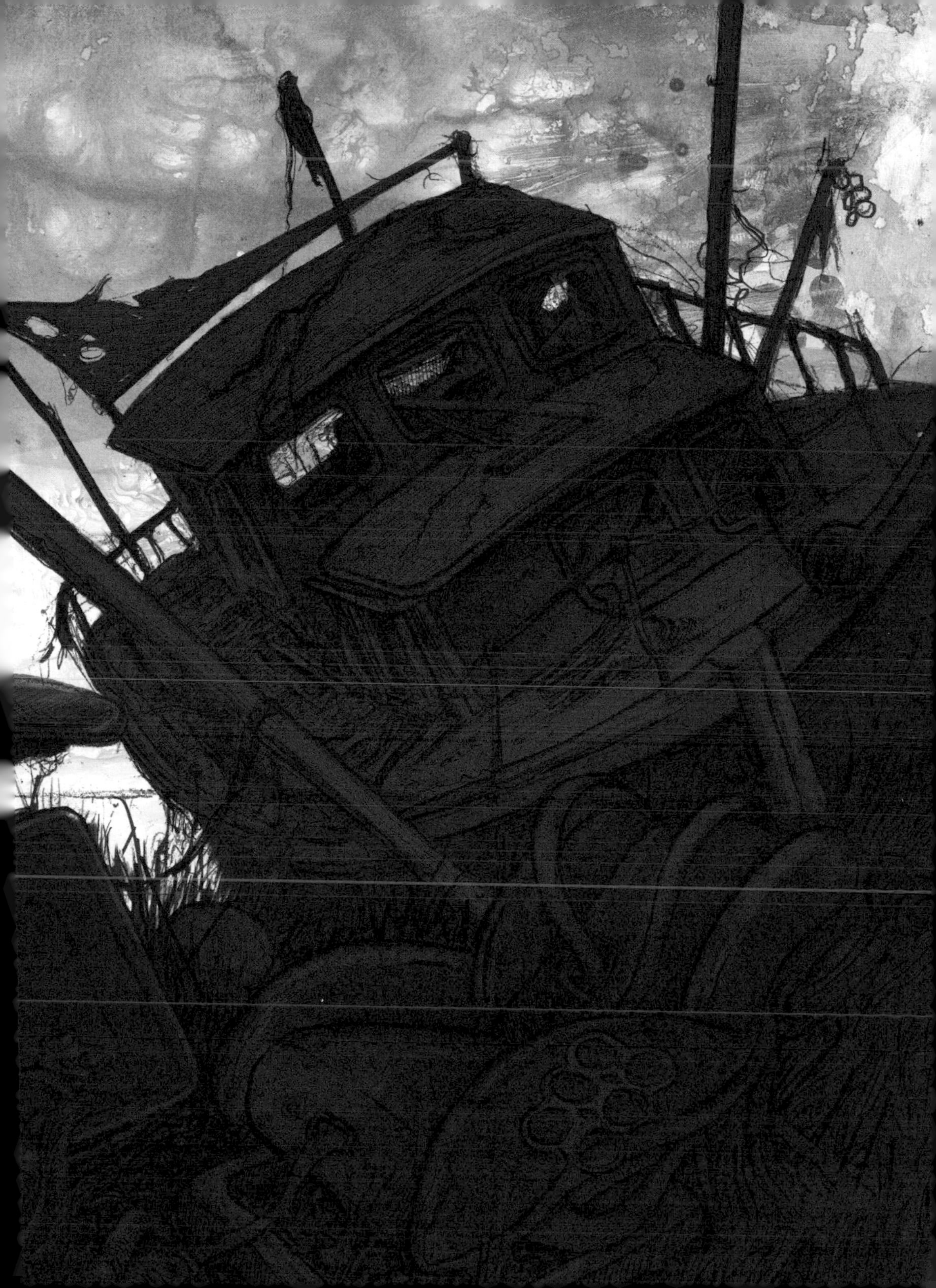

FOR NIKKI, WHO HAS CLIMBED ALL THE TOWERS, I.C.
FOR SARAH, D.R.

ISOBELLE CARMODY IS THE MULTI-AWARD-WINNING AUTHOR OF MORE THAN THIRTY BOOKS, AMONG WHICH ARE *THE OBERNEWTYN CHRONICLES, ALYZON WHITESTARR, THE GATHERING* AND THE WONDERFUL GRAPHIC HYBRID, *DREAMWALKER*, WHICH SHE WORKED ON WITH THE LATE STEPHEN WOOLMAN.

EVERMORE BEGAN AS A NOVELLA INTENDED FOR A COLLECTION, BUT GREW INTO SOMETHING LARGER AND STRANGER AND DARKER THAN EXPECTED. IT TOOK A CONVERSATION WITH ILLUSTRATOR AND GRAPHIC NOVELIST DAN REED, TO MAKE HER REALISE IT WAS A GRAPHIC NOVEL.

WHILE DAN COMPLETED HIS INCREDIBLE ILLUSTRATIONS FOR *EVERMORE*, ISOBELLE FINISHED THE SECOND IN HER *LAND OF THE LOST SERIES*, WHICH SHE ALSO ILLUSTRATED. SHE IS NOW COMPLETING THE LAST OF HER OBERNEWTYN CHRONICLES, *THE RED QUEEN*, WHILE UNDERTAKING A PHD AT THE UNIVERSITY OF QUEENSLAND.

DANIEL REED HAS BEEN A PRESENCE IN THE MELBOURNE UNDERGROUND COMIC SCENE FOR MANY YEARS, WHERE HIS MIND-BENDING SERIES *THE CRUMPLETON EXPERIMENTS* HAD AN ENTHUSIASTIC AND LOYAL FOLLOWING. HIS MORE RECENT BOOK, THE EPIC FABLE *GRUBBY LITTLE SMUDGES OF FILTH*, RECEIVED GREAT REVIEWS AND AN INTERNATIONAL RELEASE. BOTH TITLES HAVE BEEN RECOGNISED WITH LEDGER AWARDS.

IN *EVERMORE*, DANIEL'S ILLUSTRATION STYLE CREATES A RICH AND EMOTIVE SETTING FOR ISOBELLE'S STORY. INK WASHES AND PENCILLED TONES DESCRIBE THE RUINED WORLD, WHILE THE PEN AND BRUSHWORK BRINGS DETAIL AND FOCUS TO THE CHARACTERS, RESULTING IN ARTWORK THAT IS MORE AT HOME IN A CLASSIC PICTURE BOOK THAN A TRADITIONAL COMIC.

A HELEN CHAMBERLIN BOOK

FIRST PUBLISHED IN 2015 BY WINDY HOLLOW BOOKS

PO BOX 265 KEW EAST, VICTORIA, AUSTRALIA 3102

WEBSITE: WWW.WINDYHOLLOW.BOOKS.COM.AU
WWW.FACEBOOK.COM/WINDYHOLLOWBOOKS

NATIONAL LIBRARY OF AUSTRALIA
CATALOGUING-IN-PUBLICATION ENTRY
CREATOR: CARMODY, ISOBELLE, 1958- AUTHOR.
TITLE: EVERMORE / ISOBELLE CARMODY;
        ILLUSTRATED BY DANIEL REED.
ISBN: 9781922081568 (PAPERBACK)
SUBJECTS: FANTASY COMIC BOOKS, STRIPS, ETC.
        GRAPHIC NOVELS
OTHER CREATORS/CONTRIBUTORS: REED, DANIEL, ILLUSTRATOR.
DEWEY NUMBER: A823.3

DESIGNED BY DANIEL REED
COLOUR REPRODUCTION BY NUOVO GROUP
PRINTED BY DAI RUBICON